Modern Social Theory

By the same author
Existentialism and Sociology: A Study of Jean-Paul Sartre

Modern Social Theory
From Parsons to Habermas

Ian Craib

LECTURER IN SOCIOLOGY
UNIVERSITY OF ESSEX

Wheatsheaf Books

Distributed by Harvester Press

First published in Great Britain in 1984 by
WHEATSHEAF BOOKS LTD
A MEMBER OF THE HARVESTER PRESS GROUP
Publisher: John Spiers
Director of Publications: Edward Elgar
16 Ship Street, Brighton, Sussex

British Library Cataloguing in Publication Data

Craib, Ian
    Modern Social theory
    1. Sociology
    I. Title
    301'.01   HM24

    ISBN 0-7108-0183-1
    ISBN 0-7108-0178-5   Pbk

Typeset in 10 point Times New Roman by
Thomson Press (India) Ltd., New Delhi
Printed in Great Britain by
The Thetford Press Ltd., Thetford, Norfolk

THE HARVESTER PRESS PUBLISHING GROUP
The Harvester Press Publishing Group comprises Harvester Press
Limited (chiefly publishing literature, fiction, philosophy, psychology and
science and trade books), Harvester Press Microform Publications
Limited (publishing in microform unpublished archives, scarce printed
sources, and indexes to these collections) and Wheatsheaf Books Limited
(a wholly independent company chiefly publishing in economics,
international politics, sociology and related social sciences), whose books
are distributed by The Harvester Press Limited and its agencies
throughout the world.

For Benji:

Theory is good but it doesn't prevent things from existing.
(Reported comment by Charcot to Freud, quoted in Roazen, P. (1970), *Freud and his Followers*: Allen Lane. London, p. 91.)

Contents

viii   *Contents*

Preface

The best way to read this book is from beginning to end, although it is not a habit I would always encourage in sociology students. In this case it is because there are regular references to what has gone before and although Parts I, II, III and IV may be read separately without too much difficulty, this is not true for each chapter in any one part. Sections of the introductory chapters may be difficult, and they should be returned to or re-read at the end. Chapter 4, on conflict theory, and Chapter 8, on structuralist Marxism, have a certain affinity and could be read together.

This book has benefited from the wisdom of a number of people. Andrew Briggs, Sheila Strawbridge and Phil Wexler read and produced written comments on the penultimate draft (excluding Chapter 13, the conclusion). These were of considerable help and I am grateful for their time and energy. The following read and commented on parts or all of the draft: Graham Davey, Howard Newby, Allyson Purcell, Tony Tant and Mary Tomlinson. Again, I am grateful for their suggestions and encouragement. I would also like to thank Angela Bruce and Cherry Mattocks for a very efficient and speedy typing of the final Manuscript.

Finally and by no means least, I should mention the sociological theory classes I taught at Essex in 1980–81 and 1982–83; it is not often I find groups of students so stimulating and so willing to tolerate my confusions, and they must take the credit for what is good and useful in this book. Credit for the bad and useless remains with me.

Part I
INTRODUCTION

1 What's wrong with theory and why we still need it

INTRODUCTION

The very word 'theory' sometimes seems to scare people, and not without good reason. Much modern social theory is either unintelligible, or banal, or pointless. The reader does not feel she is learning anything new or anything at all; there is certainly no excitement. Even for the specialist sociology student or teacher, it requires a lot of hard work with the minimal result of simply being informed. Few people feel at home with theory or use it in a productive way.

At the same time theory increases and proliferates: it might sometimes seem that this is the result of a highly developed society allowing people to earn sizeable incomes from playing complicated games, but it would not happen if there were not real problems which force people to turn to theory. Self-indulgence is not the only reason for the existence of theory. Indeed, the problems that force people to theory do not belong solely to sociological research; they are problems we all face in our everyday lives, problems of making sense of what happens to us and the people around us, the problems involved in making moral and political choices.

So, somewhere there are real reasons leading people to produce theoretical work, and there must also be reasons why the result is so often unhelpful. The journey between the problems and the results is undertaken on sociological theory courses as well as in producing theory and it has the same pitfalls. It is not made any easier by the fact that in teaching theory we start with the result. The nature of sociology is not such that we can move directly from the more practical and informative studies of the social world to social theory. Social theory is by definition *general*, it claims some relevance to all the separate areas studied by sociologists. We can not move directly from, say, a study of workers' attitudes to a theory since any worthwhile theory must deal with much more than workers' attitudes. We have to bring the two together, use our studies of the real world as the raw material of theory and use our theory to help us understand the results of our studies of the real world. But when we learn theory, we must start with theory and that makes life difficult.

Other things make it difficult as well. Ours is not a culture that accepts easily theory in its more elaborate, worked out form. Most of us learn, almost unconsciously, to distrust it, or we become convinced that it is beyond us. *Social* theory generates its own special prejudices. Most of us know little about the natural sciences, but we will nonetheless accept that theoretical physics is a 'good thing': it seems to have useful practical results and even if we know in advance that we can't understand it, those few clever souls who can ought to be encouraged. On the other hand, social theory appears to have no practical results. Worse, it takes something we know about already in intimate detail—our own social life—and makes of it unintelligible nonsense.

If this were not enough, the teaching and learning of social theory itself operates within, and helps to create, a peculiar mystique which in turn creates a disturbing environment in which to study. The teacher of theory who, for example, is concerned only or primarily with theory, tends to receive from her colleagues a grudging respect combined with a barely veiled hostility. In departments where it is the researcher into the real world who attracts money and reputation, the theorist is a luxury, an amusement and a nuisance. On balance she is lower rather than higher in the unofficial order. Many people who see themselves primarily as theorists react to this by building a protective arrogance, returning two-fold any scorn they might receive. They refuse to compromise their concerns and indeed retreat perhaps even further into the obscure and the difficult. The process frequently starts amongst postgraduate students and it serves to make the necessary gap between teacher and student much wider than it need be at all levels. Amongst students themselves, because theory is so obviously difficult, the theorist takes on an aura that puts her apart from others; she is seen as somehow brighter, better, more able. I have no doubt that many students (and teachers) deliberately deploy this advantage, half-consciously seeking more obscure ways of expressing themselves, adopting the latest translations from Europe before anybody else, puffing out their theoretical feathers.

All these problems are there before we even start the journey. My guess is that most people start it because they have no choice, it comprises a compulsory course at some stage in their student career and they grit their teeth and get on with it. What can be done about it? It is no use pretending that theory can be made easy, but it can be made easier.

THEORETICAL THINKING

The first step is to look again at the way we approach the subject. Because we start with the result, it is too easy for students and teachers to imagine that the whole process is a matter of learning what various theorists have said, of learning *theories*. Of course, it is that, but in one sense it is the least important aspect. It is possible, in fact quite easy, once you get used to long words, to know what Talcott Parsons has to say and to reproduce it in acceptable form in essays and exam papers. And apart from the purpose of passing exams, it is quite useless. Theory is only a help if we can learn from it, and we can only learn from it if we can use it.

Another way of putting this is that it is less a matter of learning theory than of learning to *think theoretically*. It can be likened to learning a new language in a particularly difficult way, not by gradually building up vocabulary and learning the various grammatical rules, but by listening to the language being spoken, in all its complexity, its slang, dialects etc. It is only just an exaggeration to liken it to being carried off to a very different society, a tribal village in New Guinea, say, where much of what happens is unfamiliar, and having to learn the language there by listening to people speak it.

Such a process can be made easier if we have some insight into the purposes of the inhabitants, and I said earlier that the problems which lead people to theory are problems we all face in our everyday lives. I think the truth is that we all think theoretically but in a way of which we are not often aware. What we are not used to is thinking theoretically in a systematic manner, with all the various constraints and rigours that that involves; when we do see such thinking, it is, at first, foreign to us.

What, then, are the problems in response to which we all think theoretically without realising it? Most of us are affected in some way by events over which we have no control and the causes of which are not immediately obvious. Some of these are unexpected, some happen at first in a slow and less noticeable way. A member of the family might be made unemployed, for example, or fail to gain an expected place at university or college; some product or service might suddenly become unavailable because of a strike, or because of government or local authority economies; over a long period an income—wage, social security benefit, unemployment pay, pension, student grant or whatever—might buy less and less. We can do things to alleviate the effects of all of these, but they happen whether we as individuals like it or not, and it is by no means clear why they happen. There are similar, more intimate events in our personal lives: the slow changes in the relationship between parents and children or between lovers, which no-one wills but which nonetheless happen. I might suddenly find a friend has turned hostile for no obvious reason. On an even more personal level, I might fall in love at the most inconvenient and unexpected time, or find myself in the grip of some other violent emotion which comes from nowhere and seems to dominate my life. Or, an example I will continue to develop, I might find myself caught in something with a physical as well as psychological manifestation—sexual impotence perhaps.

In all these situations, we try to find some explanation. Often it takes the form of blaming somebody or thing, frequently unfairly—I lose my job because of all the blacks coming over here; I'm unhappy because my mother dominates me; I am impotent because my wife is frigid. Sometimes the blame is closer to the mark: I lose my job because of an economic situation largely created by Government policy; I am heading for a nervous breakdown because I cannot admit to certain feelings which I nonetheless have; I am impotent because women, or a woman, scare me. Sometimes the explanations are more sophisticated, but my point is that as soon as we start thinking about and trying to explain something which happens to us, over which we have no control, we are beginning to think theoretically. When something happens over which we do have control, there is no need for an explanation, it happens because I want it to happen and do something to make it happen (or do not do something which would stop it happening). There is another way of putting this that takes us closer to 'theory' as it is presented in theory courses. Theory is an attempt to explain our everyday experience of the world, our 'closest' experience, in terms of something which is not so close—whether it be other peoples' actions, our past experience, our repressed emotions or whatever. Sometimes, and this is perhaps the most difficult, the explanation is in terms of something of which we do not and cannot have any direct experience at all and it is at this level that theory really tells us something new about the world.

This will become clearer if we investigate this everyday theoretical thinking more closely. Pushing the sexual impotency example further, it might be something which happens to me unexpectedly, and perhaps I might not want to admit to it for a while. Eventually, however, I am forced to recognise it and begin thinking about it. Then I might have as my first reference some previous similar experience of my own or a close friend who has found himself in the same position. I look for common features in the situation: perhaps it is a matter of being under particular pressure at work; perhaps it happens when my wife is particularly successful in her work or gets a wage increase; perhaps if I am very frightened by the experience and need urgently to place the blame elsewhere, I might attribute it to some more intimate feature of her behaviour.

There is a second 'resource' for my explanation, which I will probably use anyway and particularly if I have no previous experience of impotency—mine or anybody else's. I can draw on some very general ideas about the world which do not come from my direct experience in anything like the same way. For example, I might assume that sexual potency—indeed a permanent readiness to exploit any opportunity that presents itself—is a fundamental part of being a man; my impotence means that I am un-manned, I no longer fall into that category. This is not an idea that comes from my experience. I do not have knowledge of the sexual cycles of all men, or any men other than myself. I have not been taught the idea in any direct way, although it might be possible to identify situations in which I have unconsciously learnt it. My main point however is that in making sense of the world, I draw on experience and on ideas about the world that have no direct relation to experience. The two intertwine: my fear and shame at being unmanned might lead me to look for something about my wife that I can blame.

Social theory is employed for the same purposes: to explain and understand experience on the basis of other experiences and general ideas about the world. Given this, it's possible to look at some differences between everyday theoretical thinking and social theory. The first is that social theory attempts to be much more systematic about both experience and ideas. In sociology the real systematization of experience often takes place in the supposed absence of theory and there is considerable debate about whether this is possible or desirable. I suspect that it would now be generally recognised that some simple 'objectivity' or completely 'unbiased' organisation of facts is not possible, but in any case the steady and systematic attempt to gather knowledge about peoples' experience can in itself produce knowledge which is at first sight strange. If I extend my concern about my impotency into a study of male sexuality even just in my own society, I might find that impotency is a 'normal' condition in that most men experience it at some time in their lives, and I will certainly find that all sorts of behaviour that I consider unmanly is engaged in by men. General ideas on the other hand are systematized through subjecting them to rules of logic—the ideas in a theory should follow from each other, not contradict each other, at the very least they should have clearly defined relationships to each other. It is important to realise that there is no conclusive end to this process on either level: we can always discover more about our world and organise it in different ways, according to different principles.

This brings us to the second difference. In the course of systematization, what I will call 'second-order' problems arise, problems about the best way of carrying on the systematization, only indirectly connected with explaining our experience as such. An example would be debates about what we mean by 'explanation', when is an explanation adequate and when is it not?

The third difference has already been mentioned. The various processes of systematization might lead us to the conclusion that things exist in the world of which we have no direct experience, and on occasion that these things are the opposite of what we might expect from our experience of the world. It is perhaps more difficult to accept this in the case of the social world, but we already accept it about the natural world and that should at least suggest that we should keep an open mind. If we believed only what we see by just looking, nobody would believe the Earth was round or that it travelled round the Sun. For most of our history, nobody did believe it (as far as we know).

Returning to our example of sexual impotency, our various systematizations might lead us to the conclusions that in most societies female sexuality has been controlled by men, and that whatever men believe about themselves, women get the blame if those beliefs are disturbed. We might then be struck by the similarity between this situation and some of the abstract ideas put forward by Marx about the relationship between social classes and set about refining and modifying Marx's ideas so that they help us make sense of the relationship between men and women. We might go further and integrate some general ideas taken from Freud and end up with a theory of something called 'patriarchy'—a model of a social organization in which men systematically oppress women. This is the opposite of my experience of my impotence: my experience and my first reaction is that my wife is exercising power over me by denying me something, she is making my life miserable. The theory of patriarchy enables me to reinterpret this reaction: what is really happening is that my wife is in some way threatening my power, perhaps she is too independent, perhaps she is simply fighting back with the weapons at hand. By blaming her, and particularly by trying to persuade her to accept responsibility, I am trying to re-assert that power.

Whether or not you accept such an explanation (and there is plenty of room for debate) every social theory considered in this book makes some propositions which are counter to our immediate experiences and beliefs, and this is in fact the way in which we learn from theory. The punk might believe that she is in full rebellion against the culture of her parents and authority, yet for the functionalist theorist, she is setting in motion a series of adjustments by means of which that culture and society continue to survive in a smoother-running way than before. The worker might believe she is getting a fair day's wage for a fair day's work but for the Marxist she is being systematically exploited. When I fail a student's exam paper, I might believe that I am applying a rule and upholding academic standards: she does not come up to some pre-determined standard, in the same way that I might say a piece of wood is not long enough for my purpose. The symbolic interactionist and (in a different way) the ethnomethodologist would say that I am creating a failure. If we are honest most of us would accept that there have been occasions on which we were really doing the opposite of what we thought we were doing; for this reason alone we should tolerate the apparent strangeness of social theory.

I said earlier that social theory can only be made easier, not easy. For example, it is not possible to trace the theories examined in this book back to everyday problems; the problems had already been subjected to many centuries of philosophical thought and developments in knowledge before the theories arose. Nevertheless they can be seen as asking sensible questions about the world (even if the answers aren't always sensible). Perhaps the best way to learn 'theoretical thinking' is not just by reading and understanding theory but by asking the theory questions and speculating on the answers. That is the way in which the book will proceed: What questions does the theory ask? What questions can we ask the theory? It should be (to begin with) above all an imaginative game. Having some idea of what Parsons says, can we, for example, explain the election of Ronald Reagan and Margaret Thatcher in Parsonian terms; or can we use Parsons to understand the increasing divorce rate or changes in the level and nature of crime. The first step is always to speculate, to try to *invent* an answer. The rigour of logic and facts will follow on all too quickly. The pay-off is that if we can do it well, if we can use our theory to find out about the world, then our range of effective action increases, we become more free.

All this could be read as an apologia for theory, a justification of its obscurities and difficulties. I nonetheless meant what I said at the very beginning—that much modern theory is unintelligible, banal or pointless. In the process of theoretical thinking, a number of things can go wrong.

THEORETICAL TRAPS

The first trap lies prior to theory proper and there have been times when sociologists have seemed especially prone to falling into it. This is the trap of only collecting facts, of becoming absorbed in technical debates about methodology and statistical correlation. The real function of theory has to do with the interpretation of whatever facts we might be able to discover and agree on, and indeed it will become apparent that in some cases we need a theory to tell us what the facts are. The first truly theoretical trap is what I shall call the '*crossword puzzle trap*'.

One of the most influential books in sociology in the last twenty years has, paradoxically, not been a work of sociology at all but a study of the history of the natural sciences: Thomas Kuhn's *Structure of Scientific Revolutions*. Kuhn makes a distinction between what he calls 'revolutionary' and 'normal' science, and it is the latter which is important for my present point. Normal science is routine science. The scientist is in possession of accepted theoretical knowledge, routine experimental procedures and the instruments necessary to carry them out. These (together with other elements) comprise what Kuhn calls a 'paradigm'. Her scientific activity consists of trying to manipulate certain features of the natural world, suitably isolated in experimental situations, to fit the paradigm. In the same way as a crossword puzzle provides a frame and a set of clues, so the paradigm gives us a general framework and indications of what the world should be like, and the scientist sets about filling in the squares in detail. Now I think there are a number of reasons why the social scientist should not employ theory in this way, however productive it might be for the natural sciences, and that is a matter of debate. The complexity of the subject matter of social science, the impossibility of isolating significant aspects of the social world in order to carry out experiments, the fact that human activity is self-conscious and reflective, all combine to make such puzzle-solving activity damaging, what some people call 'reductionist': it reduces the complexity of the real world to a set of theoretical concepts.

For example, we do not learn much about my reaction to impotence by sticking the label of 'patriarchy' on it; we need to show not only how the nature of patriarchy conditions and determines both my impotence and my reaction to it, but also the way that these processes interact with others (for example, a changing labour market which gives greater opportunity for women to embark on full time careers) in order to understand the full complexity of the situation. Otherwise something is lost. We need then, to take account of all the various links ('mediations') between what the theory tells us and the experience or event we are trying to understand.

The second trap I shall call the *'brain-teaser trap'*. I mentioned earlier that in systematizing our ideas about the world, a number of second-order problems arise, not directly connected with explaining something. I gave as an example what we mean by 'explanation'. Many such problems are very important and without doubt a number will arise in the course of this book. But many might be unsolvable, or bear little relation to what we are trying to do; they are nonetheless fascinating problems and I know from my own experience that a great deal of pleasure can be derived from tackling them—the same sort of pleasure that can be derived from the 'brain teasers' sometimes found in the 'quality' Sunday papers. I think it is a 'permissible' activity as long as it is recognised for what it is; it is when it is mistaken for the theoretical enterprise as a whole that theory seems to be (and is) irrelevant.

A good example is the debate imported into social theory from British analytic philosophy, about whether or not a person's reasons for their actions are to be considered as causes of their actions. There is a crucial issue here to do with the very nature and possibility of a social science, but the terms of the debate are so limited in their scope and exclude so many dimensions of human action that it seems to me that the real problem disappears. Indeed I think it is possible to establish elegant solutions on either side, none of which are much concrete help to social analysis and none of which are conclusive.

Thirdly, there is the 'logic trap'. This might sound odd since I've already suggested that a central aspect of theoretical thinking is the attempt to achieve logical coherence between different parts of a theory. My point is that it is possible to take this to an absurd extreme. In the course of the book there will be several examples of the way in which a theory might be demolished on logical grounds that if taken to the extreme would mean that no theory at all was possible. The main point here is that whilst a theory must strive for internal coherence, for logical order, the world itself is often illogical or logical in a different way to the theory, which must be capable of allowing for this difference. There are a number of examples of supposedly theoretical arguments which are really competitions in logic that have long left behind any concern with explaining or understanding the social world.

Finally, there is the '*description trap*'. The difference between an explanation and a description will be discussed in Chapter 2. For the moment it is sufficient to say that an explanation tells us something we didn't know and couldn't discover simply by looking; a description tells us only what we can discover by looking. A great deal of modern theory seems to me to describe something, often something we know very well, in abstract theoretical terms, and then pretend that it is an explanation. It is perhaps this which contributes most to the bad name of theory: endless pages of long words which, when we translate them, tell us the obvious. We shall see that Talcott Parsons is particularly vulnerable on this point.

So, I have tried to show why theory is necessary and some of the traps into which it can fall. However social theory is frightening for another reason: there is so much of it and so many different types. I want now to spend some time looking at the range of theories with which sociologists are presently working and at possible ways of organising them to make the task easier.

2 Cutting a path through the jungle

Anthony Giddens, perhaps the most prominent modern British social theorist, describes the present situation as a veritable Babel; that this is so must be clear to anybody who has glanced through recent introductions to theory, let alone the more advanced contributions. It has not always been the case, but neither has social theory ever comprised a single, unified body of thought accepted by everybody in the discipline and employed in carrying out and interpreting research. Ten or fifteen years ago it was possible to see and teach social theory as a debate between two opposing approaches, and although there were innumerable different views as to the best way to define these approaches the situation did not yet appear out of hand.

FROM CONFUSION TO CHAOS

Even when it was possible to organise social theory into two opposing camps, there was always a residue of confusion. It was not always clear which theory should be assigned to which camp or even where the different camps were situated. I think it is true to say that the nearest there has ever been to a dominant theory in sociology was structural-functionalism, developed in its most complete way by Talcott Parsons, but it has never been alone. In the USA, there was always a subordinate but alternative approach based originally on the University of Chicago and generally going under the name of symbolic interactionism, and beyond this, there was a radical tradition which can be traced back to Veblen, and whose most

15

prominent representative during the 1950s and early 1960s was C. Wright–Mills. The political upheavals of the 1960s led to some dramatic changes: there is now very little work continuing in the strict structural-functionalist tradition and a great deal in the symbolic interactionist and radical tradition. In Britian the main opposition was offered by what became known as the conflict approach, based primarily on the founding work of Max Weber—a tradition always fruitful in terms of research and which is still of significance today. In Britain also there was a form of Marxist theory extant, although it remained underdeveloped in the context of academic life.

It was, I think, the political struggles of the 1960s that set the cat amongst the pigeons, although a lot has happened since then. Social theory has always been fed by ideas from outside the discipline, in particular from different philosophical traditions, and in response to theoretical problems directly or indirectly highlighted by political conflict, writers turned to a variety of such traditions. This is not a history of social thought, nor a sociology of social thought: all I can really do here is sketch the developments.

One response, originating in the USA, grew out of the traditions of structural-functionalism and symbolic interactionism, although it saw itself as opposed to both. This was *ethnomethodology* and it drew upon two different sources: a linguistic, analytic philosophy (which was the dominant form of philosophy in all English speaking countries) and a very different school of European philosophy: phenomenology. As we shall see, ethnomethodology itself formed into two distinct tendencies and on its edges we can find a different, third school of phenomenology.

The two other main responses grew out of the rebirth of Marxism in academic life. There have always been national Marxisms—the theory has developed in different ways in different political contexts, and four or five different varieties of Marxist thought have fed into the mainstream of English language social theory. By far the most important of these have been the French and German traditions. In Britain the rebirth of Marxism came through the translation into English of the French philosopher Louis Althusser; interest in Althusser's work, and the work of his pupils and associates, brought with it and encouraged an interest in the tradition of thought known as structuralism. Althusser's Marxism was not the only variant of structuralism, which inspired work in anthropology and the sociology of culture. Structuralism was always a source of lively debate and over the years many of its original propositions have been turned on their head. The term 'post-structuralism' is now heard increasingly often.

In the USA where it became attached to the earlier radical tradition and to a lesser extent in Britain, the German Marxist tradition took root. Sometimes known as the Marxism of the Frankfurt School, sometimes simply as critical theory, this represented a school of thought that originated with G.W.F. Hegel—a classic German philosopher who was a crucial influence on Marx himself. Originally this generated a greater interest in Hegel's thought but this school has also undergone significant transformations, particularly in the work of Jurgen Habermas. Habermas' work has opened up yet another philosophical tradition to social thought: hermeneutics. Hermeneutics was originally a product of debates about how to interpret sacred religious texts but can now be taken as a general theory of interpretation.

The names alone on this list should be enough to intimidate anybody. I suspect social theory has always been intimidating, but now it must seem impossible to those who do not have the peculiar twist of mind that enables them to enjoy it. Even for the latter it is now difficult to find secure bearings. The tendency seems to be to find one theorists and stick to him (note, it is usually *him*), often dogmatically asserting his superiority rather than gaining sufficient understanding of alternatives and engaging in rational argument. It is not only students who are prone to this, much modern theoretical work has all the symptoms of dogmatism: unjustified assertion, over-simplification, misrepresentation. A central aim of this book is to try to introduce the various approaches in such a way that some more rational comparison is possible, and as a first way of making sense of the confusion, I have divided the book along the lines of the main streams of thought that I have just described. This will not include all the various contributions to modern social theory: there will, for example, be little mention of phenomenological Marxism or the Italian Marxist tradition originating with Gramsci; little about exchange theory or reflexive sociology or a number of other sociologies that have bloomed and vanished rapidly over the past decade; nor will I travel into the further reaches of structuralism, post-structuralism and hermeneutics. The aim rather is to give an initial insight into the most widely read and influential modern theorists.

However, matters are even more difficult since these approaches, although identifiable as distinct approaches, are themselves frag-menting. One sign of this is that the most stimulating and interesting debates in modern theory are not between different approaches but between different variations and developments in the same approach. There is not one academic community engaging in social theory, but a number of communities, each engaged in internal arguments but largely isolated from the others. Paradoxically, the only unifying theme seems to be that of fragmentation: the only thing that brings the different approaches together is that they are all falling apart. There are, I think, identifiable reasons for this, some of which I will mention in passing, some of which will be more central to the accounts of the various approaches that come later.

DIMENSIONS OF THEORY

It is useful to think of social theory as having three different dimensions, and of the theorists as doing three different things at the same time. In the first chapter, I was talking about theory as a way of establishing knowledge about the social world. This is its *cognitive* dimension and most of this book will be concerned with it. We can trace 'cognitive fault lines' in social theory which help to make sense of the process of fragmentation and I will be returning to this in the last part of this chapter. For the moment I want to concentrate on the remaining two dimensions.

To begin with, the sociologist is caught up with the problem she is trying to theorize, not just as a sociologist but as a person. There is a strong case that, however obliquely, the social theorist's experience of the world enters into her theory, can leave her blind to certain aspects of the world or affect the way in which she deals with problems. Perhaps 'her' is the wrong pronoun here since the clearest example is the way in which the mainly male sociological community has ignored or misdefined the place of women in our society. It has been usual, for example, to place a family in the stratification system according to the occupation of the male. Sexual stratification has received very little attention until recently—apart from Parsons' work on the family, where the woman's traditional role was barely questioned. In a more immediate way as well, a number of quite personal hopes and fears are embodied in the work. Alan Dawe, following the American sociologist Alvin Gouldner, has likened some theoretical work to prayer. This second dimension of theory, then, is the *affective* dimension: theory embodies the experience and the feelings of the theorist and any theoretical debate involves more than rational argument.

This second dimension muddies the waters; it cannot be held responsible for the fragmentation of theory but it can contribute to the obscurities of the arguments and sometimes to the over-emphasis of differences.

The third dimension contributes more to fragmentation. This I shall call the *normative* dimension. By this, I mean that any theory of the way the world is must make implicit or explicit assumptions about the way the world ought to be. Alvin Gouldner has referred to these as 'domain assumptions'. It follows from this that a theory must always have certain implications about political action, about what sort of actions are possible and which are desirable. Social theory, then, is not only *about* social processes, conflicts, problems, it is also *part* of those processes, conflicts and problems. I do not think that this is a bad thing; indeed such assumptions should be made as explicit as possible because if they are not argued out rationally in an academic setting, they are unlikely to be argued out anywhere. This process brings out an important aspect of any theory: its *flexibility*. A theory is always open to being used to argue different points in different ways in different situations, and the flux of normal social and political life will ensure that most theories are pushed in different ways. Marxism is the obvious example and I have already referred to the development of different 'national' Marxisms, but most of the theories we will be looking at here have become involved in debates that go well beyond their immediate cognitive dimension. Social and international conflicts always push their way into theory, often in disguised form, and sometimes split it down the middle. To develop this any further would require a political sociology of the discipline; I want to concentrate on the cognitive dimension and that involves a short excursion through the philosophy of science.

WHAT DO THEORIES EXPLAIN?

At first glance, the philosophy of social science might be even more frightening than social theory. Whereas 'theory' sometimes holds out the hope that it might be understood, the word 'philosophy' by itself defies the understanding. And if theory is such a mess, would not philosophy be even more of a mess?

The simple answer is no. Perhaps the best way of looking at philosophy is as a sort of 'theory of theory', and simply because it is more abstract, certain things appear more clearly and simply. Of course, what I called the 'brain-teaser' trap is more pronounced, and the more technical the philosophical argument, the greater the danger. However, apart from general background details, I do not want to go into the arguments. Indeed I will avoid most of them altogether—if you want to find out what they are, a number of references can be found in the further reading at the end of the chapter. What I want to do instead is concentrate on one recent development.

The philosophy of social science concerns itself with two issues: first the nature of the world, what sort of things exist and what are the different forms of existence—for example, do human beings exist in the same way as inanimate objects and if not what are the differences? These can be classed under the heading of *ontological* questions and you might think, with some justification, that the answer to the example I've just given would be obvious to anybody but a philosopher. Secondly, it concerns itself with the nature of an explanation: what methods must be employed to arrive at an explanation, what logical structure must it have, what proofs are required. These are *epistemological* questions—about the way in which we know our knowledge *is* knowledge.

In the case of the social sciences, and sociology in particular, these issues have been discussed in the context of a debate about whether the social sciences and the natural sciences are similar—whether social science should employ the same methods as the natural sciences. For a long time there were two alternatives: yes or no. Then, beginning with the work of Thomas Kuhn that I mentioned in the last chapter, it was realised that the natural sciences themselves were more difficult and complex animals than had hitherto been supposed. This opened up a third alternative: yes *and* no. In some ways the social sciences are like the natural sciences, in other ways they are not.

The arguments are, of course, still continuing, but I want to concentrate on one comparatively recent development which passes under various labels: realism, naturalism, or materialism. Each means something slightly different but the differences are not important for our present purposes. I want to concentrate on the work of Roy Bhaskar. I think there are a number of reasons why his work is fruitful, and the most important one in the present context is that it does throw some light on the fragmentation of social theory in a way that the others do not.

Bhaskar is concerned to demonstrate that the ontological and epistemological questions are inter-related in the sense that the way we gain knowledge about the world, what comprises an adequate explanation, depends on the sort of beings that exist in the world: to put it another way, the object we are studying determines the knowledge we can have of it. This should become clearer shortly.

One of the more traditional ways of dividing up social theory was to make a distinction between 'holistic' theories and 'individualistic' theories. The former start with 'society' as a whole, regarding it as something more than the sum of the individuals who make it up. The actions of individuals are then seen as in some way determined by the society of which they are a part. The latter starts with individuals and sees society as the product of individual actions. There were also those who argued that both processes go on at the same time: individuals make societies and societies make individuals. Now Bhaskar argues that all three of these positions are mistaken insofar as they regard societies and individuals (agents in his terminology) as beings of the same type, so that one can determine the other or there can be a process of mutual determination. Societies and agents are beings of a radically different type, they have different properties. The next step is to investigate those different properties.

Beginning with societies, it is possible to talk of a society as something greater than the individuals who make it up. A society exists in its own right, or *sui generis* to use Durkheim's term. The argument for this view was put forward by Durkheim a long time ago, as a demonstration that we need such a discipline as sociology to study societies. There are certain features of social existence which precede an individual's birth and continue after her death and into which that individual has to fit. We can draw an analogy with language. The English language was in existence long before I was born, and will continue in existence long after I die. If I want to communicate with any or most people in my society I must learn to speak it, and nothing I do will alter that. I do not create the language, nor does anybody else; it has, in *this* sense, an independent existence. We will see later that there is also a sense in which societies and agents *depend* on each other, without determining or creating each other.

The first property of societies is that they are *relational*: they are comprised of enduring relations of agents to each other and to the material objects that also make up the social environment. It must be remembered that relationships outlast any particular agents engaged in them so it is more useful and accurate to talk of relationships between positions rather than agents. Thus, for example, the nuclear family may be seen as involving relatively enduring relationships between three positions: mother, father, child(ren). There is a level at which these relationships remain the same whichever particular individuals fill the positions. Similarly there are basic aspects of my relationship to my students which remain the same from year to year, although I teach different students each year.

A second feature of societies is that they possess what Bhaskar calls *'ontological depth'*—they have levels of existence beyond what lies on the surface, beyond what we can see, and these underlying levels are of special significance because they can explain what we see. There is an oft-quoted passage from Marx that makes the point well: 'all science would be superfluous if the outward appearances and essences of things directly coincided'.[1] There is nothing about the outward appearances of my desk that tells me it is made up of countless millions of molecules bouncing off each other. There are, I think, two evident senses in which a process of cause and effect is at work in societies. First an underlying set of social relationships, an underlying social structure, might be seen to cause some surface set of relationships; for example a Marxist might argue that the political arguments reported in the news each day are caused by underlying economic relationships, even if the arguments are not about economics. Second, an underlying structure might be such that it has certain laws or tendencies of development; for example there might be some mechanism in the underlying relationships of a capitalist society that causes it to go through regular economic crises, or causes increased state intervention in economic affairs.

Turning now to agents, Bhaskar argues that human action does not create society but either maintains or changes it in some way—this is the sense in which the two are not independent of each other. Societies do not 'determine' agents but they only survive and change through acting individuals. Bhaskar suggests a 'transformative' model of human action: societies provide the raw material, human beings act on it, and societies come out the other end. The crucial property of human action, as far as my argument here is concerned, is that it is *intentional*, it aims at achieving something. Bhaskar makes essentially the same point in a rather different way: human beings not only monitor their action (i.e., know what they are doing) but monitor the monitoring—they can reflect on what they know they are doing, assess it, make judgements and choices. In this respect, they are crucially different to societies, which are structures of social relationships.

An important point here is that there is no simple relationship between an agent's action and intention and its effect on society or a particular social relationship. A standard example, used by several writers, is that a person might marry because she is in love, wants to please her parents or wants to gain access to regular sexual relations. The effect of that action is to reproduce the enduring social relationships of the nuclear family. There is a reverse example. I might divorce my wife because I no longer love her, because I want to live with my mistress, because I don't like her or she doesn't like me. The effect on society is to contribute towards a kinship structure in which single parent families are as common as the 'normal' lasting nuclear family. Even when my actions are directly intended to change or preserve some aspect of social structure, the result is not automatic. For example, a Government might decide to reduce public expenditure, particularly on social services, to free money for private enterprise, assuming that flourishing private enterprise society provides better living conditions for all of its members. The result might be that since there is less money available to buy industry's products, an economic recession starts and many private enterprises collapse.

The social world then is made up of two distinct and different types of being, societies and agents. It will be remembered that I said that for Bhaskar epistemological questions depend upon ontological questions. In other words this has certain implications for theory.

HOW DO THEORIES EXPLAIN?

It should be apparent by now that I am suggesting that theory is *necessarily* fragmented in that we need different types of theory to explain different things. In suggesting this, I am going some way beyond Bhaskar and possibly pushing his ideas in a direction with which he would not be happy. But on the basis of his argument, I think it is possible to suggest that the explanations of features of social structure and the explanations of human actions have a different structure. I want now to try to outline these different types of explanation, and what I am doing in effect is elaborating on the idea of theory that I presented in the first chapter, filling in some of the processes of theoretical thinking.

The work of theory in relation to societies is to identify underlying structures of relationships and to do this, the first step is to employ analogy and metaphor. A society is *like* something else. We can find a series of metaphors throughout social theory; sometimes society is likened to a biological organism; Marxism employs the metaphor of a building, base and superstructure; symbolic interactionism perhaps employs that of a conversation. In some ways this is the most imaginative stage but it is followed by increasing precision. It is not just similarities that are important but differences as well, and as the theory develops so concepts emerge that have little to do with the original metaphor. It is not just a matter of specifying underlying structures, however, since the theory must offer an explanation—in other words, it must have some conception of cause.

A digression on the idea of a *cause* is necessary since in everyday life we tend to use it as if it were unproblematic: my broken leg was caused by a car crash; the cause of the break up of my marriage was my affair with my secretary; inflation is caused by high wages. A very different process is implied in each of these explanations and a significant difference between the two types of theory under consideration lies in the type of causal explanation that each offers. It is not sufficient for a theory to suggest that something causes something else; it must stipulate how that causal process works—for example, if a firm pays higher wages it must charge higher prices to cover costs, hence inflation. (I do not believe that this explanation is right, incidentally, but it is a useful example.)

In the case of societies, a *structural* notion of cause is implied. The cause is seen not as a single event or thing, but as residing in a particular arrangement of relationships. These relationships may be seen as framing or constituting a 'causal mechanism' (rather like a light switch, perhaps) which, when set in motion, produces certain results. The theory should also stipulate what sort of conditions will set the mechanism working, or alternatively whether it will work simply by virtue of the relationships that form it. This is a difficult idea to understand in abstract terms; there will be a number of examples in Part III, but to outline them properly would require elaborating a whole theory, which I do not want to do at this stage. Instead I will offer a couple of examples which have little to do with social structures but which I hope will get the general idea across.

The first comes from music. If we can set aside developments such as the twelve tone system, all popular and most classical music we hear in the Western world is based on a limited number of notes which could be learnt in the abstract in a very short time. All music is made of the same notes; what distinguishes between pieces of music, if you like what 'causes' different tunes, is the arrangement of the notes. As a second example, most of us have been involved in a close relationship with a parent or lover or friend that has 'gone wrong' for a period, or, perhaps, for ever. We can see the surface appearances, more or less bitter arguments, nagging irritability, feelings of unhappiness, emptiness, even despair. On reflection, if we can manage it, or later, when the feelings have subsided, we can admit that it is not the fault of either partner; it is the *relationship*, some lack of balance, some 'fault' in what goes on between the partners. It might be, for example, that the 'causal mechanism' lies in the relationship between my insecurity about my masculinity and my wife's suppressed rage, which in certain circumstances will create a bitter argument about who feeds the cat.

Turning now to agents, the theoretical explanation of how and why people act has an entirely different structure and a different notion of cause. Agents, remember, reflect on their actions, make decisions, have intentions. When we talk about the cause of an action in everyday life, we refer to a number of things, but the distinctive element is the agent's intention: the state of affairs that she hopes to bring about, what she wants to achieve. The technical term for this sort of explanation is teleological: the end point, the effect, is there at the beginning, in the form of a desire which must then be put into practice. The action is explained by its end result, in a sense, the effect is the cause. There is a great deal of debate about whether this is the right way of explaining actions or whether it is possible to construct some other more conventional causal explanation and it is not possible to sort out all the arguments in this context. In practice I think a teleological explanation is implied in all forms of social theory that have anything to say about action, and I do not think it could be otherwise. This is not the only difference: to understand an action properly is to understand forms of thinking, relationships between meanings in people's heads; in other words it involves an act of interpretation in which ideas such as structural causality and causal mechanism play no role. If we are trying to make sense of a particular passage in a book, for example, these notions are of no real help.

The question remains of how we know whether a theory is right or wrong (the crucial epistemological question). The simple answer is that we don't, but we can make judgements between more or less adequate explanations offered by a theory. Such judgements are not simple, they must involve a number of aspects that are different for the different types of theory; but we must always remember that we are living in a world in which there are no final answers. As the world itself changes and becomes a different place so the theory by means of which we understand it will change.

A number of criteria by which we can make the judgement in the case of theories of society suggest themselves from what I have already said. The better theory will be able to specify in more detail the causal processes at work and the situations in which causal mechanisms come into operation. Beyond this (on the side of what in the last chapter I referred to as 'general ideas') I think logical coherence is important—a theory which regularly contradicts itself must be regarded with suspicion. On the side of 'experience' a theory must in some way be measured against evidence. It is, I think, a feature of the social sciences that this cannot be done in any rigorous and systematic way but we can always discover features of experience that suggest that a theory ought to be revised or replaced by another theory. It might be that a theory suggests that something might happen which does not happen. Much modern Marxist theory for example has been devoted to revising the original system of thought to explain the absence of socialist revolution in North America and Western Europe. *Vice versa* something the theory suggests should not happen, does happen. It is rare that a theory must be rejected—rather it is usually a matter of revision and refinement, perhaps limiting its scope, and employing supplementary explanations. All the theories we will be looking at in this book seem to me to tell us something about the world; there are some clear examples in which one theory does something better than another but whatever their deficiencies, they all have some range of applicability.

Most of what I have said also goes for theoretical explanations of action. My points about logical coherence and the relationship to evidence can remain unchanged. Detailed specification of causal processes can be replaced by detailed specification of the interpretive processes of agents. The one additional criterion is that explanations on this level always remain rooted in agents experience whereas theoretical explanations of social relationships might contradict agents' experience and employ concepts which are not available to the agents themselves.

WHY DO THEORIES FRAGMENT?

I have suggested that social theory is necessarily fragmented along the lines I have been talking about (and perhaps along others as well—I will return to this shortly). But as it stands this does not provide us with a way of making sense of the confusion I discussed in the earlier parts of this chapter. It is not possible to allocate different theories to different 'objects'—some to societies, some to agents. This sort of division would have no more success than those suggested earlier on in the discipline's history (to some of which it bears some resemblance). Perhaps it ought to be possible to carry out such a division, and if we could do so, the frontiers of theoretical knowledge would be set by the problems of passing from one sort of explanation to another, of conceptualizing the nature of the links between agents and societies. However this is not the case, and these distinctions offer us an *in*direct way of making sense of the mess.

To begin with, they indicate a dilemma. Societies and agents are two different types of being requiring different types of explanation or understanding. To understand social reality, however, we have to understand *both*: societies would not remain in existence without agents and *vice versa*. Roy Bhaskar seems to try to avoid the problem by allocating different objects to different sciences: societies to sociology, agents to psychology, and the relationship between the two to social psychology. This seems to me to be a false division since each separate science requires the others to make any sense—just as their 'objects' require each other in order to be what they are. Such an inclusive, 'totalizing' theory seems to me to be implied in the very enterprise of sociology. However, for whatever reasons, it does not yet seem possible. Nevertheless, most of the theories we will be looking at have laid claims to being such a totalizing theory, and that is precisely why the process of fragmentation has taken place, or why they have been fragmented from the start. In effect they have tried to generalize a theory appropriate to one type of object in the social world to all types of objects. The result of this is to lead to very clear inadequacies in dealing with either agency or societies or both. This attempt to totalize and its results will be a major theme throughout the book.

I suggested earlier that theory might be fragmented along other lines. By this, I mean that it is conceivable, although I do not think it has yet been established, that there might be other forms of being in the social world. I have three particular possibilities in mind. The first involves structures of social relationships at the surface level, as opposed to underlying structures. These include what most sociologists talk about under the name of *institutions* and they seem to combine qualities of agency *and* social structures. A political party, for example, has intentions, it develops policies that it desires to implement when it gains power. At the same time it has features that we would attribute to social structures: it is comprised of more or less enduring relationships and it might be possible to identify underlying structures. The second example lies on the side of agents. It is conceivable that we can identify an 'ontological depth' of the agent: in other words, an unconscious. If we take Freud seriously, it would seem that the unconscious does not work in the same way as the conscious level. In both cases the form of theory we use, the way we construct theoretical explanations, might be different. I mention this as a possibility now but it will not play any great role in what follows; it is something which is suggested, I think, by certain developments in modern structuralist Marxism. Thirdly, and this will emerge in all three sections, it seems possible to identify a level of what I will call 'general meanings', ideas which, like language, exist over and above individuals, into which we are all socialized as we become members of society, but which are different again from societies. The chapter on structuralism in Part III will deal with this level.

The discussion of theoretical explanation in the case of societies points to another form of fragmentation which I referred to in the last chapter as the 'description' trap. An explanation ought to identify clearly the causal processes and mechanisms involved; a description does not do this. All theories work with *generalizations* and *analytic abstractions*. An analytic abstraction identifies common features of objects which enable us to put them in the same class irrespective of other differences; the resulting class is a generalization. For example, we can place all organisations that produce goods for sale on the market as economic organisations—'economic organisation' becomes a class of institution. If we look at another aspect of the same organisation, we might be able to classify it as a social organisation or a cultural organisation. Descriptive theory is concerned with setting up such general classifications and not with identifying causal mechanisms. Parsons' structural functionalism is the main example and these points will become clearer in the next chapter. For the moment it is sufficient to point out that without any account of causal processes and mechanisms, it is possible to make any one class more important than the others without any decisive reason to do so. It is also possible to develop the scheme of classification to take account of anything anyone might suggest. It is rather like a jigsaw puzzle where the pieces can be put together in any order, and sections added or taken away, without the final picture looking any more or less complete. It is in fact in its identification of causal processes, giving priority to one thing rather than another, that a theory gains its explanatory impact and forms a coherent whole.

CONCLUSION

I indicated earlier that this book will be organised around different schools or streams of theory. I think each can be seen as fragmented around one or both of the 'fault lines' I have just been discussing. Mainstream or traditional sociological theory, structural-functionalism, conflict theory, symbolic interactionism, are analytic and descriptive theories that share the same basic assumption: that the proper object of sociology is social action. They then tend to generalize descriptions of social action to descriptions of social structure. 'Structuralism', as its name implies, tends to do the opposite—generalize explanations of social structures to agents, and the real problems of the approach arise when it does so. Finally critical theory and hermeneutics tend to work in the same way as social action theories but they maintain some idea of social structure existing over and above individuals: the two are brought together, but only to fall apart again.

NOTES

[1]Marx, K. (1966), *Capital*, Vol. 3, Lawrence and Wishart, London, p. 817.

FURTHER READING FOR PART I

Types of social theory

Some sense of the recent history of social theory can be derived from the various arguments about types of theory; of the following list, the articles by Benton and Sklair try to push the debate towards a realist position. Dawe and Albrow provide the most accessible starting points.

Albrow, M. (1974), 'Dialectical and categorical paradigms of a science of society', *Sociological Review*, Vol. 22, No. 2, pp. 183–201.

Bandyopandhyay, P. (1971), 'One sociology or many: some issues in radical sociology', *Sociological Review*, Vol. 19, No. 1, pp. 5–29.

Benton, E. (1978), 'How many sociologies?', *Sociological Review*, Vol. 26, No. 2, pp. 217–36.

Birnbaum, N. (1971), 'Sociology: discontent, present and perennial', *Social Research*, Vol. 38, pp. 732–50.

Bottomore, T.B. (1975), 'Conservatism and radicalism in Sociology', in *Sociology as Social Criticism*, George Allen & Unwin, London, pp. 11–16.

Corrigan, P. (1975), 'Dichotomy vs. contradiction: on "Society as construct and construction". Remarks on the doctrine of the two sociologies', *Sociological Review*, Vol. 23, No. 2, pp. 211–43.

Dawe, A. (1971), 'Review of R. Friedrichs' *A Sociology of Sociology*', *Sociological Review*, Vol. 19, No. 1, pp. 140–47.

Dawe, A. (1970), 'The two sociologies', *British Journal of Sociology*, Vol. 21, pp. 207–18.

Friedrichs, R.W. (1972), *A Sociology of Sociology*, The Free Press, New York.

Friedrichs, R. (1972), 'Dialectical sociology: toward a resolution of the current 'crisis' in western sociology', *British Journal of Sociology*, Vol. 23, No. 3, pp. 263–74.

Sklair, L. (1975), 'Ideology and the sociological utopias', *Sociological Review*, Vol. 25, No. 1, pp. 51–72.

Worsley, P. (1974), 'The state of theory and the status of theory', *Sociology* Vol. 8, No. 1, pp. 1–18.

The affective and normative dimensions of theory

Alvin Gouldner's book is the classic; Oakley and Garnsey are critiques of social theory from a feminist perspective, the Blackburn collection from a Marxist perspective.

Blackburn, R. (ed.) (1972), *Ideology and Social Science*, Fontana, London.

Dawe, A. (1973), 'The role of experience in the construction of social theory: an essay in reflexive sociology, *Sociological Review*, Vol. 21, No. 1, pp. 25–55.

Garnsey, E. (1978), 'Women's work and theories of class stratification', *Sociology*, Vol. 12, pp. 223–43.

Gouldner, A.W. (1971), *The Coming Crisis of Western Sociology*, Heinemann, London.
Oakley, A. (1974), *The Sociology of Housework*, Martin Robertson, London, Chapter 1.

The social and natural sciences: realism

Most of the reading in this section is quite difficult. Keat and Urry's *Social Theory as Science* provides the most accessible survey of the arguments. Of Bhaskar's work, *The Possibility of Naturalism*, Chapters 2 and 3, are particularly important and rather more accessible than the rest of his work. The debates in Lakatos and Musgrave illustrate a range of alternative positions.

Benton, E. (1977), *Philosophical Foundations of the Three Sociologies* Routledge & Kegan Paul, London.
Benton, E. (1981), 'Realism and social science', *Radical Philosophy*, No. 27, pp. 13–21.
Bhaskar, R. (1979), *The Possibility of Naturalism*, Harvester Press, Hassocks.
Bhaskar, R. (1978), *A Realist Theory of Science*, Harvester Press, Hassocks, 2nd edn.
Bhaskar, R. (1980), 'Scientific explanation and human emancipation', *Radical Philosophy*, No. 26, pp. 16–28.
Harre, R. and Madden, E.H. (1975), *Causal Powers*, Basil Blackwell, Oxford.
Keat, R. and Urry, J. (1975), *Social Theory as Science*, Routledge & Kegan Paul, London.
Kuhn, T. (1970), *The Structure of Scientific Revolutions*, Chicago University Press, 2nd edn.
Lakatos, I. and Musgrave, A. (eds) (1970), *Criticism and the Growth of Knowledge*, Cambridge University Press.
Sayer, A. (1981), 'Abstraction: a realist interpretation', *Radical Philosophy*, No. 28, pp. 6–15.
Thomas, D. (1979), *Naturalism and Social Science*, Cambridge University Press.
Urry, J. (1973), 'Kuhn as a sociologist of knowledge', *British Journal of Sociology*, Vol. 24, pp. 462–73.

Some more recent surveys of social theory and its problems

The items listed below are by no means easy reading.

Bernstein, R. (1976), *The Restructuring of Social and Political Theory*, Basil Blackwell, Oxford.
Boudon, R. (1980), *The Crisis in Sociology: Problems of Sociological Epistemology*, Macmillan, Basingstoke.
Giddens, A. (1979a), *New Rules of Sociological Method*, (Hutchinson, London.
Giddens, A. (1979b), *Central Problems in Social Theory*, Macmillan, Basingstoke.

Part II
THEORIES OF SOCIAL ACTION

Introduction to Part II

Part II will be concerned with theories of social action—or persons or agents. Of course, it will be a general mapping rather than a detailed exposition, taking in structural-functionalism, conflict theory, symbolic interactionism, phenomenological sociology and ethnomethodology. Of these, I will devote more space to the structural-functionalism of Talcott Parsons than to any of the others. Parsons' work dominated social theory for several decades and without doubt he is the most sophisticated and comprehensive theorist of this tradition. It will become apparent that the other approaches are in various ways fragments of the Parsonian system, despite the fact that they are often opposed to it. The lines of fragmentation are those I traced in Chapter 2. All these approaches generalize, implicitly or explicitly, a form of theory appropriate to persons to account for societies. In so doing each comes to suffer from a number of weaknesses to which one of the others may appear as a solution. We can move round from one to the other for as long as we care, without breaking out of the circle. Furthermore they all remain analytic, and mainly descriptive theories. Since they do not assign distinct causal priorities, or identify clear causal processes, it is always possible to emphasise one aspect of a theory against others without providing any conclusive reason for doing so. Parsons' system can thus be seen as a seedbed for its opponents, who are unable to break away from it.

3 Parsons: theory as a filing system

INTRODUCTION

Talcott Parsons dominated English language social theory from the end of World War II until the mid-1960s. He produced an immense theoretical framework that claimed on principle to be capable of embracing everything, and the basis of the system was laid during the economic crises of the 1930s. Alvin Gouldner, in *The Coming Crisis of Western Sociology*, argues that in fact it was developed as a response to the challenge of Marxism: whereas Marxism was a general theory of society which condemned capitalism, structural-functionalism was to become a general theory of society which did not so much justify capitalism (although it often did) as offer an explanation and understanding of its difficulties without condemning it. As we shall see, this is achieved by seeing difficulties as part of an evolutionary process leading to greater stability and integration. Perhaps luckily for Parsons, capitalism responded in an appropriate way after World War II and the period during which Parsons dominated sociology corresponds with the period of comparative stability and economic expansion. Both the theory and capitalism began to run into difficulties again in the late 1960s, and as I indicated in the introduction to Part II, very little work is now carried on directly in the Parsonian tradition. The approach however retains its interest for what it teaches us about theory and there does seem to be an unofficial revival of interest under way. It is notoriously difficult to understand — I would suggest, because of its complication rather than its profundity. Reading him, I am sometimes made to think of a filing clerk who is too intelligent for his work. To exercise his intelligence and overcome his frustration, he develops a new and complicated system which has a place for every document ever used by his firm. The problem is that he is the only person who can work it, and without him, nothing can be found.

In his early work Parsons set out to bring together the different streams of nineteenth- and early twentieth-century social thought into one comprehensive synthesis. There are still debates about the accuracy of his interpretations and critics frequently point out that he barely mentioned Marx. For our present purposes the most important feature of the synthesis is that is brings together 'holistic' and 'individualistic' theories of social action. These are approaches associated with the names of Durkheim and Weber, respectively, amongst the founding fathers of sociology. For Weber sociology should be concerned with the actions of individuals directed towards each other (i.e., social action). Such action can be seen as sets of means employed to achieve particular goals—practical purposes or the realisation of some ultimate value or a combination of both. Such action must be understood in terms of the meanings which individuals give to it. Durkheim was also concerned with meanings, but he saw the most important meanings as having an existence over and above individuals. They comprised a 'collective conscience' into which individuals had to be socialized. Thus both are concerned with meanings—with peoples' ideas, but one starts with the individual, one with the social whole. Both are theories of ideas and actions—of persons.

Here we can find the main themes of Parsons. First, he sees the social world in terms of peoples' ideas, particularly their norms and values. Norms are the socially accepted rules which people employ in deciding on their actions; values can best be described as their beliefs about what the world should be like, and they too have a determining effect on peoples' actions. The most important social processes are seen as the communication of meaning, of symbols and information. Secondly, he is concerned with the organisation of individual actions into systems of action, with employing the holistic and individualistic approaches at the same time.

The idea of a system gives us the crucial analogy or metaphor in Parsons theory: that of the biological organism or living system. He pushes this further than a simple analogy: he does not stop at saying that social life is like a living system, he says that it *is* a living system of a particular type. The problem with this will emerge later but it is fair to say that it is always dangerous to push an analogy too far: there is a world of difference between saying that 'My love is like a red, red rose' and saying that 'My love *is* a red, red rose'. The idea of social life as a system—a network of different parts—explains the 'structural' part of the structural-functionalist label that is usually attached to Parsons' work. The analogy with a biological system explains the 'functionalist' part. If we take the human body as a system, it can be seen as having certain needs, for example food, and a number of inter-related parts (the digestive system, the stomach, the intestines etc.) which function to meet those needs. A social system of action is seen by Parsons as having needs which must be met if it is to survive and a number of parts which function to meet those needs. All living systems are seen as tending towards equilibrium, a stable and balanced relationship between the different parts, and maintaining themselves separately from other systems (a tendency to 'boundary maintenance').

Parsons' emphasis is always on stability and order and indeed he sees social theory as attempting to answer the question 'How is social order possible?'—a problem named after the philosopher Thomas Hobbes, who formulated it in its clearest form. It presupposes that in the 'natural state' human beings are entirely self-seeking, that there is a war of all against all, and this natural tendency has to be moulded and limited by social organisation.

THE GRAND THEORY

Parsons' idea of theory

Parsons describes himself as an 'incurable theorist'; certainly his style conveys the sense of a terminal case. He has a particular idea of what a theory is and this explains some of the difficulty. The world that we can see is confused and confusing and to make sense of it, we must use our general ideas to organise it. Assuming that the real world is a system, then the first step is to organise our general ideas into a systematic and ordered body of abstract concepts. Only after we have done that will we be able to make propositions about the world. An abstract concept is a generalization which emphasises something important about the world. Such concepts abound in everyday life. The concept of 'red' for example, can be seen as an abstraction from all red things that we see around us. Now the logical ordering of abstract concepts is not the same thing as talking about the world we can see around us and if this is kept in mind then Parsons becomes marginally easier to read.

From Parsons' point of view the first test for such a theory is its logical coherence. If it is, as he intends, a logically coherent theory of social science then it should bring together all that we already know about the social world, and much of his work is concerned with translating other theories and research results into his own terms, to show that they fit. The assumption is one we will meet again: that despite appearances the social world is organised in a logical, rational way, and a logical, rational theory is therefore most likely to be right. Eventually, this can be confirmed by developing, from the theory, testable propositions but that stage is some way off.

The unit act and the system of action: institutionalization

In *the Structure of Social Action*, published in 1937, Parsons argued that all the major theorists he examined could be seen as moving towards what he called a 'voluntaristic theory of action', in which human beings were conceived of as making choices about, deciding between, different goals and means to achieve them. Such a conception could be the foundation of all the human sciences, and he suggested that it was possible to distil from their work a basic model of human action, defining in abstract terms all of its components. This model comprises first the human actor and second a range of goals or ends between which the actor must choose, and different means by which these ends may be reached—again the actor having to choose between them. However, the choices are not made in a vacuum. The environment is made up of a number of physical and social factors which limit the range of choices; for example, my eyesight is not good enough to enable me to become an airline pilot and in the current economic situation I cannot choose to be an engineer because no engineering jobs are available. Most important of all, the environment includes generally accepted norms and values and other ideas which influence our choice of goals and means. If I am a Roman Catholic and a gynaecologist I will not specialize in abortion, even if the option is open to me; similarly I am not able to break the informal rules that govern relationships with my colleagues (e.g., about attendance at the university) without suffering punitive criticism. The most formal and universal norms are set out in a society's legal system—I always have the option of murdering my students when they hand in late work, but I am unlikely to take it, not only because I think it is morally wrong, but because there is a likelihood of severe punishment.

The 'unit act', then, is made up of an actor, means, goals, and an environment which comprises physical and social objects and norms and values. This is an abstract description of all action and the starting point of Parsons' immense scheme, most of which can be unravelled from here. The task of the social scientist is to make sense of the ways choices are made within the constraints I have just discussed. Now Parsons is not just concerned with individual action but with systems of action and as his theory developed so did his idea of a system. Amongst the social objects in the actors' environment are other actors and for Parsons a system of action is made up of relationships between actors. The emphasis of Parsons' work here changes from voluntarism, from looking at the individual actors' choices, to looking at the way systems of action limit and even determine individual choices. This has been the focus for a number of criticisms to which I will return later. For the moment, I want to look at the way in which Parsons develops the idea of the unit act to a conception of the *social system*. This is built up around the norms and values that, together with other actors, make up part of the actors' environment. He assumes that each actor aims for maximum gratification, and if she engages in interaction with another and receives gratification, the action will be repeated. Each actor will come to expect certain responses from the other and so social rules or norms will develop, together with generally accepted values, which help to guarantee the responses. A simple example would be a love affair which develops into a marriage. As the partners gain gratification from each other so they come to expect each other to continue to act in the way which supplies gratification. The marriage will develop its own informal, and perhaps even formal, rules of behaviour. Each may come to expect the other to tolerate minor adulteries, or to share equally in the household chores and each will come to regard it as an obligation. Both may come to believe in the 'sanctity of marriage' although before the wedding, both may have laughed at the idea.

Reverting to Parsons' terminology, a system of 'status roles' develops—a network of positions to which expectations of behaviour (and rewards and sanctions for fulfilling or not fulfilling the expectations) are attached. This process is called *institutionalization*—a solidifying of relationships over time in such a way that the behaviour attached to each status role remains constant whoever is occupying it. Society as a whole, and different institutions in society, may be considered as a network of status roles, each governed by established norms and values.

The social system is not the only system contained in embryonic form in the unit act. The description of the process of institutionalization and the development of the social system which I have just described presupposes three other systems. It presupposes an actor who aims for maximum gratification (i.e., a personality system); it presupposes, as far as society as a whole is concerned, a system of wider values which give coherence to the different norms attached to different status roles (i.e., a cultural system); and it presupposes a physical environment to which society must adapt (i.e., a biological organism). This is where the filing-system requires at least sixty-four new filing cabinets. I will not bother with all of them.

Systems and subsystems: functional prerequisites

For Guy Rocher, Parsons' theory is like 'a set of Chinese boxes—when one is opened, it contains a smaller one, which contains a smaller one still, and so on'.[1] This is an apt description. I said earlier that Parsons' concepts—unit act, status roles, social system etc.—were abstractions, and there are different levels of abstraction. Going back to the example of red, there is a higher-level abstraction ('colour') of which red is one type, lower-level abstractions (dark red, light red, pink etc.) and lower-lower-level abstractions, which involve adding other qualities (dark red and round). The process can be continued until we are describing a unique object (the dark red round rubber object of six inches in diameter on the floor in front of me—in other words 'this ball'). There is here an insight into the difficulty of Parsons' theory—much of it is equivalent to describing this ball as 'the dark red... etc.'.

By talking about the development of status roles and the social system, we have arrived somewhere above the middle level of abstraction. It is possible to distinguish at least the following levels:

1   The highest level: all living systems. Sometimes Parsons writes as if living systems are a subsystem of *all* systems (i.e., everything), but that is not important for our present purposes.

2 Second-highest level: systems of action, including everything in the unit act.
3 Third-highest level: the subsystems of action; the personality, cultural, biological and social systems.
4 Fourth-highest level: subsystems of subsystems. The subsystems of the social system are the political system, the socialization system, the economy and the 'societal community' (I will explain this shortly).
5 Fifth level: subsystems of subsystems of subsystems. The most clearly worked out at this level level belong to the economy: the economic commitments subsystem, the capitalization subsystem, the production subsystem, the organisational subsystem.

Presumably the process could go on *ad infinitum*, but I will concern myself only with levels 3 and 4. The first question to ask is why at each stage we find four new subsystems, and the answer brings Parsons' functionalism into play. He argues that any system, at whatever level, must satisfy four needs or requirements if it is to survive and in each case a specialist subsystem is developed to meet each requirement. The four requirements or *functional prerequisites* are as follows:

1 Each system must adapt to its environment (*adaptation*).
2 Each system must have a means of mobilizing its resources in order to achieve its goals and thus obtain gratification (*goal attainment*).
3 Each system must maintain the internal co-ordination of its parts and develop ways of dealing with deviance—in other words, it must keep itself together (*integration*).
4 Each system must maintain itself as nearly as possible in a state of equilibrium—the examples below and later should distinguish this from 3 above; (*pattern maintenance*).

Table 1 shows which subsystem fulfils which functional prerequisite for the general system of action and the social system.

To sum up: the unit act contains in embryonic form four subsystems which can be seen as developing through a process of institutionalization; each subsystem has further subsystems of its own. At each level, the subsystems develop to meet four needs or functional pre-requisites which must be met if the system is to survive.

Table 1 Subsystems fulfilling functional pre-requisites

Major system	Adaptation	Goal attainment	Integration	Pattern maintenance
The general system of action (described in the 'unit act')	The *biological organism*, which provides the link between the physical world and the meanings (norms values etc) that make up the world of action	The *Personality system*, which is formed by socialization in such a way that it internalizes general cultural values and societal norms. It thus becomes the instrument through which the major system achieves its goals	The *social system* of status roles governed by norms which define which actions are or are not allowable	The *cultural system*—the most general ideas, ideals and values of the major system, made more concrete in the norms of the social system and internalized in the personality system
The social system	The *economy*, the link between social organisation and the physical world or nature	The *political system*—including *all* forms of decision making and resource mobilization	The *'societal community'*—the institutions of social control—ranging from the legal system to informal rules of conduct	The *socialization processes*, by means of which individuals are educated into the cultural values and societal norms of the system.

It is more important to get the general idea of all this rather than the detail.

Ways of analysing action—the pattern variables

Before moving on to look at how all this works, I want to deal briefly with one other set of variables—what Parsons calls the *pattern variables*. These illustrate even more emphatically the classifying power of his thought—on my tentative calculation, we now need 512 filing cabinets and we have not reached the lowest level of abstraction and no information about the real world has yet been collected. More importantly they bring together two different concerns in his work: the voluntaristic theory of action, concerned with individual choices, and systems theory. Both individual actions and system organisation can be seen as choosing between alternatives; remember, from the original discussion of the unit act, that all action involves choice. There are four major pairs of alternatives:

1 Particularism–universalism: I may treat an object as a specific, unique object or as one of a general class—the difference between the way I treat my children and my students.
2 Affective – affectively neutral: I may allow the full range of my feeling to come into play in a relationship (my children) or I might maintain neutral feelings (my students).
3 Quality – performance: I might value an object for its own sake (my children) or for what can be done with it, its instrumental potentiality (my students).
4 Diffuseness – specificity: I might be involved in a total re-lationship to all aspects of an object (my children) or I might be concerned with only one activity in the relationship (my students).

From the examples there is an evident tendency for clusters to develop—particularism, affectivity, quality orientation and diffus-ness tend to go together, as do the opposites but this is by no means necessary (thus adding yet again to the different combinations). It is also a matter of degree—for example, I am emotionally involved with my students but not as much as with my children.

This is as far as I want to go in elaborating the filing system as such; the pattern variables will not re-appear until I discuss the criticisms that can be made of structural-functionalism. I have included them because they illustrate certain important features of Parsons' theory.

For the time being I want to return to systems and the relationships between them.

The cybernetic hierarchy

I said in the Introduction to Part II that Parsons' theory of social action is also a theory of meanings—of norms, values, symbols and communication. For Parsons the various systems are related through the exchange of symbolic information. A symbol is seen as something not valuable in itself but because of what can be done with it. Money is the clearest example: a coin is near to worthless as a metal object, it is only valuable because we can use it to buy things. Each subsystem of the social system has its equivalent symbol: the economy itself deals in money, the political system in power, in the societal community it is influence, and in the socialisation system, commitment. Through exchanging symbolic resources each system remains in equilibrium with the others, whilst maintaining its own identity—maintaining its boundaries.

There is more than this to the exchanges between systems, however. Here we go back to the analogy between systems of action and all living systems, in fact *all* systems, because Parsons draws on cybernetics—the science of systems. This suggests that any system is controlled by that subsystem which is highest on information and lowest on energy and we can thus construct an hierarchy of subsystems, the lowest being that which has most energy but least information. Parsons himself provides the useful example of a washing machine in which the controlling timing mechanism, which has a great deal of programmed information, uses very little energy

Table 2

The general system of action		The social system
The cultural system	High on information	The socialization system
The social system	High on information	The societal community
The personality system	High on energy	The political system
The biological organism	High on energy	The economic system

(electricity) compared with the working parts it controls. Thus the lower subsystems push energy up through the system, the higher controlling subsystems pass information back down. We can thus order the different subsystems described in Table 1 in the manner shown in Table 2.

This ordering of systems, together with the postulate that all systems tend towards equilibrium, does—finally—enable us to approach the real world and organise it to some effect. We can put the filing system to work. I have not described it in anything like its full complexity—a number of the subsystems that I have only mentioned are analysed in much greater detail by Parsons, and there are other aspects to the theory. However, I hope I have dealt with sufficient aspects to convey a general idea of the enterprise without causing too many nervous breakdowns.

Structural-functionalist explanations—some brief examples
In both these examples, I will be using the term 'explain' loosely; it will emerge later that the ability of Parsons' system to explain rather than describe is a major issue for its critics.

The explanation of historical change Here Parsons draws again on the analogy with biological organisms, this time on the way a cell divides and multiplies. Most people will have seen at some time a film taken through a microscope of a cell dividing into two and then four and so on. For Parsons, the development of human society can be seen in the same way. Simple societies can be seen as the single cell, which divides first into the four subsystems of the general system of action and then in turn each of these divides. The process involves three stages: the new subsystem differentiates itself, the new arrangement goes through a process of adaptation and reintegration, and finally there is the establishment of a more general system of values at the highest cybernetic level—a system of values which embraces the new subsystem.

A more specific example can be taken from Parsons himself: the transition from agriculture-based peasant societies to industrial societies. This involves the separation of the economic from the socialization system. Whereas in pre-industrial societies the family unit was also the main unit of production, the family holding and working the land together albeit with some division of labour, industrialization separated work into factories and offices whilst family life became confined to the home. For this separation to be successful, Parsons argues that it must have greater adaptive capacity: work is carried out more efficiently and rationally in the new industrial units and productivity increases, whilst the family fulfils its socialization functions more efficiently when it is stripped of its economic functions. The process of integration involves the co-ordination of the two subsystems (presumably such developments as the laws prohibiting women and children from certain occupations) and the development of a new economic hierarchy of control since the father of the family no longer fulfils that role.[2] Both subsystems must be integrated into the wider societal and political communities and finally the value system must develop to include the new status roles, the father stripped of some previous power, the new industrial managers and so on.

Youth sub-cultures Secondly I want to look briefly at an article Parsons wrote in 1961 on American youth and youth sub-cultures[3] as it is a good illustration of the way in which structural-functionalism deals with change and conflict. In general terms he argues that the twentieth century is a period of remarkable historical change and there are reasons why youth in particular should experience the strains of such change. The strains are seen in terms of *anomie*—a state in which values and norms are no longer clear or have lost their relevance. The explanation begins with the cultural: a paradoxical feature of the American value system is that at its centre is the value of individual success and achievement. The paradox is that in the pursuit of this value, structural differentiation is hastened, society becomes more complex more quickly, and lower level value patterns become outdated. At the same time increased complexity means that individual achievement has to be limited by specialization and co-operation.

There are various ways in which youth is made problematic by this process. Training and education takes a much longer time, so during the period when they might once have moved into adulthood, youth is kept dependent on the family, despite the fact that at the centre of their lives are people of the same age outside the family, the 'peer group'. The increased specialization has isolated the nuclear family and young children are thus made more dependent on it and this can create problems later when it is time to begin leaving the family. Traditional ties are weakened by the increased complexity of social relations and this is reflected in changes in sexual behaviour, where the contrast with traditional values is most marked.

Although youth sub-cultures are much more dramatic and well established, and the conflict more intense than when he was writing, much of what he had to say then can be speculatively extended to the present. Such sub-cultures have destructive and progressive functions. On the one hand they can be simply rebellious, rejecting traditional values and the central value system and offering nothing in their place. They can also be means by which the traditional value systems are transformed and brought up to date and new values established, and they provide social support for the individual in the long period when she has outgrown her own family but is not in a position to form a family of her own. Most youth sub-cultures in fact display both aspects, and both are likely to entail conflict.

Thus change and conflict is explained in terms of continuing evolutionary adjustment of different subsystems to each other. This explanation involves relations between the cultural, social (structural) and personality systems, the explanation finding its starting point at the cultural level and its centre in the adjustments to change generated at that level.

CRACKS IN THE GRAND THEORY

I said earlier that Parsons developed the most comprehensive and worked out form of action theory, and there is a sense in which the other variants may be seen as fragments broken off his system. Now I want to look at the main fault lines along which this fragmentation occurs. Many critics distinguish between logical and substantive problems with the theory but I do not think this is very helpful: a logical problem in a theory's explanation is also a sign that it misconceives what it is trying to explain.

Here I will concentrate on the imaginative or creative aspect of the theory, the employment of the biological systems analogy, on the generalization from action (persons) to system (societies) and the explanatory power of the theory.

Structural-functionalism as Utopia: the problems of conflict and change

Conflict theorists in particular often argue that Parsons' model of social life, with its emphasis on equilibrium, balanced exchange and functional relationships, cannot make sense of social change and conflict. Dahrendorf likens it to a literary Utopia, a vision of a perfectly good or perfectly bad society; Orwell's *1984* is probably the best known example of the latter. It is a world of balance, with no sense of history and without any source of change inside the society; it shows every sign of staying exactly as it is for an indefinite period. Any hiccup or deviation from what is normal is accidental or comes from outside. Such criticism is frequently extended to argue that the theory has an in-built conservative bias: inequalities of wealth (social stratification) are seen as functional, an efficient way of keeping the system going, as are differences in status; power is distributed in the way most functional for achieving the system's goals; everything is perfect.

I deliberately employed the examples of historical change and youth sub-cultures to illustrate that this sort of criticism is misguided, although I think it does point to a real problem. Because systems have a tendency towards equilibrium and balance, it does not follow that they are always in or close to that state. We are dealing with a complex network of evolving systems, always in a process of adjusting to each other and that must inevitably involve change, disruption and conflict. It is certainly possible to develop Parsonian theory in a way that makes it more able to take account of these phenomena. Robert Merton, the second most prominent functionalist thinker or the 1950s, made a number of contributions to dealing with this problem. He argued that the emphasis on functional unity and equilibrium tends to direct attention away from questions about the *degree* of unity and equilibrium and the processes by which they come about. He also made important distinctions between manifest and latent functions (similar to that between intended and unintended consequences) and function and dysfunction (the opposite of function), both of which can be deployed to make sense of change and conflict. Alvin Gouldner, who is by no means a functionalist, pointed out that system integration may involve anything from complete dependence of the parts on each other to comparative independence. Both writers tended towards a less general level of theorizing than Parsons. Merton called it middle-range theory, dealing with different parts of the system rather than the system as a whole. Finally, Lewis Coser in *The Functions of Social Conflict*, argues that the occurrence of social conflict can be seen as having a vital integrating effect through releasing tension and setting in motion a chain of adjustments; this is along the same lines as the youth culture example.

There is, however, a way in which the criticism points to a real problem. The creative or imaginative aspect of the theory lies in its use of metaphor—social systems are like biological systems. Parsons however pushes this to an extreme which I pointed out earlier—social systems are a type of living system. There seems to me to be no reason to push the metaphor this far; to do so is to make an unjustified metaphysical assumption about the nature of the world and I think it does serve to direct attention away from things like conflict and change. Both Merton and Gouldner can be seen as developing the metaphor further, to the stage of drawing distinctions and identifying differences between social systems and other living systems. Functionalist explanations that fail to do this, and in practice there are many, certainly tend towards conservative bias (and as Gouldner has pointed out, especially in the case of Parsons, this is reinforced by the social position of the theorist), but it is not a necessary part of structural-functionalist theory. There is an important lesson for theoretical thinking here: metaphors and analogies serve to draw attention not only to similarities but to differences, and the latter are as important as the former.

Teleological and functional explanations

There is another aspect to the failure of structural-functionalism, at least in Parsons' theory, to explore the differences between biological, living systems: it results precisely in a generalization of a theory of persons to a theory of societies. Persons are, amongst other things, biological organisms; it does not automatically follow that the same is true of societies. There are a number of common criticisms of Parsons that boil down to this. One way of putting all of them is that the theory does not generate testable propositions about the world; this might be true but as I have pointed out before, this is not the only criterion by which theories can be judged, and in the case of the social world, complexity and the inability to experiment makes the formation of testable hypotheses very difficult. However, there is rather more to each of the three criticisms I am concerned with.

First of all, remember that Parsons proposes that social systems have needs which must be met if they are to survive. His critics argue that in practice this is meaningless. To establish that it is the case, we would need examples of societies which did not survive and we would have to show that they did not meet all the functional requisites. Now excluding very simple societies, it is difficult to find an example. It seems that what usually happens is that a society less well adapted to its environment is absorbed through military or economic conquest by a better-adapted society. It does not disappear but remains, perhaps in a modified form as part of the better-adapted society. Thus some native American tribes were wiped out by military conquest but others remain today as a clearly identifiable part of American society. The difference between those wiped out and those which survived seems to depend as much on the political processes of the conquering whites than anything else; and the sense in which those that remain have 'survived' is itself debatable. An even clearer example is the way in which peasant agriculture in South and Latin America has been integrated into the industrial system of North America and Europe. In fact the Parsonian position would be tenable only if different societies were like different animal species battling for survival: only the fittest would survive.

Second, the critics argue that to say that a social system has needs does not explain how those needs are met. It might be true for example that modern industrial societies need complicated educational systems (although at the time of writing the British Government seem determined to prove this wrong). Yet Britain, France and America, all societies at approximately the same evolutionary stage, have different education systems. A need can be met in any number of ways and simply stating its existence does not explain anything about how it is met.

Third, it is often argued that to explain the existence of something by the function it fulfils is to make a nonsense of the idea of cause. A function is not fulfilled until something exists. If the function is the cause of its existence then the effect—existence—must come before the cause—the function. In other words, time seems to be reversed.

I said that the first criticism would not apply if social systems were like animal species. The second and third would not apply if social systems really were like individual actors. If a social system had sense organs that could experience the need for, say, an education system like the body can experience hunger; if the experience could be communicated to a system brain, translated into symbolic thought, pondered and analysed; if the social brain could decide what sort of education system it wants and then transmit the appropriate messages along its nervous system so that an education system were constructed, then—and only then—would these criticisms not apply. But social systems do not have needs and goals like individuals.

The difference is that the human organism is made up of parts which are not capable of independent reflective thought and which are controlled by a part that is. It is only in *Peanuts* cartoons that the stomach argues with the feet and the tail demands higher status. Social systems are—according to Parsons himself—made up of parts which are capable of reflective thought as they occupy their status roles; the organic link is very different to that between parts of the body. Yet the implication that a social system is consequently different from other living systems is not taken up.

Material and normative interests

Here I want to draw on two papers by David Lockwood written during the period when Parsons was the dominant figure in sociology, and which in the present context emphasise the difference between persons and societies by pointing to features of the social world which exist but which cannot be understood by structural-functionalism.

I have emphasised throughout that at the centre of Parsons' theory are meanings—norms and values, around which the action system and the social system are organised. Lockwood suggests that there is another factor at work in social life, what he calls the 'material substratum':

...the factual disposition of means in the situation of action which structures differential (life-chances) and produces interests of a non-normative kind—that is interests other than those which actors have in conforming with the normative definition of the situation.[4]

Thus social life is structured by peoples' access to goods and property and the life which goes with the possession of goods and property. For example it is possible to argue that the distribution of property (including skills) is such in both Britain and the USA that blacks have different material interests to whites. The white material interest might be in maintaining a system of racial discrimination which keeps blacks out of certain types of jobs, and this might outweigh adherence to a core system of social values which includes racial equality. Similarly it might be suggested, with some evidence in support, that people go to work not because they adhere to a system of norms and values that says work is a good thing but because they have a material interest—at the lowest level, that of not starving. Think about it: why do *you* work?

In a second article, Lockwood distinguishes between what he calls *social* integration, which is a matter of relationships between actors, and *system* integration,[5] relationships between different parts of the system. We can talk about societies manifesting social or normative integration, but not manifesting system integration. An economic crisis, for example, may certainly be taken as an indication of a system imbalance, a lack of integration; however it may still be the case that people adhere to the values and norms of the society despite the economic hardship that they suffer. We can add to this the idea of material interests and it becomes apparent that the normative system may be used to achieve certain material interests. It may be in the material interests of large business corporations to reduce the taxes they pay, necessitating cuts in government expenditure on social services. The central normative and value system, which for example may involve a strong belief in private enterprise and the absence of state interference, may persuade those who suffer from the cuts that the cuts are justified, and even that their suffering is their own fault.

Parsons' theory, and structural-functionalism in general, seem to me incapable of grasping such eventualities despite the fact that they are immediately plausible. It can only see social life as a normative and value controlled system, not as also a 'material' system. To do that, to make a distinction between social and system integration, it is necessary to make a distinction between persons and societies.

Can structural-functionalism explain?

When I gave some examples of structural-functionalist explanation I said I was using the term 'explain' loosely. I have indicated some problems with functional explanation, and now I want to suggest that by its very nature the theory is descriptive rather than explanatory. This is indicated by the possibility of writing out vast complicated passages of Parsons' work and then rewriting them in commonsense language, adding to the clarity and not losing any ideas and taking up a few lines. C. Wright Mills does this brilliantly in *The Sociological Imagination*. It seems to me that this is possible because of the very meaning Parsons gives to theory—we break everything down into its component parts and then add them together: 'this ball' becomes the dark, red, round rubber object on the floor. My relationship with my employer is particularistic, affectively negative, performance-oriented and specific: I don't like her, but I'm having an affair with her in the hope of promotion.

If an explanation involves identifying causal processes and causal mechanisms, then the theory cannot explain. Its concepts—systems, subsystems etc.—are abstractions; causal processes and mechanisms are real. If you go back to my earlier 'explanations' I think it should be clear that they are really elaborate descriptions with an element of explanation provided by the idea of a cybernetic hierarchy and a process of evolution attached to it. It might be said that Parsons is a 'cultural determinist' as opposed to Marx's economic determinism. On closer examination, however, even this is ambiguous. Wolf Heydebrand points out that the flow is two way: energy from below, information from above, and both could be regarded as determining or causing. Taking Heydebrand's example of the police force: this must be geared to enforcing the cultural values and social norms of a society (i.e., controlled from above). At the same time its very existence depends upon an economic system which produces suf-ficient to keep a police force in existence. We cannot assign any causal priority.

I think this throws light on another criticism of Parsons already touched on several times: that as his theory develops, it changes from an individualist theory, talking about actors' choices as in the model of the unit act, to a holistic one, dealing with the way systems determine actors' choices. The vast majority of his ideas and most of his work has been concerned with systems rather than individuals and the criticism is usually made from the point of view of an action theory which concentrates on individual action and interaction. However, I do not think it is justified. He deals with both, and the importance of the pattern variables, the reason I listed them earlier, is that they enable him to deal with both. However, he cannot do so at the same time—he must switch from one point of view to the other—and this is precisely what the different variants of action theory do: structural-functionalism and conflict theory are con-cerned in different ways with systems of action; symbolic inter-actionism and more recent variants with individual interactions. Parsons cannot give priority to one or the other; in one sense, the system is the individual writ large, in another, the individual is the system writ small. No causal priority is, or can be assigned. Consequently it is possible for variants of action theory to emphasise either side over the other, and indeed for Parsons to do the same at different stages in his career.

A BRIEF CONCLUSION

All these criticisms, together with external political developments have left Parsons' system looking like a dinosaur, albeit one rather reluctant to die. Despite my comments, I think this is a pity. The system is in many ways a lesson in the activity of theorizing and its dangers. Beyond this, however, it does emphasise the large-scale systematic aspects of social existence which have come to all but disappear from currently popular forms of action theory. And above all, it has a strong claim to provide, potentially, an understanding of one realm of social existence. In Chapter 2 I mentioned an 'intermediate realm', an area of reality which displayed features of persons and societies. Organizations such as political parties, religious groups, some business enterprises, can be seen as having an independent existence and as possessing aspects of human action—goals, norms and values which unite the people involved. It might be possible to understand these organizations as forms of biological systems, and to identify with some precision the functional pre-requisites, examples which disappear because they do not fulfil the pre-requisites, the processes by which they are fulfilled, mechanisms of adjustment and integration and so on. In other words, there are occasions when groups of human beings acting together (not whole societies) can be likened to other living systems, including individual human organisms, without the dangers and inadequacies I have been discussing.

NOTES

[1] Rocher, G. (1974), *Talcott Parsons and American Sociology*, Nelson, London, p. 47.
[2] As far as I know Parsons only mentions the second of these.
[3] Parsons, T. (1964), 'Youth in the context of American society', in *Social Structure and Personality*, The Free Press, Glencoe.
[4] Lockwood, D. (1967), 'Some remarks on *The Social System*', in Demereth, W.J. and Peterson, R.O. (eds), *System Change and Conflict*, The Free Press, New York, p. 284.

[5] Lockwood, D. (1964), 'Social integration and system integration', in Zaltschen, G.K. and Hirsch, N. (eds), *Explorations in Social Change*, Routledge & Kegan Paul, London.

BIBLIOGRAPHY AND FURTHER READING

Very little of Parsons' own mammoth output makes easy reading; I have found the following comparatively accessible, and, at least, comparatively short:

Parsons, T. (1961), 'An outline of the social system', in Parsons, T., Shils, E., Naegele, A. and Pitts, J. (eds.), *Theories of Society: Foundations of Modern Sociological Theory*, Free Press, New York, pp. 30–79.

Parsons, T. (1966), *Societies: Evolutionary and Comparative Perspectives*, Prentice Hall, Englewood Cliffs.

Parsons, T. (1970), 'Some problems of General Theory in sociology', in McKinney, J.C. and Tyriakian, E.A. (eds), *Theoretical Sociology: Perspectives and Developments*, Appleton, Century & Crofts, New York.

Parsons, T. (1971), *The System of Modern Societies*, Prentice Hall, Englewood Cliffs.

His most important books are:

Parsons, T. (1951), *The Social System* The Free Press, New York.

Parsons, T. (1949), *The Structure of Social Action*, The Free Press, New York.

Parsons, T. and Shils, E. (1951), *Toward a General Theory of Action*, Harvard University Press, Cambridge.

The following are secondary sources; Rocher is the clearest:

Adriaansens, H.P.M. (1980), *Talcott Parsons and the Conceptual Dilemma*, Routledge & Kegan Paul, London.

Bershady, H.J. (1973), *Ideology and Social Knowledge*, Blackwell, London.

Devereux, E.C. (1961), 'Parsons sociological theory', in Black, M. (ed.), *The Social Theories of Talcott Parsons*, Prentice Hall, Englewood Cliffs, pp. 1–63.

Mitchell, W.C. (1967), *Sociological Analysis and Politics: The Theories of Talcott Parsons*, Prentice Hall, Englewood Cliffs.

Moore, W.E. (1978), 'Functionalism', in Bottomore, T. and Nisbet, R. (eds), *History of Sociological Analysis*, Heinemann, London, pp. 321–61.

Rocher, G. (1974), *Talcott Parsons and American Sociology*, Nelson, London.

The most useful critical essays are:

Burger, T. (1977), 'Talcott Parsons, the problem of order in society, and the program of analytic sociology', *American Journal of Sociology*, Vol. 831, pp. 320–334 plus the following debate: Parson's *Comment* 335–39; Burger's reply in Vol. 83 (ii) 1978: pp. 983–6.

Wright–Mills, C. (1980), *The Sociological Imagination*, Penguin, Harmondsworth.

Dahrendorf, R. (1964), 'Out of Utopia: toward a reconstruction of sociological analysis', in Coser, L. and Rosenberg, B. (eds), *Sociological Theory*, Macmillan, New York. pp. 209–27.

Demereth, N.J. and Peterson, R.A. (eds) (1967), *System, Change and Conflict: A Reader on Contemporary Sociological Theory and the Debate over Functionalism*, The Free Press, New York.

Giddens, A. (1977), 'Functionalism: apres la lutte', in *Studies in Social and Political Theory*, Heinemann, London, pp. 96–134.

Gouldner, A.W. (1971), *The Coming Crisis of Western Sociology*, Heinemann, London.

Heydebrand, W. and Toby, J. (1972), 'Review symposium on Parsons' *The System of Modern Societies', Contemporary Sociology*, Vol. 1, pp. 387–401.

Homans, G.C. (1964), 'Bringing men back in', *American Sociological Review*, Vol. 29, pp. 809–18.

Lockwood, D. (1964), 'Social integration and system integration', in Zollschan, G.K. and Hirsch, W. (eds), *Explanations in Social Change*, Routledge & Kegan Paul, London, pp. 244–57.

Lockwood, D. (1964), 'Some Remarks on *The Social System*' in Demereth, N.J. and Peterson, R.A. (eds), (1967). See above, pp. 281–92.

Coser, L. (1956), *The Functions of Social Conflict*, The Free Press, Glencoe.

Schwanenberg, E. (1970/71), 'The two problems of order in Parsons' theory: an analysis from within', *Social Forces*, Vol. 49, pp. 569–81.

Scott, J.F. (1963), 'The changing foundations of the Parsonian action scheme', *American Sociological Review*, Vol. 28, pp. 716–35.

Turner, J.H. (1978), *The Structure of Sociological Theory*, The Dorsey Press, Homewood.

Turner, J.H. and Beeghley, L. (1974), 'Current folklore in the criticism of Parsonian action theory' (plus following debate), *Sociological Inquiry*, Vol. 44, pp. 47–63.

4 Conflict theory: there's a lot going on out there and this is some of it

INTRODUCTION

I suggested that structural-functionalism could take account of social conflict and change; conflict theory insists that it cannot, and, in this respect I think it is simply wrong.

Why, then, devote a chapter to it? First, because it was historically important; secondly because the arguments it put forward have directly or indirectly informed much empirical research in sociology. Thirdly, because in a modified form it has important present-day representatives (sometimes known as neo-Weberians); fourth because it arose not only as a critique of Parsons but also of Marx and it tackles some of the issues approached by structuralist Marxism. The names that were associated with the approach in the 1960s were Dahrendorf, John Rex, and to a lesser extent Lockwood; the most important modern work in this tradition is undoubtedly that of Anthony Giddens. I will concentrate on two of these: Dahrendorf, emphasising the relation between conflict theory and structural-functionalism, and Giddens, emphasising the relation between conflict theory and Marxism. In both cases, my critical themes will be the same as in the last chapter.

Percy Cohen[1] represents the opposition of structural-functionalism and conflict theory as two models making a series of apparently mutually exclusive assumptions about society and social life, and this provides an excellent starting point, as shown in Table 3.

Table 3

Consensus theory	Conflict theory
1 Norms and values are the basic elements of social life	Interests are the basic elements of social life
2 Social life involves commitments	Social life involves inducement and coercion
3 Societies are necessarily cohesive	Social life is necessarily divisive
4 Social life depends on solidarity	Social life generates opposition, exclusion and hostility
5 Social life is based on reciprocity and co-operation	Social life generates structural conflict
6 Social systems rest on consensus	Social life generates sectional interests
7 Society recognises legitimate authority	Social differentiation involves power
8 Social systems are integrated	Social systems are malintegrated and beset by contradictions
9 Social systems tend to persist	Social systems tend to change

Apart from purposes of comparison, I have said all I want to about the left-hand side. On the right-hand side, the key terms are evidently 'interest' and 'power', and I suggested that Lockwood's use of the concept of interest presents structural-functionalism with situations it cannot explain. I will argue that the variants of conflict theory fail to build on this and in the end remain within the orbit of structural-functionalism compared to which they are less systematic and less inclusive. In other words, they can be seen as fragments.

CONFLICT AND AUTHORITY: DAHRENDORF

Dahrendorf emphasises from the beginning that his theory is not intended to replace consensus theory. Each theory deals with a different set of problems. Both employ the same concepts, but in opposite ways—every social element has a function, but it also has a dysfunction, consensus and coercion exist side by side. Hence the title of this chapter. Parsons' assumption is shared: our immediate experience of the world is confused and confusing and we need a theory to organise it. However, there is no one systematic theory that will take in everything. Different theories organise the same world in different ways, according to the sort of problem we want to solve.

Conflict theory is just a way of looking at the world. On Friday afternoon, the world is bright and happy, on Monday morning, it's grey and miserable.

Conflict theory thus engages with no clear metaphor for building its picture of the social world. It is nonetheless possible to suggest one from the outside: society is like a more or less confused battleground. If we watch from on high, we can see a variety of groups fighting each other, constantly forming and reforming, making and breaking alliances. For conflict theorists closer to Marxism, the groups are rather more clearly defined and the pattern of conflict more stable; others see more of a kaleidoscope. Dahrendorf falls into this latter category.

For Dahrendorf, the analogy between biological and social systems, and the idea of a social system itself, is replaced by a conception of an 'imperatively co-ordinated system'. Taken from Weber, this is, as far as I can see, a complicated term for 'authority' system or 'power' system. In some contexts, the distinction between authority and power is important: power tends towards reliance on force, authority is legitimated power—power which has achieved general recognition. In the present context, the distinction is rather less important. The crucial point is that an 'imperatively co-ordinated association' is any organisation in which authority exists (which must include, practically, all organisations) and that the very existence of authority (or power) creates the conditions for conflict. The starting point for looking at power and authority is not very different from Parsons: both see it as a necessity, although Dahrendorf would not look favourably on the term 'functional pre-requisite'. Both would agree that a 'function' of power is to integrate a unit, ensuring compliance where norms and values fail. But whereas Parsons emphasises the integrative aspect, power and authority meeting the needs of the whole system, Dahrendorf argues that it is also divisive. The reason for this is that it engenders conflicting interests and role-expectations. Power and authority are scarce resources, and those who hold them have an interest in maintaining the status quo; those who do not possess them have an interest in their redistribution, hence in changing the status quo. These, he argues, are *objective* interests, built into the roles themselves, alongside the interest or function of all roles in maintaining the organisation as a whole. The social world is thus structured into *potential* conflict groups, what Dahrendorf calls *quasi-groups*.

This is really as far as the theory goes as a theory; the next step consists of generalized empirical propositions about the conditions under which quasi-groups become conflict groups; the different conditions which result in different types of conflict; and the conditions that determine the ensuing results. Compared to structural-functionalism, then, Dahrendorf's theory is a low-level one in two parts:

1 A central theoretical proposition: that role structures generate conflicting as well as complementary interests.
2 General descriptions of conditions producing conflict.

All variants of conflict theory have a similar structure and the reason they have generated so much empirical research is that they encourage investigation into the general descriptive statements that qualify the theoretical insight.

DOES DAHRENDORF'S CONFLICT
THEORY EXPLAIN CONFLICT?

Criticisms of Dahrendorf can be divided into two: those that argue that there are features of conflict that he cannot explain; and those that argue that the theory can explain nothing. The latter is the central theoretical criticism and I will leave the former until later.

If we look again at the two parts of the theory that I listed above it is apparent that if we are to explain a real conflict, we have to describe the real conditions that produce it. The theoretical proposition only tells us that conflict is possible. Since it also tells us that consensus is possible, it doesn't tell us very much: the same thing causes opposite results. Hence we have no causal theoretical explanation at all. Peter Weingart has taken this point further. If we go back to Dahrendorf himself for a moment, we find that the 'interests' attached to roles are defined as role expectations. They are not 'material' interests in Lockwood's sense, since Dahrendorf finds such a notion inadequate for understanding the range of conflicts that occur in the real world. That part of his argument is bound up with a lengthy criticism of Marx. Each role thus has conflicting expectations attached to it. A role involving power carries the expectation that power be exercised for the benefit of the organisation as a whole and in the interest of maintaining that power. Thus the head of a nation may be expected both to put the nation's interest first and to ensure that she herself remains in power. Similarly a role without power carries the expectation that the actor will comply and that she will attempt to attain power for herself. Thus we might expect workers to work and to strike. One way in which Dahrendorf suggests we can explain what happens is that it depends on the choice of the role occupant. As Weingart points out, this attempt at explanation takes us back to 'voluntarism'—the idea that social order, the regularities of social life, depend upon individual choices. It seems to me that this is another way of saying that social order is a matter of chance, whereas one of the aims of social theory is to provide a *rational* explanation of social order (and disorder). In other words it is giving up the attempt to produce a social theory at all.

It seem, then, that this criticism is justified. What I want to do now is to compare Dahrendorf with Parsons and place the argument in the context of my overall theme of fragmentation. I have already suggested that Dahrendorf adopts a similar view of power to Parsons, and Dahrendorf himself argues that they employ the same concepts. Now the nearest that structural-functionalism comes to a proper explanation is in its theory of evolution : living systems share a property of evolving in a certain way and social change can be explained as a result of this property. Dahrendorf surrenders such an explanation by surrendering the idea of a social system : there are only 'imperatively co-ordinated associations' without any apparent systematic connection.

When Percy Cohen discusses the two apparently conflicting models I reproduced at the beginning of the chapter, he argues that the conflict is *only* apparent. Conflict can be a way of maintaining stability, as is shown by the work of Coser that I mentioned in the last chapter. In fact neither model consists of a logically necessary series of propositions and it is possible to mix them together in various ways. Beyond this, I would suggest it is quite possible to integrate the conflict model, at least in Dahrendorf's form, into the consensus model, but not *vice versa*. If we take Dahrendorf's theoretical proposition for what it is—a formal statement about types of role expectation within social systems, it might be possible to 'explain' what behaviour occurs in terms of the evolutionary process. A system of authority which serves the whole system at one stage of evolution may be rendered inefficient at a later stage. Conflict may ensue along the lines depicted by Dahrendorf, and the resulting redistribution of authority be more appropriate to the new stage. At the same time we cannot fit structural-functionalism into Dahrendorf's framework, simply because the latter is neither as systematic nor as wide-ranging. We can push an extra coat into a suitcase but we can't fit a suitcase into the coat pocket. This form of conflict theory is best seen as a special case of structural-functionalism: a fragment.

As an example which may illustrate this more clearly, we can go back to Parsons' discussion of youth and youth culture. The conflict theorist would argue that the institutions in which youth are involved, the family, school and college, the workplace—are imperatively co-ordinated associations in which power exists and conflict is always possible. It would then be a matter of identifying the concrete conditions that create conflict and the formation of a youth sub-culture. Some of these might very well fit in with Parsons' discussion—for example youth remaining dependent on their family of origin after they become physically mature and engaged in activity outside of the home. The conflict theorist however would be more specific in the conditions that he sees as important, and reluctant to fit it into the overall model of social development presented by Parsons (i.e., precisely the explanatory element of Parsons' account). Parsons on the other hand might accept the conflict theorist's list of conditions and show how they are related to his overall evolutionary framework.

My final point has to do with generalizing from a theory of persons or action to a theory of society. As with Parsons, society is seen as institutionalized action, a role structure. In his attempt to explain conflict, Dahrendorf switches from role structure to role behaviour but the two cannot be brought together in any form of causal relationship because they are not clearly separated, different phenomena. Each depends on the other without being able to explain the other.

THE PROBLEM OF INTEREST:
HALF-WAY OUT OF THE CIRCLE

I want to broaden the range of the discussion. In my introductory comments to this chapter I said that there are modern representatives of conflict theory and that they are sometimes known as neo-Weberians. It would perhaps have been more accurate to reverse the priority implicit in that statement. Conflict theory can be seen as one school of social theory based on the work of Max Weber. This particular tradition is really best understood in relation to Marx rather than Parsons, who was only a temporary target. Most of what I deal with over the next few pages should perhaps be re-read after the chapter on structuralist Marxism in Part III, but it can also provide an introduction to that chapter.

Weberian-based social theory is concerned not only with conflict but with all dimensions of class structure and the processes which determine class structure. In general, it accepts Marxist propositions about the importance of class conflict and society being comprised of social classes, but sees the Marxist model as over-simplified and too rigid. There are three aspects of Weber's work that are important in this respect. First he defines social class economically in terms of market situation, the property which a person brings to the market and the life chances that depend upon possession of that property. Owning similar property implies shared life chances and the possibility of forming a social class. This suggests that there are as many types of social classes as there are types of property (at least potentially) and can be contrasted to Marx's definition of social class in terms of the production process, which suggests only two major social classes—the owners of the means of production and the workers. Second, Weber suggests that non-economically based classes might be important, in particular status groups, based on a common life style and shared social esteem. At a pinch, Dahrendorf's authority groups might be seen as a sort of status group. Thirdly, Weber emphasises the importance of ideas in the social process, over against Marx's emphasis on economic factors: for example a class is not really a class until its members recognise it as such. Although many modern writers in this tradition might accept the Marxist definition of class and indeed Marx's economic analysis of capitalism as being superior to Weber's, they nonetheless argue that Marx did not develop an adequate theory of social action and they turn to Weber for such a theory. The work of Lockwood, Goldthorpe, Newby and many other British sociologists may be placed in this context.

The resulting model of industrial society is more complicated than that of Marx: there are more classes and more bases for the formation of groups than straightforward economic bases; and it is more fluid, there are more significant causal factors at work. The tendency is to see events as the product of several or many causes on an empirical, descriptive level. Again, there is a lot going on out there....

I want to look at Anthony Giddens' *The Class Structure of Advanced Societies* in this context. Giddens' work cuts across all the schools of theory I will discuss in this book, but this particular text bears certain interesting similarities to Dahrendorf, and raises some similar problems about the nature of a theoretical explanation. It is recognisably in the same tradition and indeed Giddens builds up a part of his argument through a critique of Dahrendorf, in particular arguing that modern societies are rather less of a kaleidoscope than Dahrendorf implies, and that the latter cannot distinguish between more and less important conflicts. More important, he implies a different conception of interest to Dahrendorf, locating it not in a role structure but in material possession of property, but he fails to develop it in the way implied in my discussion of Lockwood.

When he is developing his own theory of the class structure of advanced society he suggests a modified version of Weber's economic definition of class—he suggests that the concept of property should be extended to include the rights and capacities that ownership of the property confers. In other words, property is a material interest which brings advantages and disadvantages on the market, and it is also a social role to which expectations are attached in the form of socially recognised rights and capacities. He acknowledges that this implies a multitude of classes, at least as many as there are forms of property, but he suggests that these are then structured into larger blocks of classes and he lists the various empirical conditions that effect this process of 'structuration' and also determine levels of conflict. Thus we find the same theoretical structure as we did in Dahrendorf: a central theoretical proposition followed by general empirical propositions.

The difficulty arises with the form of explanation. The modified Weberian definition of class is intended, as far as I can judge from Giddens' argument, to be the beginning of a causal explanation but he runs into two sorts of difficulty. First, when he constructs an explanation of different social structures, the different factors of structuration play the most important part (i.e., a description of the historical development of a class structure replaces a theoretical explanation). Second there is the problem that classes are pre-supposed to exist at an economic level but do not come into existence until their members recognise their class membership; in other words classes exist before they exist. This seems to me a typical problem of Weberian explanation. Classes are defined in terms of peoples' ideas, norms and values and at the same time according to economic criteria that are not necessarily reflected in ideas, norms and values. We are half way out of the circle—the action element of the theory is modified with the introduction of material interest but not changed. In Giddens' development of Weber's definition, the two dimensions are even closer—property ownership and role expectations are two sides of the same coin, two potential explanatory levels are distinguished and then run together again.

This might be clearer if I can refer forward to my discussion of structuralist Marxism, I hope without presuming too much. There we find a clearer distinction between levels of society and a clearer distinction between societies and persons, with the idea of material interest playing a mediating role. The basic level of society is the mode of production—it doesn't matter what this means at the moment.

The way I have presented this information in Table 4 suggests that structuralist Marxism overcomes some of the explanatory problems of action theory, although it does so at the cost of creating other problems. My purpose is to show how it can be argued that Giddens runs together two different levels and thus creates problems in setting up a theoretical explanation of what happens. When in his later work he sets out to develop the notion of 'structuration' on a more abstract level, this is even more apparent. He employs the term 'structuration'

Table 4

	Level 1 (society)		Level 2 (society)		Level 3 (persons)
Marxism	Mode of production	determines	material interests	determines	Role structure, expectations and behaviour
Structural-functional-ism and Dahrendorf			(material interests)	determined by	Role structure, expectations and behaviour
Giddens			material interests	determine and determined by	Role structure, expectations and behaviour

to embrace both the action which produces structures and structures themselves and he seems to end by talking about structures not as forms of social organisation, as in 'class structure' but as the structure of rules which govern actions. His first 'new rule of sociological method' states that:

"Sociology is not concerned with a pre-given universe of objects, but with one that is constituted or produced by the active doings of subjects"[2]

Again society is dissolved into persons.

CONCLUSION: IT'S NOT SO BAD AFTER ALL

These last comments about Giddens sound very critical and to an extent are unfair in that I've been criticizing him for not meeting criteria which I have laid down and with which he might not agree. However, I hope I have shown that he has some difficulty in constructing a theoretical explanation whilst at the same time his approach goes rather beyond that of structural-functionalism and Dahrendorf's variant of conflict theory. It is difficult, because of his initial conception of class, to see Giddens as a 'fragment' of structural-functionalism. He is perhaps better seen as attempting to combine Marxism with a form of action theory via Weber but eventually ending up on the side of the latter. In fact, I think the real value of this tradition of social theory is as a corrective critique of Marxism. It does not possess the explanatory power of much Marxist theory and in that sense falls short of it (it is in fact a 'fragment' of modern Marxism), but the great danger of structuralist Marxism is that it reduces the real world to theory. I shall demonstrate this as far as possible in Part III. Conflict theory, and Weberian theory in general points instead to the complexity of the real world and actually encourages us to discover this complexity empirically rather than hide it theoretically. It is an unfortunate fact that we often seem to have to choose between a better developed theory which over-simplifies the world, and an inadequate theory—and therefore inadequate explanation—which nevertheless directs attention to the real complexity of the world. But it is nonetheless what we would expect from a study in its infancy.

It is the case that none of the forms of action theory so far examined have had much to say about acting persons, even though they are theories of acting persons. They have concentrated on the institutionalized patterns of action which they take to be society. The next two chapters will be concerned with those variants or fragments which see action as a process engaged upon by persons, and have comparatively undeveloped theories of institutions. This is in fact the direction in which Giddens himself moved after his work on class structure.

NOTES

[1] Cohen, P. (1968), *Modern Social Theory*Heinemann, London, p. 167.
[2] Giddens, A. (1976), *New Rules of Sociological Method*, Hutchinson, London, p. 160.

BIBLIOGRAPHY AND FURTHER READING

Dahrendorf
The following are the most relevant references for this chapter; the Binns reference is a discussion of the Weberian school as a whole from a rather different point of view.

Dahrendorf, R. (1959), *Class and Class Conflict in an Industrial Society*, Routledge & Kegan Paul, London.
Dahrendorf, R. (1958), 'Toward a theory of social conflict', *Journal of Conflict Resolution*, Vol. 2, pp. 209–227.
Binns, D. (1977), *Beyond the Sociology of Conflict*, Macmillan, Basingstoke.
Cohen, P. (1968), *Modern Social Theory*, Heinemann, London.
Turner, J.H. (1978), *The Structure of Sociological Theory*, Dorsey Press, Homewood.
Weingart, P. (1969), 'Beyond Parsons? A critique of Ralf Dahrendorf's Conflict Theory. *Social Forces*, Vol. 48, pp. 151–65.

Other useful works on the conflict perspective:
Rex, J. (1960), *Key Problems in Sociological Theory*, Routledge & Kegan Paul, London.
Touraine, A. (1977), *The Self-Production of Society*, Chicago University Press.

Work by Anthony Giddens
The first book is the most important; the others contain elaborations of his theory of structuration. There is little critical work available as yet but I have listed a couple of useful book reviews.

Giddens, A. (1973), *The Class Structure of Advanced Societies*, Hutchinson, London.
Giddens, A. (1976), *New Rules of Sociological Method*, Hutchinson, London.
Giddens, A. (1977), *Studies in Social and Political Theory*, Hutchinson, London.
Giddens, A. (1979), *Central Problems in Social Theory*, Macmillan, Basingstoke.
Urry, J. (1977), 'Review of *New Rules*', *Sociological Review*, Vol. 25, pp. 911–15.
Tyriakian, E.A. (1973), Review of *Class Structure*, *American Journal of Sociology*, Vol. 83, pp. 1022–25.

The neo-Weberian work on class structure

There is a large amount available, and the theory tends to be hidden amongst the empirical studies. In general terms they are concerned with peoples' perceptions and actions within the class structure, rather than the nature of the structure itself, although, as in Giddens work, the two tend to be run together. The following are good examples of the tradition:

Bulmer, H. (1975), *Working Class Images of Society*, Routledge & Kegan Paul, London.
Goldthorpe, J. (1978), 'The current inflation: towards a sociological analysis', in Hirsch, F. and Goldthorpe, J.H. (eds), *The Political Economy of Inflation*, Martin Robertson, London, pp. 186–216.
Goldthorpe, J. (1980), *Social Mobility and Class Structure in Modern Britain* Clarendon Press, Oxford.
Goldthorpe, J. *et al.* (1970), *The Affluent Worker in the Class Structure*, Cambridge University Press.
Lockwood, D. (1958), *The Blackcoated Worker* Allen & Unwin, London.

5 Symbolic interactionism: society as conversation

INTRODUCTION

Symbolic interactionism is the least-developed theory discussed in this book. Paul Rock calls it a 'deliberately constructed vagueness'; there are various varieties and the existence of the approach seems to have depended more on informal verbal tradition rather than established textbooks. The centre of its development was the University of Chicago sociology department around the 1920s and amongst the founding thinkers who I will not discuss were Robert Park and W.I. Thomas. It drew on the uniquely American philosophical school of pragmatism, on a sociological interpretation of ecology (the study of the relationship between an organism and its environment), and on the field methods developed by anthropology, now generally known amongst sociologists as participant observation. As later functionalists noted, it was strong on empirical research and weak on theory, and it has always produced a range of field studies of social behaviour in different situations. As the anthropologist will live with a tribe in New Guinea, so the interactionist will find and live with a social group in her own country. Insofar as it has a founding thinker who can be regarded as the major theorist, it is George Herbert Mead. All modern discussions of the approach give Mead a central place and the vagueness that I referred to is best illustrated by the fact that his central work, *Mind, Self and Society*, was compiled from his students' lecture notes after his death.

To place symbolic interactionism in the context of the previous chapters it is best to go back to Parsons and the idea of the unit act. This involved a set of assumptions about the social actor: she makes choices between goals and means towards these goals in a situation of both physical and social objects—the latter including social norms and cultural values. The process of institutionalization involves actors gearing their actions to each other to provide mutual satisfaction, and if that is successful, the actions become stabilized into a pattern of status roles—a role structure. These are seen in terms of the expectations that people have of each other (i.e., in terms of meanings or symbols). Now I said in relation to both structural-functionalism and conflict theory that the approach can focus on either role structures and social systems or role behaviour and social action. I suggested that they had difficulty in bringing these together in any sort of overall causal explanation (even though they might want to do so) because the theory could not properly separate them from each other. Social systems and role structures were sometimes seen as the result of social action and sometimes *vice versa* but they are basically the same thing: a theory of persons generalized to a theory of societies. Symbolic interactionism does not make this switch: it stays with social action and although implicitly it sees social structures as role structures in the same way as the other approaches, it does not concern itself with analysis on the systems level. In Parsons' terms, it stays with the unit act, the way actors make choices, and in this sense, it too can be seen as a fragment of his action theory.

There are several forms of interactionism, but the tendency I will concentrate on is known as the Chicago school, the major second generation figure of which is Herbert Blumer. I will concentrate on this school because I think it offers the most distinctive contribution, and the one that is most difficult to assimilate to structural-functionalism, even though it shares the same propositions. Here the analogy of the conversation is most appropriate: the social world shows the same qualities of flow, development, creativity and change as we would experience in a conversation around the dinner table or in a bar (at least in the early stages). In fact the world is made up of conversations, internal and external. This tendency is, I think, closer to the spirit of the originators of the approach, with their optimism about social progress and democracy, and their view that social development is caused by and causes the development of individual creativity. It is also closer to its social basis in American life, with its emphasis on egalitarianism, individual liberty and social mobility.

How close it is to the full reality of social life is, of course, another matter.

THE ASSUMPTIONS OF SYMBOLIC INTERACTIONISM

The most economical formulation of interactionist assumptions comes from Herbert Blumer:[1]

1 Human beings act towards things on the basis of the meanings that the things have for them.
2 These meanings are the product of social interaction in human society.
3 These meanings are modified and handled through an interpretive process that is used by each individual in dealing with the signs each encounters.

They correspond roughly with the three sections of Mead's *Mind, Self and Society*. Mead's starting point is the discussion of the crucial feature that separates human beings from other animals. Like many other thinkers, he settles on language or the 'significant symbol' and he is concerned to elaborate the implications of this. Animals engage in conversations of gestures but it would be wrong to say that they communicate like human beings. When one dog snarls at another and the other backs away, one dog is feeling aggressive and one dog is feeling scared, but there is no mutual understanding. When I want to warn off a student, perhaps because he is taking up too much of my time, I do not (usually) bare my teeth and snarl; I present him with a reason which I believe he will understand. The difference is that, unlike the animal gesture, the significant symbol brings out the same reaction in myself as it does in the other and *vice versa*—each of us, in the exchange, puts ourself in the position of the other. Dogs, as far as we know, are not capable of identifying with each other in this way, and it is language, the significant symbol, that makes the difference.

Another way of putting it is that the significant symbol is a shared meaning. It is developed in the course of interaction, which itself is a matter of people seeking to achieve practical results in co-operation with each other. Mead is describing something like the process of an intimate relationship between two people where the participants develop an almost private language in the course of their daily activities—but for Mead this is a general social process. Social interaction produces meanings, and meanings make up our world. There is a sense in which we create our world by giving meaning to it: a piece of wood is a piece of wood; in our daily activity it becomes a table. The word 'table' means the role it plays in our interaction: something to eat off, work on, use as a barricade against the bailiffs. Such meanings change and develop and as they do so, the world changes and develops.

The significant symbol provides humans with the ability to 'pause' in their reaction and rehearse it imaginatively. The symbols enable us to stand back from the objects in the world and carry out thought experiments; that is what is happening every time we think about doing something. It is the existence of language which enables us to stand back, to consider and choose. This brings us to the interpretive process mentioned in Blumer's third assumption. So far I have been talking about 'external conversations'—the processes of interaction in which we create, together, our shared world. The internal interpretive process is also a conversation, between two different parts (Mead called them 'phases') of the self. The significant symbol, remember, brings out the same reaction in myself as it does in others; it enables me to look at myself as others look at me. The '*Me*' is precisely that: myself as others see me; the second phase, the '*I*', is the part that looks at myself ('I am thinking about myself') and Mead sees this as the source of originality, creativity and spontaneity. The internal conversation provides a channel through which all the external conversations, or patterns of interaction, must pass. This conception of the self also involves a description of the process of socialization. In the life of the infant, initially random gestures are narrowed as she comes to recognise those that have a meaning for others. Then through play she learns to take the role of individual others, and as she grows older, she learns through games to co-ordinate her activities with others and to see herself as the group sees her. Through peer groups (friends) she comes to see herself in an increasingly wider context until she takes on what Mead calls the 'role of the generalized other', until she can view herself as the society as a whole views her. Another way of putting it is that she takes on a sort of social conscience.

The various forms of symbolic interactionism place emphasis on different parts of the theory. The Chicago school concentrates on the flow of interaction and interpretive processes, looking at the way in which meanings develop and change; the 'Iowa school', the leading figure of which is Manfred Kuhn, tries to change these insights into measurable variables. Assuming that the self is stable and relatively unchanging. His Twenty Statements Test (The 'Who Am I?' test) asks people to choose the series of twenty statements which most accurately describe themselves, and he proceeds to relate the results to the social positions of the respondents. Mead's ideas are not really used as a theory, to explain what is observed, but rather as a simple description of what is observed. Another variation, usually labelled 'role theory' looks at the way in which the internal conversation of the self mediates the presentation of the self in role structures. Ralph Turner's work is the most systematic in this area.

As an example, however, I will look briefly at the work of Erving Goffman, who falls half-way between the Chicago school approach and the more systematic form of role theory. It is often labelled the 'dramaturgical approach', a term which he applies to himself. Roles—the expectations which others have of our behaviour in specific circumstances, are seen as like scripts which we then enact, and Goffman is concerned to show how we act, the way in which we manage our performance. Thus, in the 1950s, American women at college would act stupid to impress their boyfriends; Shetland Islanders, where Goffman did much fieldwork for his most famous book *The Presentation of Self in Everyday Life*, would let the outward appearance of their cottages decay lest the landlord assume they were wealthy enough to pay higher rent. All aspects of life are seen in these terms, from the most private to the most public. It is not just after she has spent the afternoon in bed with her lover that my wife tries to impress me with her care and concern for me when I get home. That 'impression management' is going on all the time, as if we were all advertizing agents for ourselves. We use our physical surroundings as props and we maintain areas of privacy 'backstage' where we can relax from our performances (the toilet, for example).

This can be seen in the context of Mead's discussion of the 'I' and 'Me'. Goffman is describing the ways in which the 'I' presents the 'Me'. The difficulty is that we never find out what the 'I' is—and Mead didn't tell us either beyond saying that it was the source of creativity and originality. Everything is reduced to acting: the self has no substance beyond what is expected of us on different occasions, and we have as many different selves as there are different occasions.

This leads on to one of the main criticisms of symbolic interactionism which I will discuss shortly.

Goffman's work is mainly descriptive: *The Presentation of Self in Everyday Life* is a classification of the techniques and strategies of acting. This indicates something of the nature of interactionism as a theory: it is not rigorous and does not involve logical deduction. Rather it provides a series of ideas which the researcher may use in her work as very general guides. The explanation that the researcher develops is of a comparatively low level; in Goffman's case it simply presupposes Mead's I/Me distinction without discussion, and then employs it to redescribe various actions using the theatrical analogy.

Goffman at least sees all action in these terms. Many other interactionists would argue that any explanation can only be appropriate to the particular situation which it explains; we cannot make generalizations about social life. Society seen as a conversation is in constant flux and cannot be forced into generalized abstractions. Nevertheless, it does seem to me that Mead's insights provide a basis for an elementary teleological explanation of human action, revealing a logic to what people do that is not at first apparent. The sociologist can show the way in which people assess the world and choose between different courses of action, when often to the immediate perception of the observer, no choice is involved. Thus, in *The Outsiders*, Howard Becker is able to show how marijuahana use is less a matter of physical addiction than a learning process—people have to learn from others what the effects are before they themselves can experience them. We can then describe this learning process in terms of new meanings developing from the interactions and choices of the new and experienced smokers. Interactionism looks for what Paul Rock calls the 'occasional rationality' of the action, the specific perspectives, meanings and choices involved in each situation.

ARE SYMBOLIC INTERACTIONISTS BLIND AND STUPID?

The most regular criticisms that you are likely to come across in the rapidly growing literature on symbolic interactionism is that it ignores the wider features of social structure and thus cannot say anything about power, conflict and change, and that its theoretical formulations are hopelessly vague. These points are usually made as if they were self-evident: any idiot can see social structures and their effect, and only a fool would be content with vague theoretical formulations.

As a rule neither argument takes account of the interactionist defence of their position. If we start with the argument that its concepts are vague, it seems to me that in fact this is a necessary aspect of the approach's distinctive contribution to sociology. If the aim is to reveal the 'occasional' logic of peoples' action, and if it is the case that social interaction is in constant flux, then the theoretical starting point must be flexible and 'sensitizing' (i.e. vague) or we would lose vital aspects of what we are studying. It is at this level of analysis that we are most in danger of doing violence to what we are studying if we have to force it into a well worked-out elaborate theory.

Whereas the role theory tendency in interaction does take account of social structures, from the point of view of the Chicago school an explicit case can be made against taking social structures into account. They are abstract entities, the argument goes, we can engage in abstract and interesting arguments about them (the brain-teaser tendency) and we can reinterpret the world in their terms (the crossword puzzle tendency) but we can never arrive at any satisfactory conclusions about them and we are likely to miss what is going on under our noses. Paul Rock makes the point clearly:

The character of society is so obscure that scientific attempts to discuss it are generally absurd. Although loose working definitions might be used to guide analysis, it is misleading to assume that larger systems of society can ever be mapped. Indeed it is not entirely reasonable to suppose that society and its 'structures' are organised. If they are, then they can be known only to analytic *a priori* conjectures which are forever uncertain or to synthetic *a priori* understanding which is entirely unscientific. The sociologist therefore hesitates to write of society as a viable analytic topic at all. When he does so, it may only be to represent it as a shapeless conglomeration of fluid exchanges.[2]

This is, I think, a strong case. It corresponds with my argument in the Introduction to Part II, that at least to begin with a theoretical explanation is a matter of imaginative explanation. I argued that this could be made less speculative as it is subjected to criteria of rationality and evidence; Rock does not believe that this can be done in any useful way.

How do we decide? I think the argument against Paul Rock can be based on something that he himself says. He acknowledges that sometimes the people we study might employ the term 'society' and we can investigate its meaning to them, and the way the meaning of the term develops in their interaction. I said in the opening chapter that everybody, in their everyday lives, is a theorist and in day-to-day interaction it is reasonable to suggest that people talk about 'society' because they are aware of the effects of something that they cannot identify in any clear experiental way. To suppose 'society' to be a fiction, to suppose that it is unorganised etc., is to ignore the experience of its effects amongst those we study. In other words, it is to do precisely the opposite of what symbolic interactionism sets out to do. We can grant to Rock that our knowledge of 'society' will always be somewhat tentative and that we should not absorb processes of interaction into a rigid theory, but not that we should have no theory of society. From my introduction it would follow that the criticism that symbolic interactionism does not take into account wider social structures might be true but how they should be taken into account is a major problem area—not a simple matter as the critics suppose it to be.

There are two further points that I want to make about the approach, one of which can be often found in the critical discussions and one of which has to do with the general theme of the book. The first is that it is often pointed out that interactionists see people as purely cognitive beings, as if we understand people when we understand what they think they know about the world, their meanings and self-conceptions. Yet people also have emotions and it is arguable that unconscious processes occur as well and it is a criticism that symbolic interactionism has nothing to say about these. This points to the fact that a theory of persons must also deal with different levels of the personality and relationships between them; in other words, the personality needs to be given substance. We can acknowledge, with Goffman, that we act, but we are more than actors. Even when we deal with meanings and symbols, some approaches I will be looking at later show that interactionism underestimates the complexity of meaning formation. In the next chapter it will become apparent that the way people form and develop their view of the world can be seen as subjected to certain rules and that there are general processes of meaning formation that are not investigated by interactionism. And in Part III it will become apparent that meanings or symbols themselves might be seen as possessing an organised structure, even as comprising yet another type of reality in the social world.

Secondly, what I have said suggests that interactionism offers the beginnings of a teleological, as opposed to a straightforward causal explanation of people's actions. But as it stands, it is a comparatively unworked out explanation—interactionists choose to remain closer to the flux of interaction processes at the expense of developing their theory further and that perhaps is a necessary choice, at least given the present state of knowledge in the discipline as a whole. The danger, however, is that the choice tends to leave them in some cases engaging in purely descriptive work. In the case of Turner's form of role theory, we are left with something like the conflict theories I discussed in the previous chapter: the theoretical insights are provided by Mead and there follows a series of descriptive empirical generalizations about what factors influence the way people enact roles. The same is the case with Goffman: there is the central theoretical insight about self-presentation followed by a catalogue of different ways in which people present themselves in different contexts. If Parsons' work can be likened to a filing *system*, then Goffman's sometimes seems like a collection of index cards that can be arranged anyway we want. All actions can be understood via the theatrical analogy and we may list them in any order we desire.

SUMMARY CONCLUSION

Symbolic interactionism, then, is a theory of persons, of social action, which in its most distinct form does not attempt to become also a theory of society. Its explanations of action—its theoretical component—remains fairly simple, but this can be seen as a conscious choice in favour of grasping some of the complexity of real situations. The theoretical task that it points to is the development of a more sophisticated theoretical explanation, which takes in more aspects of persons' actions, without losing the complexity of the real world.

NOTES

[1] Blumer, H. (1969), *Symbolic Interactionism: Perspectives and Method*, Prentice Hall, New York, Chapter 1.

[2] Rock, P. (1979), *The Making of Symbolic Interactionism* Macmillan, Basingstoke, pp. 227–9.

BIBLIOGRAPHY AND FURTHER READING

Central works of symbolic interactionism
Included here are each of the three tendencies I identified. Mead and Blumer are the best starting points.

Blumer, H. (1969), *Symbolic Interactionism: Perspectives and Method*, Prentice–Hall, New Jersey.

Denzin, N.K. (1971), *The Research Act in Sociology: A Theoretical Introduction to Sociological Methods*, Butterworth London.

Faris, R.E.L. (1967), *Chicago Sociology 1920–32*, University of Chicago Press.

Glaser, B.G. and Strauss, A.L. (1967), *The Discovery of Grounded Theory: Strategies for Qualitative Research* Weidenfeld & Nicholson, London.

Kuhn, M.H. (1964), 'Major trends in symbolic interaction theory in the past 25 years', *Sociological Quarterly*, Vol. 5, pp. 61–84.

Manis, J.G. and Meltzer, B.N. (1972), *Symbolic Interaction: A Reader in Social Psychology*, Allen & Bacon, Boston.

Mead, G.H. (1934), *Mind, Self and Society*, Chicago University Press.

Rose, A.M. (1962), *Human Behaviour and Social Process: An Interactionist Approach* Routledge & Kegan Paul, London. See particularly the paper 'Role taking: process vs conformity', by R.H. Turner.

Useful introductions and critical discussions
Meltzer and Petras is the most useful and accessible; Rock is comparatively advanced but provocative.

Fisher, B.M. and Strauss, A.L. (1979), 'Interactionism', in Bottomore, T.B. and Nisbet, R. (eds), *A History of Sociological Analysis*, Heinemann, London, pp. 475–97.

Meltzer, B.W. and Petras, J.W. *et al.* (1975), *Symbolic Interactionism: Genesis, Varieties and Criticisms*, Routledge & Kegan Paul, London.

Rock, P. (1979), *The Making of Symbolic Interactionism*, Macmillan, Basingstoke.

Turner, J.H. (1974), 'Parsons as a symbolic interactionist. A comparison of action and interaction theory', *Sociological Inquiry*, Vol. 44, pp. 28–94.

Turner, J.H. (1978), *The Structure of Sociological Theory*, Dorsey Press, Homewood.

Critical papers are included in the Manis and Meltzer reader and there are useful references in Meltzer and Petras. On Goffman see:

Ditton, J. (ed.) (1980), *The View From Goffman*, Macmillan, Basingstoke.

Interactionist studies which make good starting points:

Becker, H. (1963), *Outsiders: Studies in the Sociology of Deviance*, Macmillan, Basingstoke.

Goffman, E. (1971), *The Presentation of Self in Everyday Life*, Penguin, Harmondsworth.

Goffman, E. (1968), *Asylums*, Penguin, Harmondsworth.

Goffman, E. (1968), *Stigma: Notes on the Management of Spoiled Identity*, Penguin, Harmondsworth.

Humphreys, L. (1970), *Tearoom Trade: A Study of Homosexual Encounters in Public Places*, Duckworth, London.

Plummer, K. (1975), *Sexual Stigma*, Routledge & Kegan Paul, London.

6 Society as a conspiracy: phenomenological sociology and ethnomethodology

Although phenomenological sociology and ethnomethodology share certain features, only the latter label designates a 'school' in a strict sense. Both emerged in the late 1960s, initially in the USA, and ethnomethodology became something of a cult for a few years. The common features of the two approaches stem from their debt to a European school of philosophy known as phenomenology. The very possibility of developing philosophical phenomenology into a sociological theory has been questioned, but the validity of the logical connections between the two is less interesting than the shared spirit of investigation.

The founding father of phenomenological philosophy was Edmund Husserl whose most important work was published in the last decade of the nineteenth century and the first decades of this century. Husserl was concerned to develop a radical philosophy in a literal sense of the word: a philosophy that goes to the roots of our knowledge and experience. In particular, he argued that scientific knowledge had become divorced from the everyday experience and activities in which it is rooted, and he saw the task of phenomenology as restoring that connection. Half a century later, sociologists were to use the same argument against established social theory and in particular structural-functionalism: it has become divorced from everyday social experience.

Phenomenology is a form of idealism, concerned solely with the structures and workings of human consciousness and its basic though often implicit presupposition is that the world we live in is created in consciousness, in our heads. Of course, it would be absurd to deny that there is an external world, but the argument is that the outside world only has meaning through our consciousness of it. The sociologist — or any scientist for that matter — is only interested in the world insofar as it is meaningful and must therefore understand how we make it meaningful. This is achieved through setting aside what we normally assume we know and tracing the process of coming to know it. This setting aside of our knowledge is sometimes referred to as the 'phenomenological reduction', sometimes as 'bracketing' and in the more technical literature as the *époché*. I will look at it in more detail shortly when I discuss the work of Alfred Schutz; for the moment, I want to make two points. The first is to emphasise the similarity between the approaches I have discussed so far and the concerns of phenomenology. They all see meanings — norms, values, beliefs etc. — as the central focus of the sociological enterprise. They are all theories of persons and of action. Secondly I think that in its sociological form, phenomenology loses some of its most interesting aspects. I have discussed it so far purely as a theory of cognition, of knowing; many phenomenological philosophers, including Husserl, have concerned themselves with a much wider range of experience, with emotions, the imagination, hallucination and so on. This side has been lost in phenomenological sociology.

PHENOMENOLOGICAL SOCIOLOGY:
THE COMMON SENSE WORLD

The most significant theorist of phenomenological sociology was without doubt Alfred Schutz, a pupil of Husserl who emigrated to the USA after the rise of fascism in Europe and made a career as a banker and part-time teacher. He came under the influence of pragmatist philosophy and symbolic interactionism and perhaps the best way of approaching his work is as a more systematic and penetrating form of interactionism. In his classic work, *The Phenomenology of the Social World*, however, he was concerned with combining the insights of phenomenology with sociology through a sociological critique of the work of Max Weber.

He argued that the phenomenological reduction, the setting aside of our knowledge of the world, leaves us with what he called a 'stream of experience'. The label phenomenology means the study of the way in which phenomena—the things of which we are conscious—appear to us, and the most basic way in which they appear is as a continuous flow of sense experiences which we receive through our five senses: sight, hearing, touch, smell and taste. Setting aside all I know about my desk and the objects on it, my first experience is of different colours and textures; out of that experience of sense impressions I build up the different objects—the desk itself, the typewriter, the paper, the book. The basic stream of sense experiences is meaningless—they are just there; the objects are meaningful—they have uses, names, different parts, and they signify certain things about me, that I am an academic and a writer, and certain things about other people that follow on from my being an academic or writer. Phenomenology is concerned to identify this passage from a world of meaningless sense experience to a world of meaningful objects, a passage which occurs initially in our separate individual consciousnesses and then collectively, in the interaction between consciousnesses. This passage is one in which consciousness *acts* on raw sense data to create meaning, in the same way that we may see something ambiguous in the distance and, without going any nearer, identify it through a process of relating it to its background. It seems to be moving, so it is a person and not a tree. Similarly we may be bemused at first sight by an abstract painting, but the longer we look at it and the more we think about it, the more sense we come to make of it. This brings us to one distinct difference between phenomenology and other forms of action theory: 'action' so far has referred to peoples' actions in relation to each other and their environment. For phenomenology action also and even primarily refers to internal processes of consciousness, whether they be individual or collective. Once action is transferred into our heads it becomes difficult to break out again and this has consequences for the attempt to extend phenomenological sociology to a theory of society as well as of persons.

According to Schutz, the way in which we construct meaning out of the basic stream of experience is through a process of typification. This involves building up classes of experience through similarity. Thus in my stream of experience I notice that certain objects have particular features in common, that they move from place to place perhaps whilst their surroundings remain constant. This gives me the most abstract category of 'living beings'; then I notice that amongst these there are some who emit consistent noises of a type of which I am capable; thus, from 'living beings' I sort out 'other people'. I then distinguish different classes of other people: blacks and whites, men and women. Finally I identify those characteristics which distinguish specific others: my mother, my friend. Thus we build up what Schutz calls 'meaning contexts', sets of criteria by means of which we organise our sense experience into a meaningful world. I am employing such criteria when I look in front of me and see a book. All I can actually see are two sides of a red and white object; through the employment of well-established criteria, I 'constitute', make this sense experience into a book. Our meaning contexts are organised together, again through a process of typification, into what Schutz calls 'stocks of knowledge'. The stocks of knowledge are not stocks of knowledge *about* the world, they are, to all practical purposes the world itself. When I look at my desk, I see a book; the book is created in my consciousness but I see it in the outside world. These stocks of knowledge are therefore taken for granted. I do not think about how I move from sense experience to seeing a book, I just do. The basis of our social world is made up of such taken-for-granted knowledge. We each organise the world of commonsense knowledge on the basis of the 'here and now', of what we are doing in a particular time and place, or to use another of Schutz's terms, on the basis of our 'project'. My world involves for example a series of taken-for-granted assumptions about the nature of the opposite sex: that they tend to have higher voices, breasts, different genitalia, that they move in a certain way, that they have certain concerns and ways of behaving which I might regard as natural or instinctive, that they have certain abilities and inabilities. A threat to some of these assumptions is likely to prove more disorientating than a threat to my political beliefs, even though I never think about the former and regard the latter as very precious. This helps to explain the violence of some male reaction to feminism. Different aspects of these taken-for-granted assumptions will be important at different times depending on my 'project', on whether, for example, I'm dealing with a woman as a stranger, a colleague or a lover.

Why, then, have I chosen to call this chapter 'Society as a conspiracy'? All I have said so far indicates that phenomenology sees the world as a personal invention, I have been talking about my stock of knowledge as my world organised according to my project. The point here is that after a certain stage of development, the typified stock of knowledge which comprises my world is shared by other people. We share a commonsense, taken-for-granted world that Schutz, following Husserl, calls the 'life world', which is the basis of all our social activities. We construct and change it in our social interaction and pass it on from generation to generation through our socialization processes. It is as if, without knowing it, we conspire to create a stable world out of the jumble of sense experiences and out of our separate individual experiences. Since we are separate individuals, we each have a separate stream of experience which depends upon our own particular positions in the world. Out of these separate streams, we must construct, through typification, a shared world—a social world and the sociologist is concerned with this world and its construction. The sociologist is distinguished from other people by her own project and consequent organisation of the shared stocks of knowledge. Her project is to construct a rational and therefore objective account of the social world. To do this, she must construct 'second-order typifications': typifications of our commonsense typifications which order the social world in a rational way; we can then use this rational model to predict how people behave if they behave rationally and to indicate the irrationality of their action if it does not fit the model. Schutz talks about social theory as creating a world of rational puppets who can be manipulated by the theorist to provide knowledge about the real world: we can say that if people have certain goals and behave rationally, then they will act in such a way; if the situation changes, then their action will change in this or that way. Again the cognitive emphasis of Schutz's work is clear.

Phenomenological sociology has the peculiar ability to be exciting and tedious at the same time. Particularly in the context of structural-functionalism it is a refreshing change, moving away from highly abstract theoretical categories which have little to do with the social life that most of us experience, and plunging straight into the everyday world. It can be obvious and new at the same time: obvious because it seeks to describe what we already know, our commonsense knowledge; new because the more profound areas of our commonsense knowledge are rarely put into words. Theoretically, it can prove extremely tedious, engaging in a process of classification similar to that of Parsons, but at a much lower level of abstraction. *The Phenomenology of the Social World* in this respect is one of the most boring books I have read, and this has to do with the sort of theoretical work it engages in. Like other forms of action theory when compared to structural-functionalism it works at a comparatively low level with some theoretical propositions pointing the way to empirical description; like some symbolic interactionists it engages in low-level classification, setting out the different areas and forms of organisation of commonsense knowledge. It only goes beyond classification in the conception of the project, which offers a rather more complete framework for teleological explanation than any of the other theories. In the course of his work Schutz offers a programme for understanding social action which is able to make a number of important distinctions and clarify certain processes of interpretation. Whereas the other theories tend to take the meaning of an action as unproblematic once it is discovered, Schutz lays down certain procedures by means of which we can clarify and check that meaning. He indicates first of all that it must be done in the context of the project: we don't begin to understand the meaning of an action until we discover what that action is intended to achieve. We then undertake a process of elaboration by relating that intention to a range of pre-established and taken for granted meaning contexts, and thus it emerges that we are not dealing with one meaning but with a complex of meanings. He also makes an important distinction between 'because motives' and 'in-order-to motives'. The former refer to our past experience, the latter to the goal of the action. Whilst it is the most complete analysis of action, and thus of persons, we have so far come across, however, it remains at a purely cognitive level. It assumes a simple relationship between beliefs, knowledge and actions and, as I have said before, there is overwhelming evidence that no such simple relationship exists. Like symbolic interactionism it possesses no independent conception of society in which to situate individual interaction. The existence of society is reduced to the stock of knowledge.

If we stay at the level of the stock of commonsense knowledge, we are directed to fairly small-scale studies of particular situations, the sort of empirical work at which symbolic interactionism excels. Gererally Schutz's work has been used to provide further sensitizing concepts, often implicitly. I am not aware of any one empirical study that uses it systematically except through the development of ethnomethodology, which I will be discussing shortly. There is however one writer, Peter Berger, who has made systematic attempts to extend phenomenology to a theory of society. The central work, which he wrote with Thomas Luckman, is *The Social Construction of Reality*, which explicitly sets out to combine a holistic and individualistic analysis. Shared and taken-for-granted commonsense meanings are still seen as the basis of social organisation, but they are more concerned with shared and explicit over-arching meanings that develop out of commonsense meanings. They argue that human beings have very few stable and specific instincts; the stability of social life must therefore come from the social environment which they themselves create and in this environment, it is the over-arching values and meanings, initially religious, which provide the real focus of social organisation and which are shared by everybody. Berger and Luckman are concerned with the way in which these meanings develop and are 'objectivated' in social institutions and thus socialize new members of a society.

Overall this leaves us with an approach similar to structural-functionalism. Ideas, cultural values and norms, are seen as the centre of social organisation, into which new members are socialised. Berger and Luckman spend rather more time talking about the development of these values out of the social interaction of individuals, but the end picture of social organisation is the same. The crucial difference is that structural-functionalism has a great deal to say about institutional organisations and the systematic relationships between institutions, whereas for Berger and Luckman this tends to be secondary. It is fairly simple to place this approach in a structural-functionalist context as yet another fragment, concerned with the cultural system, which for Parsons is one of four systems, even if it is the most important. I said earlier that once phenomenology has placed action 'inside the head', it finds it difficult to break out again, and indeed in sociological literature Berger is regarded primarily as a sociologist of knowledge rather than a theorist of society.

If Schutz's importance were to be measured by its direct influence on the activities of sociologists, he would not have deserved so much space. The same would be true of phenomenology as a whole; the importance of the ideas I have discussed rather abstractly lies in their contribution to an apparently radical and new development in social thought: ethnomethodology.

ETHNOMETHODOLOGY: DOING

For some time, ethnomethodology was a thorn in the side of the sociological establishment: it appeared to undermine all existing forms of sociological work and indirectly challenge the integrity of established sociologists. There was a period at the beginning of the 1970s when a number of sociology departments in universities in the USA and Britain were split by arguments, and there are stories of ethnomethodologists being fired from sociology departments because they were ethnomethodologists. After an initial cult popularity, the movement subsided somewhat and although a number of sociologists still identify themselves with the approach, it has settled into being another of the discipline's many aspects. The analogy I drew with viewing society as a conspiracy is even more apt in the case of ethnomethodology. Like phenomenology, ethnomethodology sees social organisation as something which has to be established out of different experiences of different individuals. However, whereas Schutz would argue that order is the result of shared commonsense knowledge, ethnomethodology argues that such knowledge is itself inherently unstable, something which is created anew in each new encounter. We conspire together to create the impression of shared commonsense knowledge. In a classroom we all assume that we are reasonably intelligent people engaged in a process of learning and teaching and rarely, if at all, do we need to articulate those assumptions. For Schutz the existence of such assumptions explains the orderly proceeding of the class. For an ethnomethodologist, such assumptions do not exist in any substantial way and in each and every class we are conspiring together, of necessity in a taken-for-granted way, to give each other the impression that they do exist. We are 'doing' a class—my students are 'doing' being a student and I am 'doing' being a teacher. Every stable social interaction is an *achievement*, something done, and ethnomethodology seeks how it is done. Hence the name—*ology* (the study of), *ethno* (peoples) *methed* (methods)—for creating social order.

The intellectual origins of ethnomethodology lie not only in phenomenological sociology as developed by Schutz but also in the tradition of linguistic philosophy that originated with Ludwig Wittgenstein. It used to be common to distinguish between 'situational' and 'linguistic' ethnomethodology but I think such a distinction is misleading since the central insights of the approach have to do with our use of language to make situations stable. Paradoxically the clarity of expression associated with linguistic philosophy is transformed by ethnomethodology into the most convoluted jargon to have appeared in an area where jargon is the norm. As time has passed, it has become clear that the verbiage hides two important ideas which have led to some interesting work and a lot of nonsense — or more charitably, a lot of routine work dressed up in a jargon that makes it seem nonsense. These ideas are built into a criticism of established sociology and this provides a good entry to the substantive contribution of ethnomethodology.

The usual way of putting this criticism is that other forms of sociology take as a resource what should be taken as a topic. At some level, different in each case, the meanings employed by those we study, their norms, values, attitudes and beliefs, the rules which govern their conduct are treated as if their meaning were unproblematic. The work of explanation then employs those very same meanings as its basis — the sociologist conspires with the people she studies to produce yet another impression of social order. This is where the important insights of ethnomethodology come into play. The first is that of the inherent *indexicality* of meaning. Language works rather like an indexing system in a library, constantly referring us to other works on the same topic, works by the same author and so on; the meaning of each term in a language refers us to its context, the situation in which it is used and the words around it. This is most obvious with pronouns such as 'you' — which 'you' I am talking about is clear only in the situation in which I use it. However, the same is true of any word or statement; when we listen to somebody talk we are always having to wait to understand what they are saying: if you go back and read the first sentence of this paragraph it is by no means clear what I am talking about; in the process of reading you suspend judgement until I explain what I mean. However the same is true of any sentence or phrase taken in isolation and the process of explanation has no end. It is always possible to ask 'What do you mean?' to any reply that you get. We cannot, therefore, take any meaning for granted yet we all behave as though we can.

The second significant idea approaches the question of how we can behave as though meaning were clear: it points to the *reflexivity* of our talk about our actions and situations. When we describe a situation, we are at the same time creating it, making it appear solid, meaningful and rational. When I write: 'I am writing a book on sociological theory' I am not just describing what I am doing, I am at the same time justifying what I am doing, telling myself and others how to approach what I am doing, removing areas of doubt and uncertainty. The term 'reflexivity' sums up the activities that, in everyday interaction, we employ to correct 'indexicality' and establish a sense of social stability. Harold Garfinkel, the generally recognised founding father of ethnomethodology, first followed Schutz in referring to them as 'background expectancies', taken-for-granted forms of commonsense knowledge. His earlier work took the form of experiments to establish the existence of such expectations and of indexicality. He would send his students out to do things that would challenge background expectations, for example to go into a department store and try to bargain for goods, or to go back to their family home and behave as if they were lodgers. He regarded the resulting social disorder as proving his claim. To demonstrate indexicality he asked them to clarify the meaning of a transcribed conversation between a husband and wife and, of course, no complete clarification was possible. He could always ask 'What do you mean by this?'.

Later he came to talk less about background expectations and more about 'practices' and rules, emphasising the point that maintaining an impression of social order is a never ceasing activity. Such activities are difficult to grasp at first, simply because they are, in Garfinkel's view, a taken for granted basis to all our actions; it is rather like paying constant attention to the process of breathing or the way in which we put one foot in front of another. A couple of examples should suffice. The first is 'glossing'. If we use the word at all in our everyday speech, glossing usually refers to something like 'avoiding the issue' or trying to talk our way around the issue. The first part of this paragraph was glossing—I could not give a literal definition of these practices so I talked about how hard it is to understand them. If the argument about indexicality is correct, then all talking is glossing. One of the most interesting ethnomethodologists Aaron Cicourel, sums it up thus:

We can perhaps achieve glimpses of our glossing activity by making it clear that every attempt to stimulate or avoid the glossing activity is itself a glossing operation. This means showing the absurdity of efforts to be uncompromisingly literal in our description of observed events or activities in which we participate[1].

In the process of glossing, it seems we have recourse to certain implicit and taken-for-granted rules (as opposed to taken-for-granted substantive knowledge). An example of such a rule is the *et cetera* clause which is an addendum to all rules of social behaviour which says something like 'except in reasonable circumstances'. For example, when I give a lecture there is an informal (and sometimes formal) rule that I am the one who does the talking and everybody else keeps quiet. The *et cetera* rule allows people to break the first rule 'in reasonable circumstances', by asking a question, perhaps, or carrying on a short whispered conversation with a neighbour. The next step would be to look at ways in which the *et cetera* rule is invoked.

Again we are left with a low-level theory—a few theoretical insights which point towards empirical investigation. Although there have been attempts to develop the theory further—I shall look at these shortly—the emphasis of ethnomethodology has been on empirical work. It involves a sort of empirical application of the phenomenological reduction: the researcher pays no attention to the substance of what people say (that would be to engage in the conspiracy of giving an impression of social order) but looks at the way they say it, trying to identify the rules and practices by means of which the impression of order is given. The result is a startling departure from what we would normally expect. Another early ethnomethodologist, Harvey Sachs, employed his research time in a Suicide Prevention Centre studying the way in which people opened telephone conversations. Much ethnomethodological research seems to spend a great deal of time and energy to come up with taken-for-granted rules that are in fact no surprise to anyone: amongst Sachs' conclusions, for example, were the propositions that in conversations, generally only one person speaks at a time and when more than one person speaks at a time, it will be only briefly. There are, I think, good reasons for this comparative poverty of research findings: reflexivity refers to a process in which the product is a sense or order of apparently substantive meanings, and the starting point is the absence of that sense; we can find out very little about the process itself without knowing about the starting point and the end point. It would be like trying to understand the production process in a factory without bothering to find out what raw materials are used and ignoring the finished product, and in this case there would appear to be no raw materials. This is precisely what a lot of empirical ethnomethodology manages to do, and for this reason a lot of sociologists dismiss it. I think this is mistaken: like any other theory ethnomethodology opens some doors and closes others. I want now to examine its theoretical status rather more closely.

THE WAY OUT OF COGNITION

I think the best way to approach ethnomethodology is as a theory of 'social cognition' which in turn must have its place in a general theory of persons or action. It is a theory of the way in which we come to agree on what makes up the social world. Aaron Cicourel seems to me to have made the most theoretical progress in this direction and his work points to more interesting possibilities. He argues that the sense of social structure we seek to establish in our interaction is the product of what he calls 'surface' and 'interpretive' or 'deep' rules (drawing here on the work of the linguist, Chomsky). Surface rules are the norms of social life that the other theoretical approaches have taken for granted. Ethnomethodology has, I think, established conclusively that such rules can not be taken for granted but are at least interpreted and reconstructed in different ways in different situations. This reconstruction is carried out by an underlying structure of interpretive rules which he seems to think are innate properties of human beings. We do not learn them, they are instead the basis for learning. This in itself is sufficiently interesting but Cicourel goes further in indicating why such an underlying structure of interpretive rules should be necessary. Our perception of the world works through all of our five senses: we can see the world, hear, feel, taste and smell all at the same time and the things and events of the world are perceived simultaneously. Language, however, enables us only to talk about one thing at a time and there is a process of translation from our other non-linguistic experiences of the world into our descriptions. This is why describing an event is always creating that event, never simply a matter of recording it. Here at last, there is a pointer out of cognition, since not just our minds but our emotions are involved in our experience of the world. The connection between the word and the perception, and the word and the feeling, have been barely touched on by social theory; yet all empirical investigations concerned with what people say assume that the relation presents no problems.

One of the points to emerge from phenomenological sociology in general and from Cicourel's work in particular, points to another part of the social world which seems to comprise a separate area of study: the realm of general meanings. The existence of such a realm is disputed by ethnomethodology in some of its forms; to accept a realm of general meanings is seen as entering into the conspiracy to give an impression of social order. However, whilst it might be true to say that an impression of social order is constructed afresh in each social interaction, we do not invent meaning each time; what we do is give a specific situation-related version of a general meaning. General meanings are tools we employ in different ways in different circumstances, rather as we might use a hammer for knocking in a nail, pulling out a nail, or smashing a window to escape from a fire. These general meanings are Cicourel's surface rules or Berger and Luckman's over-arching symbols, socially shared and established, similar to language itself. Thus, if not exactly pointing beyond cognition in this respect, ethnomethodology again points to an area of investigation and a problem for action theory: what is involved in employing a general meaning in a particular way.

Having said all this, it is still the case that ethnomethodology closes some extremely important doors. I argued in the case of symbolic interactionism that to assume that there may be no such thing as a society when the experience of those we study suggests that there is such a thing is to do violence to the experience of those we study. Ethnomethodology deliberately sets out to do such violence: the perception of 'society' as a social structure over and above social interactions is a result of a conspiracy. To investigate society in such a sense is simply to take part in the conspiracy. For reasons I have already suggested, it seems to me we can accept that social interaction involves creating an impression of social order, but this in no way invalidates the arguments that I used in the Introduction to Part II about the existence of societies as separate and different objects of study. If we accept the ethnomethodological argument on this point, then we cannot approach any of the major social problems such as unemployment, crime or war, that are crucial features of our lives. It is not true that opening the door to the indexical and reflexive features of interaction closes the door to more conventional forms of sociological study; rather it should add a new dimension to them.

NOTES

[1] Cicourel, A.V. (1973), *Cognitive Sociology*, Penguin, Harmondsworth, p. 109.

FURTHER READING

On phenomenological sociology
The two books co-authored by Peter Berger are very readable starting points but Schutz provides the real flavour of the approach. The other works listed are mainly introductory articles or readers (Psathas is more advanced) and there is little to choose between them.

Berger, P. and Luckman, T. (1967), *The Social Construction of Reality*, Allen Lane, London.
Berger, P. and Kellner, H. (1974), *The Homeless Mind*, Penguin, Harmondsworth.
Filmer, P. et al. (1972), *New Directions in Sociological Theory*, Collier MacMillan, London.
Lassman, P. (1974), 'Phenomenological perspectives in sociology', in Rex, J. (ed.), *Approaches to Sociology*, Routledge & Kegan Paul, London, pp. 125–44.
Natanson, M. (1970), 'Phenomenology and typification: a study in the philosophy of Alfred Schutz', *Social Research*, Vol. 37, pp. 1–22.
Gorman, R. (1977), *The Dual Vision*, Routledge & Kegan Paul, London.
Psathas, G. (1973), *Phenomenological Sociology: Issues and Applications*, John Wiley, New York.
Schutz, A. (1962/6), *Collected Papers*, 3 vols, Martinus Nijhoff, The Hague.
Schutz, A. (1972), *The Phenomenology of the Social World*, Heinemann, London.
Wolff, K.H. (1978), 'Phenomenology and sociology', in Bottomore, T.B. and Nisbet, R. (eds), *A History of Sociology Analysis*, Heinemann, London.

Ethnomethodology
Attewell offers a good survey and Leiter a good introduction. The rest is the hard stuff. Douglas contains a useful discussion of the difference between ethnomethodology and symbolic interaction.

Attewell, P. (1974), 'Ethnomethodology since Garfinkel', *Theory and Society*, Vol. 1, pp. 179–210.
Cicourel, A.V. (1973), *Cognitive Sociology*, Penguin, Harmondsworth.
Cicourel, A.V. (1964), *Method and Measurement in Sociology*, The Free Press, New York.
Douglas, J.D. (1971), *Understanding Everyday Life*, Routledge & Kegan Paul, London.

Garfinkel, H. (1967), *Studies in Ethnomethodology*, Prentice–Hall, Englewood Cliffs.
Leiter, K. (1980), *A Primer on Ethnomethodology*, Oxford University Press.
Sudnow, D. (ed.) (1972), *Studies in Social Interaction*, The Free Press, Glencoe.
Turner, R. (1974), *Ethnomethodology*, Penguin, Harmondsworth.

Useful critical studies

Giddens, A. (1976), *New Rules of Sociology Method*, Hutchinson, London, Chapter 1.
Goldthorpe, J.H. (1973). *A Revolution in Sociology, Sociology*, Vol. 7, pp. 449–62.

Part III
SUMMARY AND PREVIEW: FROM ACTION TO STRUCTURE

Introduction to Part III

All the approaches dealt with in Part II were based on the same
starting point: a model of human action that makes reference to
peoples' intentions, the means available to carry them out, and the
meanings in which they formulate their intentions and select what
seem to be the appropriate means. It is recognised that peoples'
surroundings limit their choices, and that the surroundings may be
interpreted in different ways. Each approach works with an explicit
or implicit idea of social structure as a system built up out of the
actions and interactions of individuals. This is most explicit and
worked-out in structural functionalism: indeed it is so thoroughly
worked-out that we saw the emphasis of Parsons' work shift from
consideration of interaction and choice to an analysis of the ways in
which social systems limit and determine interaction and choice. I
suggested that such a switch was built into his theory, given that there
is no clear distinction between action and social structure or system.
In effect they are the same, one is a congealed version of the other, and
we can look at this same thing from one perspective or the other, from
the point of view of the individual or the system, but not from both
points of view at the same time. I also suggested that the various
inadequacies in the structural—functionalist conception of social
system can be traced to the view that the system is congealed action;
most important it could not distinguish between what David
Lockwood called social integration and system integration. In other
words there is no conception of a social structure underlying peoples'
actions and meanings, but separate from them.

  The other approaches did not have such a thorough conception of
the social system and in this sense they can be considered as fragments
of structural-functionalism. Conflict theory certainly focusses on the
system level, but its analysis is much more limited and descriptive; its'

one advantage over the more complete analysis of structural-
functionalism is that it points to the complexity of the social world
instead of over-simplifying it by forcing it into abstract theoretical
concepts. Symbolic interactionism and ethnomethodology both
concentrate on the aspect neglected by Parsons, individual interaction as opposed to system analysis, and at first sight they appear
opposed to Parsons. However, they both imply a similar notion of
systems as congealed interactions, even though, in the case of
ethnomethodology, it does not remain so for longer than the course
of the interaction. They both take the alternative perspective to that
of most of Parsons' work and they both present a more elaborate
view than Parsons. Symbolic interactionism tries to make sense of the
flux and flow of everyday life and is closer to the world that most of us
experience; ethnomethodology offers a more rigorous and carefully
worked-out idea of the structure of action, but both suffer from not
having any worked-out conception of social system. I have tried to
show that none of the three other approaches are fundamentally
incompatible with structural-functionalism; they take an aspect of
the latter and move it to the centre of the analysis.

The other dimension of fragmentation has to do with there being
different types of object in the world, each requiring different types of
theory to understand it. In the Introduction I concentrated on the
distinction between action and agents on the one hand and societies
on the other. In the course of Part II, I have pointed to further
distinctions on the agency side. I suggested, for example, that
structural functionalism might be an appropriate theory for looking
at active organised groups in the process of establishing themselves.
Such groups are halfway between individual interaction and established structure; they might contain aspects of both and yet be
different from either. I also indicated that there might be different
aspects to the analysis of action; generally these approaches concentrate on the social processes of cognition, of how we come to
know, at the expense of processes of emotion and of unconscious
levels of the person. Finally, in my criticism of ethnomethodology I
suggested that there might be a level of 'general meanings', that the
ideas which we share as members of society might make an object of
study, with its own type of theory.

This leads on nicely to the general approach labelled 'structuralism'. There are two aspects of the approach I want to discuss. The
first and most important is as a theory of social structures that exist

independently of our knowledge, and, in one sense, of our actions—the aspect of social life that is absent from all variations of action theory. I will look at this through the work of modern Marxist thinkers such as Louis Althusser and Nicos Poulantzas. Before I move on to this however I want to look at the other aspect: structuralism as a theory of general meanings. Here we find the notion that our ideas, the way we think, have an underlying structure which in fact determines what we think. As I write this book, it might seem to me that I am thinking creatively and freely; nobody is looking over my shoulder telling me what to write. A structuralist would argue that everything I write is predetermined by the ideas I start with. I want to deal with this aspect of structuralism for two reasons: first it provides an introduction to a method employed by structural theorists of society and helps us to make more sense of them; secondly this approach does seem to me to tell us important things about the world in its own right. After dealing with structuralism as a theory of general meanings, and then as a theory of social structure I will go on to look at the way this approach has fragmented. The process is the opposite one to that of action theory. Whereas the problem with action theory is that it tries to move directly from interaction to social structure, the problem with structuralism is that it tries to move directly from social structure to interaction: it sees our actions as determined by social structures rather than as affected by but different from social structures. As this problem has come to be seen as more acute, so structuralist theories of society have lost their distinctiveness: they too end by saying 'there's a lot going on out there....'.

Before moving on to structuralism, however, it is necessary to make some distinctions. The difficulty with words such as 'system' 'structure' and 'society' is that their meanings overlap without being exactly the same. So far, I have been careless in their use because the differences have not been all that important, but it is now time to try to use them more precisely. I will use *system* to refer to the structural-functionalist idea of social organisation as congealed patterns of interaction; the approach should really thus be called 'system-functionalism'. I will use *society* as I used it in Chapter 2, in the discussion of Bhaskar, to refer to an aspect of social reality which is distinct from agency and action and needs to be understood in a different way. Finally I will use *structure* to refer to the underlying models of the world that structuralists seek to identify.

7 The world as a logical pattern: an introduction to structuralism

THE BACKGROUND

'Structuralism' is a form of theory which has come to be influential in a number of disciplines: philosophy, social theory, linguistics, literary criticism, cultural analysis, psychoanalysis, the history of ideas, the philosophy of science, anthropology and others. It is difficult to provide a definitive definition, not least because during the 1960s and 1970s, it became a fashionable cult. Originating in France, where it has generally been the case that intellectuals play a greater part in public life than in Britain and America and their work sometimes attracts a following amounting to a sub-culture, the movement also gained a following amongst young academics in Britain and America. Thus it took root in an intellectual climate very different to that of France. Traditionally British (especially) and American universities have been suspicious of ideas originating from France and Germany, they are seen as vague and jargon-ridden speculations and structuralism came under attack for precisely these reasons. The response of the disciples in these countries has been similar to the reactions I talked about in the Introduction: they retreated into their own world, made a virtue of jargon and complication, and tended towards dogmatism. In turn their critics became more bitter and destructive. As with the struggle over ethnomethodology, people lost their jobs. As recently as 1980, Colin

McCabe, a structuralist literary critic was fired from his post at Cambridge University precisely because he was a structuralist (although he was almost immediately offered a chair at another university). Much recent writing on structuralism carries the mark of these battles.

As a school of thought, it can trace several lines of descent. One line runs through British and French anthropology and will be of comparatively little import to what I have to say here. Another runs through the central tradition of French sociology: Comte in the early nineteenth century, Durkheim around the beginning of this century, taking in particular the idea of society existing over and above the individual and 'social facts' as consisting of 'collective representations'. A third line is the philosophical tradition originating with Kant, the crucial idea being that human beings possess rational faculties with which they impose order on the world. Yet another, and substantively the most important, is through the school of structural linguistics and the work of Ferdinand de Saussure and the Russian Formalist school of literary criticism. If there are many roots, I have already indicated that there are many branches, and the leading figures are still French: Claude Lévi-Strauss (anthropology), Louis Althusser (social theory and philosophy), Roland Barthes (literary criticism and cultural studies), Christian Metz (film criticism) Jacques Lacan (psychoanalysis), Michael Foucault (the history of ideas) and Jacques Derrida (philosophy).

Intellectual cults, like other modern cults, tend to pass quickly, and perhaps it was because of the intensity of the debate that the proponents of structuralism were the first to develop in such a way as to undermine its own foundations. The names associated with what is now known as 'post-structuralism' are also associated with the original movement—Foucault and Derrida in particular. I will be following through one branch of this development in Chapter 9, that in relation to the structuralist Marxism of Althusser. For the moment, however, I want to focus on structuralism as a theory of general meanings rather than of societies.

A FIRST APPROXIMATION

The first model I will take throughout this chapter is language. Structuralism regards all human products as forms of language and this includes what I called 'general ideas'. My argument in relation to ethnomethodology was that when we talk to other people we use terms which already have a general meaning and we give them a specific, context-bound meaning. I suggested that these general meanings might be considered another realm of social reality and I want now to suggest that structuralism contributes to our under-standing of this area. We can take a set of general ideas, a particular theory, or perhaps what we call 'commonsense', and look for an underlying structure, a rationale or logic to them. Hence the title of this chapter—the world as a logical pattern. Just as we might look at all the different actions and choices of a friend and seek an underlying logic in order to understand her, so we might do the same for all the different statements that, say, a Christian makes.

This is not to say that I think structuralism is unreservedly a good thing. I would like to make a distinction between structuralism as a method and as a set of metaphysical assumptions. By method, I mean a procedure, a way of looking at or thinking about the world which enables us to discover things that we did not initially know were there. This sometimes involves making certain assumptions about the world. For example, if I am making a journey by train or plane and I want to discover how long the journey will take, I assume that the transport will run on time, that I won't be struck down by lightning when I leave and so on. The assumptions become metaphysical if I assume that they *really* are the case, that all trains *do* leave on time, that I shall *never* be struck by lightning and so on. As a method I think structuralism is useful, it can tell us things about the world that we could not find without it. As a set of metaphysical assumptions, I think it is a disaster and an absurdity. Paradoxically the metaphysical assumptions have become most closely identified with and most clearly distinguish the school as a whole and I want to begin by looking at them—this will give us a view of the carcase of the animal as a whole; then I will look at the method, trying to distinguish the edible parts and the points at which they are connected to the carcase. From the point of view of many structuralists, I *will* be doing a butchering job, since the metaphysical assumptions are the most vital part of the approach.

THE METAPHYSICAL ASSUMPTIONS

By 'metaphysical assumptions', then, I mean statements about the nature of the world that cannot be proved and eventually have to be

taken on faith when in fact there are decisive arguments against
taking them on faith.

The world as a product of ideas

I have mentioned several times the view that the world we see around
us is a product of our ideas—this in turn has its roots in Kant's
philosophy or a distorted form of it. This is very much an assumption
of structuralism, and in claiming to show the underlying structure or
logic of general ideas, it is also claiming to show how we—or rather
our ideas—produce the world we see. Thus when Lévi-Strauss, for
example, claims to have discovered the underlying structure of
kinship systems in tribal society, he is claiming to have discovered the
underlying structure of kinship terminology, the ideas with which
these societies talk about kinship. Again I must repeat the same
argument: there is a degree of truth in this view—people with
different ideas do, to an extent, live in different worlds. But the world
always offers resistance to these ideas and then it becomes a matter of
approximating one to the other. Structuralism in its extreme form
does not consider this resistance: it does not matter to Lévi-Strauss
that kinship behaviour is different from what the terminology would
lead us to expect.

This assumption often takes the form of an attack on any attempt
to prove theories by testing them; after all, if our theories produce the
world, there is no point in testing them against the world. We will find
only what we have put there in the first place. Any approach which
sees some form of empirical testing as playing a role (such as the view
I am arguing for) is dismissed as 'empiricist', one of the dirtiest words
in the structuralist vocabulary.

The world as a logical pattern

The structuralist emphasis is always on the logical order or structure
underlying general meanings. It is sometimes assumed that this
'structure'—which I will discuss in more detail shortly—matches the
'structures' of the world, sometimes on the grounds that since the
mind is part of the world, the ideas that it produces will have the same
structure as the world. This is a sort of wager which we must make
against our intuition—since the real world gives evidence of being

illogical—and it leaves structuralism open to what, in the Introduction, I called the 'logical trap'. Any theory which is not entirely
logical must be wrong, and since no theory is entirely logical, we fall
into a bottomless pit.

'The death of the subject'

'The death of the subject' is the slogan most closely associated with
structuralism. 'Subject' means what I have referred to as agency,
action and persons. The idea being attacked is that people are the
authors of their thoughts and actions. It is assumed instead that
people are the puppets of their ideas, and their actions are determined
not by choice and decision but are the outcome of the underlying
structure of ideas, the logic of these ideas. If for example, I am a
Christian, I do not speak about Christianity, rather Christianity
speaks through me; some structuralists reach the extreme of saying
that people do not speak but rather they are spoken (by the
underlying structure of the language), that they do not read books
but are 'read' by books. They do not create societies but are created
by societies.

Again I can offer a 'moderate' argument: it is true that we are
always limited by our ideas, that they stop us saying certain things
and perhaps force us to say things that we do not exactly mean. We
are all engaged in a constant struggle with our ideas. But it does not
follow that our ideas, or rather their underlying structure, turn us
into puppets. Choice, intention, goals and values still have a role to
play and need to be understood; they are not entirely pre-determined.

I will now turn to structuralism as a method, showing the origins of
each of these metaphysical assumptions but also distinguishing the
usefulness of the method. When we come to look at structuralist
social theory in general in the next two chapters, these assumptions
will appear again frequently, as they generate the tensions and
difficulties that lead to the fragmentation of the approach.

Structuralism as a method

By 'method' here I mean that structuralism can act as a guide to the
analysis of general meanings: it gives us some idea of what to look for
and how to find it. I will begin with linguistics as a basic model and go
on to look at how the model has been extended.

The linguistic model

Ferdinand de Saussure is often regarded as the founding father of modern linguistics. Putting it over-simply, prior to Saussure, linguistics had been concerned with how a language develops over time; Saussure argued, like Durkheim in sociology, that we do not know how something works by tracing its history. Just as we can only understand a society by looking at the relationships between the different parts, so we need to look at the relationships between the different parts of language. The attempt to understand something by looking at its history has been labelled 'historicist', and, next to 'empiricist' is the second dirtiest word in the structuralist vocabulary.

Speech and language The function of language is to enable people to communicate, and we need to look at the way in which the different elements of a language contribute to communication through their relationships to each other. We cannot do that by looking at individual acts of speech, we need to look at the language as a whole, hence the distinction between speech and language. The individual speech act, what I say when I open my mouth, is always to some extent unique, and it cannot therefore be the object of a science. Language, on the other hand, is constant and possessed by everybody who speaks it; it is the raw material out of which we form our sentences. Each language is made up out of a finite number of sounds and rules about combining sounds, rather like the rules of grammar we learn at school. Speech refers to the apparently infinite number of sentences we may produce using these sounds and rules. Games provide helpful examples: the language of chess, for instance, consists of the board and the pieces and the rules of the game and these are the same for every game; the speech act is the individual game which is different from the other individual games.

The language is, then, the underlying structure or logic behind speech.

The sign The elements of this structure or logic are 'signs'. In everyday life, we tend to use the word in different ways: a cross on a chain around my neck is a sign that I am a Christian; dark clouds are a sign of rain; a red light by the side of the road is a sign that traffic must stop. The American philosopher, C.S. Pierce, one of the few non-European ancestors of structuralism, distinguished three types of sign: the *icon*, where the relationship is based on similarity, the cross around my neck is similar to the cross on which Christ was crucified; the *index*, where the relationship is causal, such as that between clouds and rain; and the *sign* proper, where the relationship is a matter of social convention or agreement. This is often called an *arbitrary* relationship, meaning that there is no necessary connection between, for example, the colour red and the instruction to traffic to stop. The colour could be blue, orange or purple; it just so happens that everyone agrees that red means stop or danger and this is an external reality imposed on individual members of society. If I were to decide that, for me, red means go and green means stop, I would not remain a member of society for very long.

Signs, the basic units of language, are arbitrary. There is nothing intrinsic in the word 'dog' that means that it has to refer to some hairy four-legged creature; we might as well call such animals 'professors' but we don't. The sign has two aspects, a *signifier* and a *signified*, the relation between them often being likened to that between two sides of a sheet of paper. The signifier is the 'material' element, the physical sound of 'dog', or the marks on a sheet of paper. This element is meaningless without the signified which is the concept the sounds refer to. Both are necessary to each other: the concept cannot be articulated without the sound.

It is important to remember that the signified is the concept not the object. We tend to assume that words are attached to objects like labels but structural linguistics breaks this connection, insisting on the difference between the concept and the object. There are various pithy ways of pointing this out: the concept of a circle is not round; the concept of a dog does not bark. This is a first step along the road to the metaphysical assumption that the objects we see in the world are created by our language or ideas. It is, I think, a justified step, in that it is simply the case that words do not 'grow out' of things naturally and are different from the things they denote.

Syntagm and paradigm   To say that the relationship between the sign and what it points to is arbitrary is only half the story. It is not a matter of agreeing the meaning of each sign in a language separately; rather they are all agreed as a structure of a whole—the red of the traffic light is part of a structure that includes green, red means stop because green means go and vice-versa. *The meaning of the linguistic sign depends upon its relationship to other signs.* We only know what 'three' means because of its relationship to 'one', 'two', 'four' etc. If we regard a simple sound as a sign, in English the words 'dog' and 'god' are made up of the same signs, but they have different meanings because the sounds have different relationships to each other. Similarly, Althusser argues that the word 'alienation' has a different meaning in Marx's later work to its meaning in his earlier work because it is related to different concepts.

We find the significant elements of a language by a method of 'concomitant variation'. We take a sentence or a word and in a sort of thought experiment, we vary each element, replacing one by another, and if there is a significant change in meaning, we have found a significant unit. If, taking the word dog, I substitute 'h' for 'd' and get hog, I have found a significant element. Structuralists often organise these elements as opposing pairs (binary oppositions)—d/h, for example. Lévi–Strauss would claim that the human mind is such that it orders the whole world into such opposites. Whether this is true or not is less important than the fact that here already we are beginning to get to the rules which govern relationships between signs, and thus govern what meanings can be produced. They can be analysed on two levels—the *syntagm* and the *paradigm*—and the first is more clearly a matter of rules than the second.

The syntagmatic level refers to what sounds or signs can or cannot follow each other in the 'syntagmatic chain'. Thus in English we do not usually find the combination 'hd', though we might find 'dh'. Odd little rules at this level are sometimes taught at school as an aid to spelling: 'i before e except after c'. The rules of grammar are again the appropriate model. The syntagmatic level can be seen as a horizontal axis of language, the paradigmatic level is the vertical axis. The paradigm consists of the set of words connected with the word in question by rules of similarity of sound or meaning. In the same system as 'dog' we can find 'hog', 'bog', 'cur', 'bitch', 'golden retriever' etc. Every time we use a word, we select from such a paradigm (see Figure 1).

This is as far as it is necessary to go with the linguistic model. We can see how the metaphysical assumptions are rooted in the method without following logically and necessarily from it. It seems to me justified to look at the language rather than speech but it does not follow that speech is determined by language and that we must disregard the speaking subject. Similarly, it is reasonable to suggest

PARADIGM	The	cur bitch dog hog cog bog	sat on the mat

SYNTAGM

Figure 1. Sometimes the paradigm too may be described in terms of opposites (e.g., dog/cat, dog/bitch etc.).

that the meaning of a word or sign depends on its relationship to others, and that it stands for a concept rather than an object, but it does not follow that it has no relation to an external object or that it creates that object. So far I hope I have demonstrated that structuralism seeks the underlying structure of a language—the basic elements and the rules which govern their relationships—the logic underlying a language.

The linguistic model extended: semiotics
'Semiotics' is the name given to the 'science of signs' (or general meanings)—not just of linguistic signs. I want to look at a couple of examples of structuralist analysis in this area—Roland Barthes on modern myths, and Will Wright's analysis of Western films—to emphasise what I see to be the benefits of this type of analysis.

The extension of the linguistic model into a general theory or science of signs is not precise—linguistics is used more as an approximate analogy as will become apparent when I look at the examples. It is based on the assumption that all human products are at some point a means of communication and can thus be analyzed like language, with a similar distinction between language and speech. Thus Lévi–Strauss claims to reveal the basic unit or 'language' of kinship systems, of which the different kinship systems of each tribe are the equivalent to speech acts. As we shall see in the next chapter, Louis Althusser identifies an underlying social structure or 'language' of capitalism of which the individual capitalist societies are 'speech acts'. Semiotics proper deals with a more diffuse area of cultural products. Barthes, for example, talks about the language and speech of food. The elements or signs are the individual foods. At the syntagmatic level there are rules governing which food may or may not accompany other food. In Western societies, we do not usually combine sweet and savoury items, pour custard over fried chicken or gravy over ice cream. If we eat such foods at the same meal, they must follow each other, savoury first, sweet after. The paradigmatic rules give us a choice of combinations, which meat with which vegetables. The individual meal, with its particular choices of food and methods of preparation is the speech act, employing the elements and rules. The assumption is that, in principle, any human product may be analyzed in this way.

Modern myths   In looking at the structure of modern myths,[1] Barthes deploys the concepts of sign, signifier and signified, but tends to assume that the signifier may point not just to an idea but to a real object. He borrows from Lévi–Strauss's work on mythology in tribal societies, where it is seen as a means by which a society organises its world, comes to terms with its problems, maintains an image of itself and ensures that individuals embrace that image. As an example of Barthes' analysis, I will take a newspaper picture, not all that different from one of Barthes' own examples, some variant of which appears in the British press each year at the end of August. At that time, the Notting Hill Carnival takes place in London; Notting Hill is an area of racial tension and the Carnival is primarily a West Indian event, based on carnivals in the Caribbean, although all races take part. There are often minor or major incidents of rioting as the day draws on. The picture, however, shows a white policeman and a black (of either sex) embracing and/or dancing together. Sometimes the black is wearing the policeman's helmet.

We can see this picture as a sign, combining a signifier (the material element, the patterns of ink on the newspaper) and a signified (a policeman and a West Indian apparently enjoying themselves). This picture is also part of a myth, it has another meaning beyond the signifier which helps make it up. The picture as a complete sign is incorporated into another language as a signifier for another signified—a set of beliefs which are, to say the least, debatable and sometimes contradicted by other events on the same day. These mythical beliefs comprise the image the society has, or would like to have of itself as a society in which people of different races co-exist happily, where black customs contribute to the quality of white life, in which there is no mistrust between blacks and the white police, and the latter are sufficiently confident to surrender their sign of authority (the helmet) in order to enjoy themselves.

The alternative way of talking about this picture as a sign is to take it up as a *signified* into another language (a 'meta-language'); in other words, it is to analyze it rationally, which is what I have been trying to do. It is easy to see, in this example, how this modern myth obscures a possibly threatening reality. What this analysis shows is how the 'meaning' of the picture is produced on two different levels. It shows the machinery at work behind what we might otherwise take for granted. There are plenty of mythical elements at work in our public life: the signs used by politicians to gain support, 'democracy', 'the silent majority', the 'evil of communism', are all mythical signs that mean much more than they say. The structure of myth and metalanguage can be represented diagrammatically as shown in Figure 2.[2]

The Western[3]   Wright described the 'language' of the Western, its underlying structure or logic. In fact, he deals with four types, while I will discuss only two—the classical plot and the 'vengeance' variation, as shown in Table 5. The basic elements of the Western, the 'signs', can best be seen as the characters: The hero(es), society (sometimes different aspects of society, e.g., ranchers versus farmer)

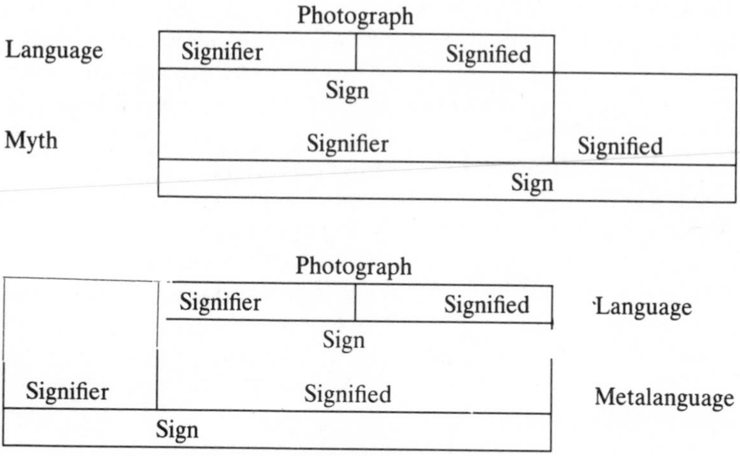

Figure 2

and the villain(s). Wright lists a set of 'narrative functions' for each type of plot, each function describing relationships between or qualities of the elements. The functions can be considered as themselves more complex signs. We arrive at these by the method of concomitant variation—if Wright's analysis is correct then changing any one element will change the meaning of the plot. After you've read the next couple of pages it might be useful to come back and experiment in this way.

As Wright presents them, the narrative functions are really a descriptive list but we can re-write them as rules, often simply by replacing 'is' with 'must be': 'the hero must be unknown to society', for example. They cover the succession of events, the syntagmatic level; each function enables the next to take place. In the classic plot, for example, nothing can happen until the hero arrives and is distinguished from the society, and then the conflict between the society and the villain may develop. Rewriting these as rules would provide a blueprint for a Western movie. All sorts of variation would be possible without affecting the basic plot—different types of fight, various sexual relationships and so on.

Turning to the paradigmatic level, we again enter the realm of mythology. Wright arranges this level in terms of oppositions which present problems that the plot sets out to solve. He identifies four, the last being the least important: inside society/outside society, good/bad, strong/weak, and wilderness/civilization. These are first of all oppositions which can be read off from the films themselves, qualities signified by the characters. According to Wright, they are also ways in which members of modern societies see their world—they divide it up into good and bad, strong and weak, what is inside and outside society. This creates a tension: how do we come to terms with a society divided in this way. The Western offers us a solution, not necessarily one we can practice in real life (although Wright suggests that it offers a model for individual action) but one which relieves the tension. It seems to me that what emerges from Wright's discussion is that the major opposition is not one of those listed above but that of individual/society: the Western offers a model for the resolution of the tensions between the two, different types of Western offering different types of solution. The word 'code' is often used by structuralists, less in a precise technical sense but rather with the implication of a hidden message: the Western is a code for these tensions and their resolution.

Table 5

The classical Western*	The 'vengeance' variation†
1 The hero enters a social group	1 The hero is or was a member of society
2 The hero is unkown to the society	2 The villains do harm to the hero
3 The hero is revealed to have exceptional ability	3 The society is unable to punish the villains
4 The society recognises a difference between themselves and the hero; the hero is given a special status	4 The hero seeks vengeance
	5 The hero goes outside of society
	6 The hero is revealed to have a special ability
5 The society does not completely accept the hero	7 The society recognises a difference between themselves and the hero; the hero is given a special status
6 There is a conflict of interests between the villain and the society	8 A representative of the society asks the hero to give up his revenge
7 The villains are stronger than the society; the society is weak	
8 There is a strong friendship or respect between the hero and a villain	9 The hero gives up his revenge
	10 The hero fights the villains
9 The villain threatens the society	11 The hero gives up his special status
10 The hero avoids involvement in the conflict	12 The hero enters society
11 The villain endangers a friend of the hero	
12 The hero fights the villain	
13 The hero defeats the villain	
14 The society is safe	
15 The society accepts the hero	
16 The hero loses or gives up his special status	

* Examples of the classic Western include: *Cimarron* (1931); *Destry Rides Again* (1941); *Duel in the Sun* (1947); *Shane* (1953); and *Cat Ballou* (1965).
† Examples of the vengeance variation are: *Red River* (1949); *Apache* (1954); and *The Man from Laramie* (1955).

THE ADVANTAGES OF THE STRUCTURALIST METHOD

I want to use the Western as an example of what the structuralist method enables us to discover. First of all, the very idea of an underlying structure or logic: it enables us to organise and classify material in a way that would not be possible if we dealt with all aspects on the same level. We could watch Westerns until we went blind without finding any way of classifying them if we treated each incident and character equally. In one, the hero falls in love, in another he doesn't, in one the villains are killed, in another they escape. There could be as many labels as there are types of film. Of course, structuralism does not offer a fool-proof method of classification, but then neither does any other method: what it does do is guide us towards the core, the most important and central aspects of what we are studying, beneath the surface flux. The fact that it is not just the basic elements but also the relationships between them, or rather the rules governing them means that the 'machinery' of the Western is laid open for inspection. We come to understand how the Western works. Particularly important here is the organisation of the paradigmatic level into oppositions which the 'syntagmatic chain' puts into motion and attempts to resolve. Structuralism takes the lid off the way in which cultural products work, the way they communicate.

It also presents us with a different and, I would argue, more useful conception of structure. Action theory possesses a concept of system, but that is seen in terms of the elements rather than the relationships between the elements; structuralism gives priority to the relationships. If we were to concentrate on the elements of Westerns, we would attempt to classify them by the roles of hero, villain etc., and different roles would entail a different type of Western. We would examine the roles in terms of the qualities and actions of the individual(s) concerned and these might not differ significantly from one type to the other. Wright shows that the elements might remain the same for each type, but the relationships between them give them a very different meaning.

This view of structure introduces the idea that there are different levels: a level which is more or less observable at first sight and a level which is less observable which has to be sorted out. We can compare this to the functionalist notion of system which deals with one level only (one level of reality, that is, functionalism deals with a number of levels of abstraction). Another way of putting this is that structuralism enables us to make the sort of distinction that David Lockwood was getting at in his differentiation between social and system integration; and it also suggests that the underlying level is more important, that it has some explanatory power when we look at the surface level.

THE DRAWBACKS OF THE METHOD

Reductionism

All the drawbacks of the method are associated in some way with the metaphysical assumptions that have come to characterize structuralism; they represent the tendency of the method to lead towards the assumptions. Thus to be able to distinguish an underlying structure or logic which has an explanatory importance can tempt the theorist to reduce the world to this level and thus lose dimensions of meaning that exist at the surface level. For example, the various surface-level incidents of the Western might add dimensions of meaning that do not change the underlying meaning but nonetheless add to the complexity and richness of the film. These incidents might have to do with sexual or racial relations, with historical events or situations and so on.

The tendency to reductionism, to losing secondary but nonetheless significant aspects of what we study is built into the separation of language and speech, since these aspects occur at the level of speech. The reduction can go much further than the underlying structure. It would be possible, for example, to describe the relationship between the syntagmatic chain and the paradigmatic oppositions as an algebraic equation; this could be done for each type of Western and we could then develop a higher level equation to describe the rules of transformation between the different types. I am not, you will be glad to hear, going to attempt this, but it can be done. Lévi–Strauss sometimes comes close to it. In the process *all* meaning seems to be lost and we end with a formal equation that is of no use to anybody. I should point out that Wright does not engage in this exercise and in fact moves in the opposite direction that I am implicitly recommending: towards the complexity of the surface level.

The problem of change

The problem of change stems from the criticism of historical development that I mentioned at the beginning and the tendency to regard the 'subject' as determined by underlying structures. Structural analysis is intended to replace historical accounts and the structure revealed is static—a set of relationships between elements. Wright, for example, is able to identify a classic plot and three variations, but at the level of structural analysis he cannot show why the variations develop and the classical plot changes. To do this properly he looks at social developments outside of the film itself which in this context is a return to the subject, to speech. Many structural linguists have argued that change in language can only be understood by reference to speech and the subject; structuralists at the heart of the modern movement, however, rule out this possibility and they are left to talk about 'transformations' as rather magical events with no real cause. Wright's explanation of the development of different types of Western also presupposes a world existing outside of the structure of ideas encoded by the Western, a world which effects this structure. This again would not be allowable to the strict structuralist who would have to assume that the external world is completely defined by the structure of ideas.

FROM GENERAL MEANING TO SOCIAL STRUCTURES

In this chapter, I have looked at structuralism as a way of identifying the underlying structures or logic of general meanings; we all have to live in and work by this structure even if it cannot be seen as determining precisely what we think or do. I have dealt with it only as a fragment of social theory, however, concerned with just one area of the social world. I now want to move on to structuralism as a general social theory, attempting to embrace the whole; in other words, moving back to the realm of Grand Theory and Parsons, although the Grand Theory is of a very different type. The metaphysical assumptions of structuralism will play a much greater role here since I think the fragmentation of the approach owes much to their existence.

NOTES

[1] Barthes, R. (1970), 'Myth today', in *Mythologies*, Jonathan Cape, London, pp. 109–59.
[2] Adapted from Barthes, R. (1970), *ibid.*, pp. 115.
[3] Wright, W. (1975), *Six Guns and Society*, University of California Press, Berkeley.

FURTHER READING

There are now numerous introductions to structuralism; Hawkes is probably the most accessible, although my personal favourite is Jameson—this is the most difficult but employs some useful images and sensible criticisms. Kurzwell provides the best general survey of individual writers.

Blonsky, M. (ed.) (1979), *The Essential Semiotics Reader*, Basil Blackwell, Oxford.
Clarke, S. (1981), *The Foundations of Structuralism*, Harvester, Brighton.
Culler, J. (1976), *Saussure*, Fontana, London.
Ehrmann, J. (ed.) (1970), *Structuralism*, Doubleday Anchor, New York.
Gardner, H. (1982), *The Quest for Mind*, Quartet, London.
Hawkes, T. (1977), *Structuralism and Semiotics*, Methuen, London.
Jameson, F. (1972), *The Prison House of Language*, Princeton University Press.
Kurzwell, E. (1980), *The Age of Structuralism*, Columbia University Press.
Lane, M. (ed.) (1970), *Structuralism: A Reader*, Jonathan Cape, London.
Robey, D. (ed.) (1973), *Structuralism: An Introduction*, Oxford University Press.

Of structuralist works relevent to the ideas of this chapter, Barthes' *Mythologies* is probably the best to start with, although all the works listed are worth reading. And of course there is Wright.

Barthes, R. (1967), *Elements of Semiology*, Jonathan Cape, London.
Barthes, R. (1977), *Image—Music—Text*, Fontana, London.
Barthes, R. (1972), *Mythologies*, Jonathan Cape, London.
Barthes, R. (1975), *S/Z*, Jonathan Cape, London.
Wright, W. (1975), *Six Guns and Society: A Structural Study of the Western*, University of California Press, Berkeley.
If you're interested in literary structuralism, see also
Lodge, D. (1981), *Working with Structuralism*, Routledge & Kegan Paul, London.

Most examinations of the relation between structuralism and sociology are not very helpful; of the following Badcock is the best, though it has little to do with the material dealt with in this chapter.

Badcock, C. (1973), *Levi-Strauss: Structuralism and Sociological Theory*, Hutchinson, London.
Bottomore, T.B. and Nisbet, R. (1979), 'Structuralism', in Bottomore, T.B. and Nisbet, R. (eds) *A History of Sociological Theory*, Heinemann, London, pp..557–98.
Goddard, A. (1976), 'On structuralism and sociology', *American Sociologist*, Vol. 11, pp. 133–39.
Runciman, W.G. (1979), 'What is structuralism', *British Journal of Sociology*, Vol. 20, pp. 253–65.

8 Structuralist Marxism: the world as a puppet theatre

THE TARGETS OF STRUCTURALIST MARXISM

For structuralist Marxism, the 'death of the subject' became an over-riding priority: the theory's claim is that the experience we have of being the authors of our action is in some sense mistaken or 'ideological' and that what really happens is that underlying social structures determine our actions, work through them and that our actions serve to reproduce and maintain these structures, or, on occasion, to transform them through revolution. Human beings become the puppets of social structure, which in turn becomes a sort of machine in permanent motion, and I want to argue that despite the usefulness of its analysis of social structures, the theory begins to break down when it approaches the realm of action, when it describes the strings which work the puppets.

This is the first chapter to deal with a theory in which the cognitive aspects, concerned with knowing the world, are intimately and often explicitly bound up with the political aspect, the attempt to change the world. There is already a tension here: if we are the puppets of social structures, how can we change those structures. This tension will reappear regularly. For the moment, I want to look at the practical, political context of structuralist Marxism: it is perhaps too easy for those of us who live in the West to think of Marxism as a monolithic entity in both theory and practice: a totalitarian regime matched by a dogmatic set of assertions about the world more akin to religion than science. It is worth remembering that no regime is so monolithic that no opposition exists, there is always some debate and conflict and in countries such as France, Italy, Germany and Spain where there are, or have been, large socialist and communist parties, these conflicts have been intensified and the debates more wide ranging. Over recent years, this has been so for two reasons: the parties have had to separate themselves in the public mind from the discredited regimes of Eastern Europe, and secondly they have had to come to terms with a situation in which parliamentary democracy seems to be well established and the possibility of a socialist revolution to have disappeared. The communist parties have had to appeal to the electorate for their survival.

The emergence of 'Eurocommunism' over the past few years is only one result of a long and painful debate amongst European communists. The arguments sparked off by tactical debates about political survival have also been carried on in terms of theory, about how Marxism can tell us about the world, and, indeed, about the nature of the world (i.e., modern capitalism) itself.

Like structuralism, structuralist Marxism originated in France and in this chapter I will look at the work of Louis Althusser, the most prominent figure, and, in less detail, of Nicos Poulantzas. In the context of modern socialism, Althusser and Poulantzas are representatives of a more orthodox and traditional form of Marxism, which they see as a science, giving us a scientific knowledge of the world that can be employed in developing a political strategy for bringing the working class to power. The representative of the working class is the Communist Party, the bearer of knowledge and decider of tactics. We find in their work the same tendencies to dogmatism (we are right) and authoritarianism (the Party knows best) that have unfortunately become the hallmarks of traditional Marxism. At the same time they have produced a remarkably sophisticated and stimulating interpretation of Marxism that has been, in different ways, influential on both sides of the Atlantic. In Britain it has led to increased sophistication in some original work in the philosophy of science in particular: Bhaskar's work, discussed in the introduction, owes much to the debates stimulated by Althusser. In the USA it has helped to generate a rich empirical investigation of class structure through the work of Erik Wright. It is a tragedy that the productive lives of both Althusser and Poulantzas have ended in immense personal disaster; it is a sign of the bitterness of the debates that their more unscrupulous opponents have tried to attribute these disasters to their theory and politics.

Their sophisticated form of orthodox Marxism has been developed against two targets, usually graced with the labels 'voluntarism' and 'economism'. Economism is a crude form of orthodox Marxism. It entails the assumption that everything originates at the economic level of society: that a particular form of economic organisation determines the nature of the rest of society, its political organisation, its ideas of itself and so on. There is also an assumption that the progress of history is determined by this same economic organi- sation, that the development from capitalism to socialism has something inevitable about it. 'Voluntarism' on the other hand works with the assumption that people determine what happens, not economic organisation; that human beings are free agents who have lost their freedom to a particular type of social organisation—capi- talism. Socialism will come when people realise this and seize back their freedom. This point of view owes much to Marx's earlier works, in particular the *1844 Manuscripts* and it became very important after 1960 amongst French Marxists arguing for radical changes in Communist tactics and organisation. Althusser was thus trying to separate himself from the orthodox tradition of Marxism and at the same time defend it—another manifestation of the tension I men- tioned at the beginning.

I ought to note two points before continuing. The first is that Althusser has always denied that he has been influenced by structu- ralism, which he calls an 'ideology'. I suspect this denial is itself of a political nature, but in any case the influence should be apparent in my account of his ideas. Secondly, in the early 1970s he published a small book *Essays in Self Criticism* in which he makes a number of modifications to the framework of ideas he built up during the 1960s. I will barely refer to this at all: it seems to me that the most important modifications lose the originality of his theory and leave him with little new to say. The important and instructive criticisms have come from those who have tried to develop and employ his work.

THE NATURE OF THEORY

The way in which I shall proceed in this chapter is through as straightforward an exposition of the ideas as possible beginning by looking at Althusser's conception of theory itself, which reveals some of the tensions which have led to the fragmentation of the approach. It is worth bearing in mind throughout this chapter that with structuralist Marxism we are back in the world of generalizing theory *à la* Parsons, attempting to develop concepts that will grasp both societies and agency. Parsons starts with agency, structuralist Marxism with society: each founders when it tries to move from one to the other. Like Parsons, Althusser is an obscure and difficult writer: in some of his work the aim of communication has been given up for the empty aim of being precise over what is by nature imprecise. But unlike Parsons, Althusser can often bring a real passion and concern to his theory which is all too often lost on his followers.

One reason for his obscurity might be that there is a tension in his work between two different views of theory. It is a tension which runs throughout his books, between on the one hand the need to find some way of testing a theory against 'facts', even if the theory talks about things we cannot see, and on the other, the view that our ideas about the social world actually create the facts that we see in it. This latter view is similar to the structuralist view discussed in the previous chapter. Althusser seems to argue on occasion that the world we see is in some way 'created' by the structure (or 'problematic') of the theory we employ. Each scientific theory creates its own world of 'theoretical objects' and he argues that one of the defining features of a science is that it produces a world of theoretical objects—different from the world we see in everyday life, but a world seen by the scientist in her scientific work. The problem with this approach is that each theory creates its own world, we cannot discover a 'real world' outside of theory which we can test our theories against. In other words, we cannot judge between theories: each belongs in its own world and is, presumably, right for that particular world. This poses an evident problem for a Marxist trying to establish that Marxism is *the* science of society; *the* theory; Parsons, after all, introduces 'theoretical objects', such as the general systems of action, and its various subsystems. How do we choose between them?

The other view of theory in his work is an answer, at least in part, to this problem. Despite the fact that a theory creates its own world of 'theoretical objects', these nevertheless have some relationship to real objects which have an independent existence in the world—independent both of the theory and of whether we can actually see them. This view comes very close to the one I have been arguing for since the beginning of the book: theory identifies real but unobservable social structures the nature of which explains what we can observe. It still leaves the problem of how we know that our theory is right, or at least better than others; how do we know that we have identified real underlying structures, or, in Althusser's terms, 'appropriated' them? Since a theory creates its own theoretical objects which are 'appropriations' of unobservable structures, we cannot test the theory directly against what we can see, so what do we do?

For Althusser, this is tied up with the problem of how we identify a science, of what is scientific and what is not. A science does not present us with a 'truth' once and for all, but goes through stages of development or 'revolutions' the first of which marks its foundation as a science, the moment when it creates its 'theoretical objects'. Beyond this, he suggests two criteria by means of which we can distinguish a science or show that one theory is more scientific than others. One of these criteria is, I think, not very helpful, the other helpful but partial, and the partiality contributes eventually to the undermining of his theory. The first he refers to as the 'openness' of the theory's 'problematic'—the body of concepts which make it up. If a theory is a body of concepts by means of which we understand the world, it does so by enabling us to ask questions about the world in terms of these concepts—it enables us to pose problems, hence 'problematic'. According to Althusser a closed (non-scientific or 'ideological') problematic asks questions but presupposes the answer. If we take Christianity as an example, it leads us to ask questions such as 'If God is good, what is the meaning of suffering'; the answer is presupposed because if we are not to challenge the whole belief system, we must find some answer that preserves the idea that God is good. Now it seems to me that this is true of any theory, whether scientific or not. For example, Marxist theory leads us to ask why there has been no revolution in the advanced capitalist countries; an answer in terms of the functional equilibrium of different subsystems would challenge the basis of the theory, which assumes quite clearly that capitalism is subject to regular crises. The answer must involve instead reference to the development of the capitalist mode of production, class struggle and so on—it must involve the conceptual tools of the theory and uphold the more basic propositions to which those tools lead us.

Althusser's second criterion has to do with what he calls the 'order of exposition' of the concepts in a theory. You might, correctly, find this ambiguous; as far as I can understand it, he is arguing that the more 'logically' or 'rationally' related the theory's concepts to each other, the more each depends upon and can be derived from the others in some particular order, the more scientific is the theory. I have already argued that logical or rational coherence is one of the means by which we can judge a theory but that there are other ways, equally useful. These can include the scope of the explanation it offers—how much it can cover—and the extent to which it can be directly or indirectly confirmed by our observation. All these play a part and it is never a matter of simply accepting or rejecting a theory on the basis of any or all of them. I have also argued that the problem with this, apart from what we may mean by 'logical' or 'rational' coherence, is that the world itself is not necessarily a logical and coherent place and it is doubtful whether a fully coherent theory could be produced; it would be like the seamless web with no beginning and no end. It is in the search for such a theoretical web that his followers, particularly his English followers, began to fragment the theory; Althusser himself left them little else to go by.

For Althusser, then, theory creates its own theoretical objects which nonetheless 'appropriate' real but unobservable objects (i.e., underlying social structures). A scientific theory is rationally and logically coherent in its production of theoretical objects. I should emphasise that Althusser is talking about the theory and not the theorist, who is as much the puppet of the theoretical structure as we all are of social structures. He tries to show that in the course of Marx's work we find the theoretical revolution (the 'epistemological break') which founded a science of society, and that the conceptual structure of this science can be found in his later work, especially *Capital*. This is a vital part of his case against humanism: the earlier works on which it is based are not scientific. He does not claim, like other modern Marxists, to be developing or interpreting Marx, but rather to be presenting what Marx really said. This gives much Althusserian work the air of biblical exegesis, the attempt to discover revealed truth. Althusserian social theory to an extent rests its claim to validity on the grounds that 'this is what Marx really said', but there is no reason to take this too seriously. We can regard Althusser as a developer and interpreter of the Marxist tradition and thereby get more out of his work than we could in engaging in arguments about sacred texts.

ALTHUSSERIAN SOCIAL THEORY: BASIC CONCEPTS

Practices and structures

We can now turn to the basic concepts—or less charitably, jargon—of Althusser's social theory, trying as far as possible to avoid the less attractive aspects of his style. These are the concepts that make up Marx's scientific problematic and I will proceed by looking at the most general ideas first, setting out a 'map' of the social machine that works the human puppets. I will begin with the ideas of 'practice' and 'structure' and then move on to the ways in which these are brought together in Althusser's model of social organisation, or the 'social formation'. I will then look in more detail at the basic level of the social formation, the economic structure, and the way in which this enables us to distinguish between different types of society.

'Practice' is the term used to refer to human action and it plays the important role in his theory of removing from the beginning the aspects of agency which I have argued are important, such as intention and choice. A practice consists of three elements and the model for all practices is economic practice, the act of producing something out of something else. There is the raw material, the means of production, including labour power and available tools, and there is the finished product. The determining element in a practice is seen as the combination of labour power and means of production, the former acting as a sort of fuel for the latter; agency is simply the power which moves material things. There is certainly a sense in which Althusser produces a metaphorical description of many work processes, people do become dominated by their tools, they become the energy that keeps the machine going; for many industrial workers there is no question of choice or intention. There is, however, a difference between a metaphorical description of the work process, which may also be used as a basis for criticizing capitalist society, and a basis for social theory.

Be that as it may, human action is seen as a number of practices analytically distinguishable from each other but modelled on economic practice. *Political* practice works on the raw material of social relations, by means, presumably, of political organisation; *ideologi-*

cal practice works on the way people see themselves and their world; *theoretical* practice works on ideology by means of the theory's problematic in order to produce knowledge, the scientist providing the 'thinking power'. The analogy with economic practice is not always entirely clear, because, I would suggest, agency is much more important at the political and ideological levels. I will return to this later; for the moment I will stay with theoretical practice because it underscores a significant difference between theory as conceived by Althusser and theory as conceived by exponents of action theory. For the latter, theory is an elaboration of commonsense knowledge, a matter of making explicit what people know already. For Althusser theory is a transformation of the commonsense or ideological world, the finished product is radically different from the raw material. If we are going to produce a theory of social structures as opposed to agency, then it should be apparent from what I have said before that Althusser's conception is closer to the one we need.

There is no *a priori* reason why the list of practices should not extend indefinitely; Althusser himself has added artistic practice to the list. However three are particularly important because they provide the basis of the analysis of society: economic, political and ideological. Each of these practices takes place in structures, sets of relationships constructed around the basic elements of the practice, the raw material, means of production and finished product. The structures in which these three practices are placed comprise the basic levels (or 'instances') of society—the economic, political and ideological levels. All societies can be seen as comprising these three levels; they make up the 'social formation', a structure of structures. The basis for arguing that there are three levels is that Marx said so. I do not want to dispute this: it seems to me quite a useful way of looking at the world with a pay-off which will emerge shortly. For the moment, it is worth pointing out that 'political' and 'ideological' should be given a wider meaning than we give them in everyday speech. Most organisations can be treated as political and ideological and the latter refers to all our ways of seeing ourselves and the world. Such a division of society into three levels covers most of what we would want to talk about in social theory.

Structural causality and over-determination
One important difference between Althusser and the more orthodox structuralists is that he does work with an idea of causality, as

opposed to 'rules of transformation'. There is, however, the same emphasis on the importance of relationships and the 'causes' about which Althusser writes lay not in distinct things (or the elements of the structure), nor, of course, in peoples' intentions, but in the relationships between the elements. My discussion of causality in Chapter 2 owes much to Althusser, with the difference that I maintained that the teleological notion is essential for understanding agency whilst Althusser takes the opposite view.

Now I argued earlier that Althusser was fighting on two political and theoretical fronts, that he was arguing against the crude forms of orthodox Marxism and against humanist Marxism. For the moment I want to deal with the first argument, against crude Marxism. The idea of structural causality is already something of an advance, since Marxists have always had a tendency to write as if the economy were a thing with a simple linear causal influence on everything else, as if the economy were the billiard cue and the political and ideological levels the billiard balls that it sets in motion. Althusser thus draws attention to the fact that these three levels *are* structures, that they have different elements and relationships between them and that we must take care to analyse them. They are not simple. He also goes on to argue that the political and ideological levels are not produced as the simple effects of the economic level. Each has its own real existence and is related to the others in various ways ('complex' is a favourite word). There is a useful architectural analogy here which comes orginally from Marx and takes us some of the way to understanding Althusser's view. We can look at the relationship between the floors of a multistory building: it would be nonsense to say that the first and second floors are caused by the ground floor, even though they rest upon it, have some sort of relationship to it. Each is separate from the floor above and below it, and what goes on on each floor is not determined by what goes on below it. The first floor might be a shop, the second floor offices and the third floor living quarters. Althusser's term for describing this relation where there is a causal connection but not complete dependence is 'relative autonomy'. The political and ideological levels are neither completely dependent on the economic nor completely independent. If we take this building as a single enterprise, the office work which goes on on the second floor obviously depends upon the sort of trading that goes on in the shop but there are various ways in which it might be organised, and the work relationships there may develop in ways not influenced by the economic activity going on below. Similarly, if the owners live on the third floor their standard of living and way of life has its limits set by the nature of the business they run but there are choices within these limits and the development of a marriage and family life has its own dynamics.

Althusser's next step away from crude Marxism is to argue that the causal processes are two-way: the political and ideological levels effect the economic. Returning to the example, decisions based on administrative criteria in the offices may have an effect on the trading in the shop—a 'streamlining of the management structure' for example, might lead to increased turnover. Similarly if the business is jointly owned and the marriage fails, the settlement between the partners might have an important effect on the nature of the business. This, however, is as far as we can take this analogy; to follow Althusser's argument further we need to return to a more abstract level.

It has always been the case that Marxists have seen the economic level and its development as determined by a contradiction—usually identified as that between the forces and relations of production. It is not necessary to know the technical details of the arguments, but the basic idea is that the productive forces of capitalism, its ability to produce wealth, are immense and continue to grow; on the other hand the relations of production, the fact that the wealth is privately owned and appropriated, restrict their growth. This sets up a dynamic in the system which, amongst other things, leads to a recurrent crisis—the system produces too much, so production falls and unemployment rises. The contradiction, which is a matter of the *relations* of production, is then the causal factor. Now Althusser argues that the causal factors at the other levels can also be seen as contradictions and what happens in the day-to-day life of a society is a result of the way in which the development of contradictions in the underlying 'structure of structures' come together. This he calls *over-determination*; in one sense it is another word for 'a lot going on out there', but in certain cases it means something more. This is when it is used to refer to the way in which the contradictions at the different levels come together to reinforce each other or to inhibit each other's development. In the first case, the result is revolution and the emergence of a different form of society; in the second case, it is stagnation and decay. Russia and India respectively are often given as examples.

The Russian Revolution is a particularly good example of 'over-determination'. It is especially useful for Althusser because he can draw on the 'sacred texts' of Lenin, although perhaps a better and clearer account can be found in the first chapter of Trotsky's *History of the Russian Revolution*.[1] Over-simplifying, the argument is that we can identify first the contradiction at the economic level: in the still small but rapidly growing Russian capitalism the contradiction between the forces and relations of production led as always to a class conflict between workers and owners. Coupled with this, in the much larger sector of feudal agriculture, a different economic contradiction produced a conflict between peasants and landlords. Based on this were other contradictions and conflicts, between Russian capitalists and Russian landlords, the latter threatened by the growth of capitalism, and between Western financiers who were backing Russian capitalism and some sections of Russian capitalism who desired to control their own industries, as well as the more traditional Russian feudal aristocracy. All these can be considered as primary and secondary economic contradictions. At the political level there was a conflict between the defenders of the old regime under the Tsar, authoritarian and heirarchical, and those who wanted to move towards some form of political democracy. This conflict is based on the economic level in that feudal regimes are authoritarian and hierarchical whilst the development of capitalism often, but not always, tends to encourage political democracy. But it also had its own developmental logic of conflict and compromise. On the ideological level, the conflict was between those influenced by modern Western scientific ideas and those who supported the traditional religious beliefs of Russian feudalism. This conflict too is related to the economic conflict but with its own logic of development. These separate logics of development would mean that, for example, people whom one might expect to be one side because of their economic position would take the opposite political or ideological standpoint. Russian society was riven by contradictions in a way that was by no means simple. The factor that brought these contradictions to breaking point, causing a fragmentation out of which the Russian Revolution emerged, was the Russian defeat by the Germans in World War I.

'Determination in the last instance' and 'structure in dominance'
To understand the meaning of these rather daunting phrases we have

to remember the other side of Althusser's political battle. Despite attacking the cruder forms of traditional Marxism, he was still defending a Marxist orthodoxy against humanist revisions which tended towards abandoning the view that the economic level had any priority at all. He needed still to argue that despite the comparative independence and causal effect of the ideological and political levels, the economic level still has some priority in determining what goes on (and consequently in understanding what goes on). His way round this dilemma is summed up in the phrase 'the economic is determinant in the last instance', a phrase from Engels, which Althusser immediately qualifies by pointing out that 'the last instance never comes'. This seems to amount to saying that the economic contradiction is the most important but that it is never found in its pure form, it is always overlaid by other contradictions. I hope that the next few pages will establish that in trying to understand the general shape and development of different types of society, this is quite a useful approach; however, it sets up a number of tensions that I have already mentioned, between the 'dependence' and 'independence' of the different levels which, if one is demanding logical consistency, act in a destructive way.

One way in which Althusser both distances himself from crude Marxism but maintains the idea of the causal importance of the economic level is through arguing that different types of society are distinguished by the 'dominance' of different structural levels. By this he means that in the day-to-day internal development of a society one particular level or levels is most important. In fuedal societies this role is shared by the political/ideological levels, in early capitalist societies it is the economic, and some would argue that in late capitalist societies the political level is dominant. It is, however, the structure of the economic level which determines which level, including the economic, is dominant. It is as if the economic level hands over its power to one of the other levels, or keeps it to itself, for the duration of that type of society. To make this clearer entails looking at his analysis of the 'mode of production', or the economic level; this, remember, is the most basic of the underlying structures of society.

The mode of production
A lot of what I have to say here comes less from Althusser's own work than from that of Etienne Balibar, one of the co-authors, with Althusser, of *Reading Capital*, a central source of structuralist

Marxist theory. We have already seen that economic practice involves a raw material, a means of production, including labour power and a finished product. In the analysis of the economic level, these elements are grouped together as one element, the means of production, to which two other 'elements' are added: the 'labourer' and the 'non-labourer'. The 'labourer' refers to the person (or people) who transform the raw material into the finished product, who work directly upon the goods produced. The 'non-labourer' refers to those who do not work directly on the product, even though they might work—in effect the non-labourer refers to the owner of the means of production in most societies. These are sometimes called 'positions' to emphasise that while the personal characteristics of those who occupy them are not important, the positions they occupy are. Thus a society in which there is a high degree of social mobility, in which people can move from 'labourer' to 'non-labourer' with relative ease, is still capitalist since it is the existence of the positions that define it as such.

This is, of course, a misleading way of putting it because what defines a society as capitalist or otherwise is not the simple existence of the positions or elements (they are present in all types of society) but the relationships between them. There are two important relationships between these elements. The first is that of ownership—the 'labourer' or 'non-labourer' may own the means of production. The second is in effect the relationship of 'control'—referring to which position, labourer or non-labourer, has the power to work the means of production. This should become clearer as I work through some examples of different types of society, since variations in the way in which the three elements are joined together by these two relations enable us to distinguish between different types of society. Four types of society can be distinguished immediately:

1   *Feudalism.* The non-labourer is the feudal lord, the labourer is the peasant. The lord effectively owns the land (although he cannot dispose of it at will—in theory it is held in trust from the king who in turn holds it in trust from God). The peasant family on the other hand controls their piece of land in the sense that they choose when to work it, what to grow etc. This is no big deal, since we are talking about a subsistence economy with few crops which have to be worked during all daylight hours.

2   *Capitalism*. The non-labourer is the factory owner, the labourer
    the worker. The non-labourer owns the means of production and
    controls them—it is the owner who decides what to produce,
    when it will be produced and so on.
3   A *transitional* mode of production between capitalism and
    feudalism, often referred to as a period of 'cottage industry'. This
    was the form taken by the textile industry during the industrial
    revolution in Britain. The worker and family still control and
    work a piece of land but their income is supplemented by
    producing goods on machinery (a loom for example) which they
    own and keep in their cottage. The worker or the labourer
    therefore owns the means of production. The non-labourer is
    usually a merchant who buys the raw material, farms it out to his
    workers and takes the finished product; in this sense the non-
    labourer controls the use of the means of production. When the
    machines are moved into one place, factory production and
    capitalism proper emerge.
4   *Socialism*. The labourer owns and controls the means of pro-
    duction through an extended form of participant democracy.

I want to make three points about this conception of the
underlying economic structure before moving on to look at its
relationship to other structures. The first is pedantic: Althusser
argues that one reason why this theory cannot be regarded as
structuralist is that the elements themselves change with the relationships. The means of production under feudalism is land, under
capitalism, machines. For orthodox structuralism the elements are
constant-'d' 'g' and 'o' remain the same in dog and god. This might
be true but seems to me unimportant in the face of the shared feature
of giving priority to the relationships rather than the elements.
Althusser would certainly argue that it is the change in the
relationships that leads to the development of the elements since
the opposite would lead him back to crude economic determinism.

The second point is that the model as it stands can only distinguish
between four modes of production and these by no means cover all
societies we know about. Something that Marx called the 'Asiatic
mode of production' is a particularly thorny problem—it is, like
feudal society, pre-capitalist, but the state appears to play a very
important role. Those followers of Althusser who demand complete
logical consistency have tried to argue that there are societies without

modes of production on the basis that the theory cannot describe them. I do not think this is very helpful. The proper theoretical alternative is to look for other elements, or, more important, relationships that might help us distinguish other types. Nicos Poulantzas, for example, has distinguished between 'juridical' and 'real' ownership—ownership as defined in law and in practice. In Eastern European societies juridical ownership is in the hands of the labourers, real ownership in the hands of the state bureaucracy who control and reap the benefits of the means of production. Such a system might be called 'state socialism' or 'state capitalism' depending on how sympathetic you are to the regimes in question.

The third point is the classic structuralist problem of change. These models are static models of different types of society; if the argument was that these models identified mechanisms which led the society to change then it would take us back to crude economic determinism. Althusser cannot resort to agency to explain change since he is arguing precisely against such a position. As a result it seems to me to remain unexplained on a theoretical level, although it can be described—which was what I was doing in the earlier reference to the Russian revolution. Why these contradictions should come together in such a way at such a time is explained by the Russian defeat, not in terms of some theoretically identified mechanism. The 'transitional mode' is an attempt to come to grips with the problem but succeeds in producing another intermediate static model. Here we come back to another form of the basic tension which contributes to undermining the theory as a whole.

We can now move on to look at the causal mechanism framed by these economic relations and the way in which it affects the relationship of the economic, political and ideological levels together. The best comparison is provided by feudalism and capitalism, and the assumption is that in both systems an economic surplus is produced (i.e., more than is strictly necessary to keep all or most members of that society in existence). In class societies, which include all but socialist societies, this surplus is appropriated by the non-labourer. The causal mechanism we are looking for is the mechanism of appropriation, the means by which the non-labourer takes the surplus.

In fuedalism the non-labourer owns the land but the labourer controls it. The labourer may produce sufficient to keep the family in existence, but since he controls the land, it does not follow automatically that a surplus is produced and handed over to the lord. In practice this is ensured in various ways: the peasant might have to pay an annual tax to the lord, or work on the lord's land or work in the lord's household for so many days in the year; to do this the peasant has to be persuaded that it is the right thing to do, a moral obligation or duty, or he has to be forced to do it under threat of judicial punishment. The theoretical explanation of this is that the relations of production are such that the non-labourer must assure appropriation of a surplus through political and ideological structures. Hence the nature of the economic level places the political and ideological levels in dominance.

We can compare this to capitalism in which the non-labourer owns *and* controls the means of production. When the worker goes to work, she must produce goods of sufficient value for her own keep (her wages) and a surplus at the same time—she cannot decide to go to work to produce just enough for herself, the employer would fire her, or, if everybody did it, go out of business. The worker cannot use the factory for her own purposes, only for the employer's. She has to work the length of time the employer stipulates or she leads an impoverished existence amongst the unemployed. If the worker works, she produces a surplus which is automatically appropriated by the employer since he controls the product. The mechanism of appropriation thus operates at the economic level, and the economic level, as well as remaining determinant in the last instance, is also dominant. The economic structure is the most important cause of developments in the day-to-day life of the social formation.

It seems to me that what we have here is as good a theory as is available for distinguishing in general terms *between* different types of society, and for delineating the *internal* relations of the 'structure of structures', of the social formation. I have already indicated some of its problems, enough to show, I think, that it is not a perfect theory. It is open to further development and some problems such as that of change might remain beyond its scope. However, *as far as it goes*, it is useful, and that is perhaps as much as we can ask from any theory at the moment.

IDEOLOGY AND POLITICS: PUSHING THE THEORY BEYOND ITS LIMITS

I will now look at the structuralist approach to the other levels, the political and ideological, the parts of the machine that are engaging most directly in working the puppets. This will lead directly on to Althusser's view of ideology—the puppet's strings.

It has always seemed to me that the logical way in which to develop the theoretical basis—the fruitful logical way, that is,—would be to attempt to analyse the underlying structures of the political and ideological levels, with their respective causal mechanisms, and identify the way in which they in turn act upon the economic level. This has not happened; when they turn to the other levels, Althusser and his followers deal not with underlying structures but with the surface institutions. I can suggest a reason for this: to identify underlying structures at these levels that do not originate at the economic level would involve granting some independent structure to agency, since in politics and ideology the problem of agency is posed most clearly: the material world of nature and machines can exercise some control over human beings; in thinking and political action human beings attempt to control the material world. To recognise independent structures at these levels would be to grant too much to the humanists so they resort to a form of economic determinism in which the underlying economic structure produces surface political and ideological institutions. It is not a straightforward economic determinism—there are some peculiar contradictions involved.

In this section I want to explore this by looking at Poulantzas' work on social classes, and the work of Poulantzas and Althusser on the state and the 'ideological state apparatuses'. Returning to the metaphor of the puppet theatre, we are moving close to the puppets, reaching now the second level of the machinery that works them, the first level being the mode of production.

Social classes

The analysis of class structure is one area where Althusserian theory has made positive contributions, although not as radical as it claims. Nicos Poulantzas has undoubtedly contributed most. Certainly the analysis of class structure is more sophisticated than that offered by cruder forms of Marxist analysis, without breaking down into the kaleidescope of distinctions offered by theorists such as Dahrendorf. The basis of the argument is that social classes are determined not just by the economic structure but by political and ideological structures as well. The advances, however, seem to me to have been in understanding class determined by the economic level and this is what I will look at first.

The extreme version of crude Marxism would hold that capitalism produces two classes, owners and non-owners, bourgeoisie and proletariat, with a third class—the petit-bourgeoisie, small scale producers—gradually squeezed out. The first contribution that structuralist Marxism makes is to point out that modes of production can co-exist in the same social formation, and the problem of the way in which they are 'articulated' has received considerable attention. This means that different social classes belonging to different modes of production can exist in the same society. Poulantzas talks about 'petty commodity production', which seems to be a modified transitional mode, continuing into capitalism in order to explain the continued existence of the petit-bourgeoisie. Beyond this, however, he suggests that we can identify 'class fragments' determined by secondary economic criteria. Amongst the non-labourers we can distinguish owners of land, of industrial capital and finance capital who at different times might have conflicting political and ideological interests as well as conflicting economic interests. He goes on to suggest a difference between a 'reigning class' who hold political office and a 'hegemonic' or ruling class as that class in whose interests political decisions are taken. In Britain for the last part of the nineteenth century for example, the landed aristocracy held political office but exercised it in the interests of the industrial capitalists. On the side of the labourers, we can distinguish between skilled and unskilled workers, conflicts between which have been important in the development of the British trade union movement. Poulantzas' debate with the English Marxist Ralph Milliband[3] illustrates the difference, and, if you can cut through the jargon, the increased sophistication of this type of analysis over more conventional Marxism.

So far, so good: we have a relatively complex model of the class structure. When Poulantzas turns to the political and ideological determinations of the class structure however, he seems to end up back at the economic and I have already suggested a reason why. He discusses as some length the 'new petit-bourgeoisie'. These have a different economic position to the 'traditional petit-bourgeoisie': they are not owners of family enterprises but workers in such areas as advertising, non-productive workers. Yet they can be categorized as petit-bourgeoisie because ideologically they have much the same beliefs as the traditional section of the class. When we look at why they have these beliefs, however, it seems to be the case that they stem from an economic position—a different economic position nonetheless causes the same set of political attitudes. Poulantzas also talks about 'social categories' which are determined by their position in political institutions, such as state bureaucrats and intellectuals and the military. In certain situations he argues, these social categories can play a crucial role: they are particularly important in fascist regimes, for example. However, he also argues that in times of crisis they tend to divide along the lines of their class of origin, the social class from which they came. Thus again economic determination takes on major importance. I will not go into these arguments in any detail: what I hope I have shown is that we can, using structuralist Marxism, gain a more complex and useful model of class structure than we can from cruder forms of Marxism and from conflict theory; but that despite itself, despite the intentions of the theory, an economic determinism emerges. This is not necessarily mistaken—it still gives us a sort of skeletal analysis of the class structure; but by itself it cannot explain the complexity of political groupings that we find in modern society and which the conflict theory can at least describe. To go further we would need a more detailed theoretical analysis of underlying structures at the political and economic level.

The state and ideological state apparatuses

More conventional Marxists, crude or otherwise, would trace political conflicts from classes defined by economic structures, but most would acknowledge that all sorts of other factors need to be taken into account before we can fully understand the political life of a society. For the structuralists this issue seems to have become a touchstone by which one can judge the 'crudity' of a theory—in such a way, eventually, that any attempt to relate political conflict to economically defined classes is dismissed as crude or deterministic. This is despite the paradoxical fact that they have produced a comparatively complex and useful model of the class structure based on economic definitions and that they seem unable to get away from it. There are some even odder paradoxes.

The state has become a key area for investigation largely under the influence of structuralist writings. It will soon become apparent that the term 'the state' means much more in this context than it does in everyday language. This is clearest in Althusser's paper on ideology and ideological state apparatuses. Earlier I recounted the argument that what is distinctive about capitalism is that the 'mechanism of appropriation' is guaranteed by economic relations. Althusser argues that, though this is the case, there are many other features required by those relations which are not guaranteed at the economic level itself. For example, labourers require to be fed and housed from day to day if they are to continue 'in working order'; they need to be trained in the requisite skills in general terms—they need a certain level of ability in reading and writing, for example—and in more specific skills; their children must be reared and trained to provide future labourers; they need to know their place, so that they do not become discontented or paralysed by hopeless ambitions or by resentment at being told what to do. All these things are necessary, they are the 'conditions of existence' of the continuation of capitalist relations of production.

For Althusser, as for Poulantzas, the role of ensuring these conditions is fulfilled by the state; the state comes to be seen as the centre of the social formation and the continued existence of capitalist relations of production. It does so in two ways: in extremes it uses force: the army, the police, the 'repressive state apparatuses'. Most of the time this is not necessary, because of the more or less efficient working of the 'ideological state apparatuses' which ensure that people do what the underlying structure demands they do. These apparatuses are all institutions which ensure that the conditions of existence I listed above are actually met, and they include as well as obvious 'state institutions' such as the education system, many institutions we would normally regard as private: the media, the church, the family and even trade unions. All these work to ensure the continuation of capitalism.

One line of criticism is that this argument blurs very important distinctions between state and private institutions, but more telling is the argument that Althusser's explanation is functionalist and, in fact, not an explanation of much at all. To say that the economic level requires a number of conditions to be met is not an explanation of how they are met; they need not be met at all, and they may be met in various ways: witness the different education systems in North America and different European countries. To state the need for something is not to explain that it is met or how it is met—this is as true for societies as for individuals. I need vast sums of money but I do not get it. Lurking behind this explanation is an economic determinism; the implicit assumption, which cannot be made explicit since it is precisely what Althusser is arguing against, is that the existence of these institutions is determined by the economic level.

A further problem for both Althusser and Poulantzas is that Marxists have always argued that the conflict between social classes is carried on in many of the state institutions they discuss; if this is so, and both would like to maintain that it is, where does such conflict originate? It cannot come from the ideological and political appa-ratuses themselves since they exist to ensure the smooth running of the system, and they would not be doing that if they generated conflict; and it cannot come from economically determined classes, that would be to grant too much to crude Marxism. 'Class struggle' is introduced from nowhere. The tension this creates in the theory leads Poulantzas in particular in two directions: one is to a more orthodox, though by nò means crude, Marxism influenced by the Italian theorist Gramsci, and the other is towards some of the ideas of post-structuralism, which I shall touch on in the next chapter.

The subject: the puppet's invisible strings

Althusser's discussion of the ideological apparatuses leads us on finally to the stage presentation of structuralism's puppet theatre. His discussion of the 'ideological state apparatuses' is a step on the way to his discussion of the subject and subjectivity, or more appropriately the death of the subject. In the last chapter, I dealt with this in terms of the experience we have of being the authors of our action being in some way mistaken or misleading. Althusser desires to explain how such an experience occurs and why it is misleading, why we are really puppets. Why my belief that I am writing this book (when it is really social theory writing itself through me) is mistaken. In fact he develops a subtle argument around this issue, claiming that the experience is both necessary and misleading: in doing so, he makes the core of what we mean by 'ideology' this experience of being the authors of our actions. He terms the experience 'imaginary', borrow-ing a term given a technical meaning by the French psychoanalytic structuralist, Jacques Lacan. Lacan sees the experience as a pre-condition for calling ourselves human; the gaining of the experience of being a subject marks our entry into society and culture. It occurs during a period of childhood in the first years that he calls the 'mirror stage'—a stage which runs conjointly with the stages of development that Freud described. The idea is that the new-born child experiences itself as a bundle of conflicting and very strong drives pulling it in opposite directions. Most psychoanalysts would agree with this, seeing the process of growing up as learning to control and channel these drives. For Lacan the process is gaining the experience of being a subject. It happens through the infant seeing a mirror image—not necessarily in the mirror, but perhaps through the parent in the way that G.H. Mead saw the 'Me' as being produced. For Lacan it is the 'I' that is produced: in the image the child sees a being not torn apart by powerful drives, but in control of itself. Anyone who makes a habit of looking in a mirror will understand that sometimes the image seems to possess everything that the viewer lacks. The infant, argues Lacan, tries to become like this image, it tries to become this subject which is 'imaginary', whilst underneath the contradictory drives continue to exist in some form. Most of us go through periods of stress when they come to the surface.

Lacan is concerned with the structure of the unconscious which underlies this imaginary experience of being a subject. All I want to say is that it would certainly give us a more sophisticated conception of agency than we met amongst action theorists. This however is not Althusser's concern. His argument is that this imaginary sense of being a subject comes from the ideological apparatuses. They exist before the person is born and they map out our lives for us—we are born into a role already waiting for us in the family, in the school, at work and so on. The idea is in fact very much like that of Parsons' 'status role'. Our sense of being a subject and many other aspects of our ideas stem from the actions (or practices) which await us and which we are compelled into performing. Althusser quotes the Jansenist theologian Pascal to the effect that one does not believe in God and then kneel to pray; one prays and through praying comes to believe in God. Through acting in the prescribed way in the roles in which I am placed, I come to believe that I am the author of my actions.

WHY THE THEATRE MACHINERY IS INTERESTING

Here we have the puppet theatre in full view: the strings originate at the economic level, the mode of production; they pass through the state and the ideological state apparatuses, a second level of machinery that services the mode of production, keeping it in operation. And they finally work the puppets through an imaginary sense of being free, of choosing, of acting. There is a fatal flaw in this argument that I will postpone to the next chapter; for the moment I want to recap on the usefulness of the machinery:

1   It gives us a model of society that enables us to make distinctions that, for example, Parsons cannot make, and which does adequately separate society and agency, even if problems arise when we reach the latter.

2   It provides a way of looking at different types of society and the way in which two or more modes of production might conjoin in one society.

3   It provides a more complex model of class and political structure than crude Marxism, without giving way to the flux of events as does conflict theory.

4   It at least enables us to start thinking about processes of reciprocal determinations between the economic, political and ideological levels; and there is a way forward here if it were to prove possible to identify underlying structures at the political and ideological levels, together with the relevent causal mechanisms.

5   Despite the fatal flaw in its conception of the subject, it can hint at a more profound conception of agency than we have met so far through its reference, via Lacan, to the unconscious.

On the other hand tensions have emerged, originating in the tensions in Althusser's political battles, and at the very heart of his conception of Marxism. These can be summed up in the theme of this book as a whole, the tension between the analysis of social structure and the analysis of social action. Althusser's sophisticated structural determinism leaves us with a number of problems in explaining change, conflicts which do not appear to be related to the economic contradictions and also in explaining human action itself. These are in addition to the specific theoretical tensions and problems I discussed in the section on the nature of theory. In the next chapter I will look at the way in which these problems have led to the fragmentation of the approach.

NOTES

[1] Trotsky, L. (1967), *History of the Russian Revolution*, Vol. 1, Sphere Books, London.

[2] The term is often used to refer to all three levels rather than just the economic level (which is the sense in which I am using it here) and 'social formation' is used to refer to combinations of modes of production. Such a usage goes further in avoiding simple economic determinism.

[3] See Further reading for this chapter.

FURTHER READING

The structuralist Marxist tradition
All work in this tradition is difficult; from Althusser the best starting points are the essays 'Contradiction and overdetermination' and 'On the materialist dialectic' in *For Marx*; the ideology essay is in *Lenin and Philosophy*; the *New Left Review* article is probably the best starting point for Poulantzas.

Althusser, L. (1969), *For Marx*, Allen Lane, The Penguin Press, London.
Althusser, L. and Balibar, E. (1970), *Reading Capital*, New Left Books, London.
Althusser, L. (1971), *Lenin and Philosophy*, New Left Books, London.
Althusser, L. (1976), *Essays in Self-Criticism*, New Left Books, London.
Poulantzas, N. (1975), *Classes in Contemporary Capitalism*, New Left Books, London.
Poulantzas, N. (1976), *The Crisis of the Dictatorships*, New Left Books, London.
Poulantzas, N. (1974), *Fascism and Dictatorship*, New Left Books, London.
Poulantzas, N. (1973a), 'On social classes', *New Left Review*, No. 78, pp. 27–54.
Poulantzas, N. (1973b), *Political Power and Social Classes*, New Left Books, London
Poulantzas, N. (1978), *State, Power, Socialism*, New Left Books, London.

For the differences between structuralist and more orthodox Marxism, see the debate with Ralph Miliband in

Blackburn, R. (ed.) (1972), *Ideology in Social Science*, Fontana, London.
Poulantzas, N. (1976), 'The capitalist state: a reply to Miliband and Laclau', *New Left Review*, No. 95, pp. 63–83.

Other works influenced by the tradition
Balibar, E. (1977), *On the Dictatorship of the Proletariat*, New Left Books, London.
Castell, M. (1977), *The Urban Question: A Marxist Approach*, Edmond Arnold, London.
Godelier, M. (1977), *Perspectives in Marxist Anthropology*, Cambridge University Press.
Macherey, P. (1978), *The Theory of Literary Production*, Routledge & Kegan Paul, London.
Wright, E.O. (1978), *Class Crisis and State*, New Left Books, London.

Useful introductions
Callincoss, A. (1976), *Althusser's Marxism*, Pluto Press, London.
Geras, N. (1977), 'Althusser's Marxism: an assessment', in *Western Marxism: A Critical Reader*, New Left Books, London. pp. 232–72.

9 The fragmentation of structuralist Marxism: there's a lot going on out there Mark 2

INTRODUCTION

In the last chapter I argued that despite certain advantages in the way that structuralist Marxism conceptualized societies, problems begin to arise when the structuralist form of analysis attempts to deal with agency, with human action. I tried to demonstrate this in relation to the political and ideological levels where I suggested the alternatives were to grant some form of autonomy to agency, or to resort to a deterministic model, based on the economic level. I suggested that both Althusser and Poulantzas take the second option, producing a sort of economic functionalism rather than a system functionalism—whereas Parsons attempts to explain institutions in terms of their function for the whole system, Althusser does so in terms of their function for the economic level. I likened Althusser's system to a puppet theatre with various levels of machinery, working a set of invisible strings which give the appearance that the actors work of their own volition. Finally I suggested there was a crucial flaw in his explanation of the working of these invisible strings.

In this chapter I will look at the way the theory has fragmented. The first focus will be the attempts to develop Althusser by British thinkers, in particular Paul Hirst and Barry Hindess. Their work provides an example of what happens when social theory falls into the logical trap. They leave us without any way of distinguishing levels of

147

the social formation, and, as with conflict theory, we end with the statement 'there's a lot going on out there'. This will lead on to the main themes of post-structuralism, a more specifically French development which comes from rather different intellectual origins. Finally I will look at a full-scale attack on the whole structuralist movement by E.P. Thompson, an English Marxist historian who was the first to use the machine analogy, and I will try to use the attack to sort out the contradictions and failures of the approach as a whole.

THE FAULT-LINES OF STRUCTURALIST MARXISM

Hindess and Hirst, two British sociologists who contributed to the introduction of Althusser's work to an English speaking public, also managed over a period of less than ten years during the 1970s, to dismantle it. The culmination was a wholesale revision of Marxism in a two-volume work written with Anthony Cutler and others, *Marx's 'Capital' and Capitalism Today*. Here I will deal only with the arguments relevent to Althusser, and the way in which they play on the tensions I have already noted.

The most important fault lines have to do with the attempt to force a theory of societies onto other inappropriate areas of social reality. The most important of these is that of agency, the problem being that the subject never quite manages to give up the ghost; beyond this, however, the area I referred to as that of 'general meanings' proves troublesome as the metaphysical assumptions of structuralism re-assert themselves. The specific political factors at work in this British development have to do with the attempt to explain conflicts that have arisen around race, sex and nationality, since it proves very difficult if not impossible to make sense of these issues using traditional Marxist, or Althusserian Marxist, economic categories. This prepares the ground for collapsing the idea of the social formation, with the economic level 'determinant in the last instance'. Once this happens, developments of orthodox structuralism are taken up as a way of getting to grips with 'free-floating' ideological and political issues. Perhaps the best way of describing the fragmentation is as a slide from a theory of societies to a descriptive theory of the intermixing of general meanings.

I will begin by returning to what I called the 'fatal flaw' in

Althusser's argument about the subject and subjectivity. To summarize the argument again: the 'ideological state apparatuses' arise to fulfil certain needs at the economic level; they involve 'material practices', courses of action carried out by the individuals placed into them, born into them in the case of the family. Through engaging in these institutional practices, already mapped out before the person takes up position, the agent comes to see herself reflected as the author of her actions, and experiences herself as such. The experience is real, but imaginary and hides the deeper reality that she is the bearer of underlying structures. Now the flaw in this argument is that neither Althusser nor Lacan is proposing a view of the unsocialized individual as a *tabula rasa*—a blank slate upon which society writes whatever it desires. We are not the *simple* product or 'effect' of underlying social structures. Both argue that the experience of subjectivity, of being the author of one's actions, comes from recognising an image of oneself—in a mirror, to use Lacan's metaphor, or in a 'material practice', and then identifying with that image. Now this presupposes that the individual already possesses certain characteristics of subjectivity; she must be able to recognise an image and identify with it, and if she is the author of these actions, there is no *a priori* reason why she should not be the author of others. If Althusser's theory is intended to explain why, as he puts it, people 'work by themselves', it seems to presuppose what it is trying to demonstrate. The explanation only holds if individuals already possess that quality. The subject refuses to lie down.

This point is argued with considerable subtlety by Paul Hirst.[1] The conclusion I would draw from it is that we need to maintain some notion of the subject as the author of actions, even if it is modified or 'de-centred' to use another favourite structuralist term. However, this is not Hirst's conclusion; he is firmly committed to abandoning such a notion. His way out will emerge shortly but I want to leave this argument for a while. It is sufficient to note for the moment that the space between society and agency proves an unbridgeable gap.

I now want to turn to other tensions in Althusser's theory that encourage the process of fragmentation. These lead in one way or another to examples of what I called in the introduction the 'logical trap': the idea that one can know what the world is like through logical theoretical argument alone. In the criticism of Althusser's theory, this takes the form of posing either/or questions and coming down on one side or the other. The important point is that the logical criticisms we will be looking at arise around the different areas of social reality that the theory attempts to embrace, in particular social structures and general meanings.

The first such criticism focusses on what I have already identified as a tension in Althusser's view of theory. This involves a combination of the structuralist metaphysical assumption that a theory (or a language) creates its own objects, its own world, and that theory nonetheless 'appropriates' a real external object, in this case underlying social structures. The criticism, as simply as I can put it, is this: if the theory creates its own objects, and if we can only judge a theory by its rational or logical coherence, we have to make the implicit assumption that the world is logically coherent if we are to maintain a realist position. This assumption involves the view that our theory and the external world should be of the same structure, we can match one against the other, and is (God forbid) therefore empiricist. This sort of argument can lead to an attack of vertigo unless you take it slowly. In effect, the critics are saying: *either* a theory creates its own objects, *or* it somehow describes objects in the external world. The latter has already been ruled out of court, therefore the former must be the case. We are left with the fairly simple view that the world is a product of our ideas; in other words, we are left only with general meanings.

Now it seems to me that it is quite reasonable to suggest that a theory does not refer necessarily to observable objects in the world, but it does not follow that it does not refer to any external and independent object. We cannot *see* a mode of production, but it is reasonable to suggest that it exists as an underlying structure. Althusser is trying to grasp and master a subtle problem and he does so by introducing a tension in his explanation. Logically, the tension may be called a contradiction and resolved on one side or the other, but such a resolution does not help us to understand the world any better. As I have argued frequently before, the resolution suggested here ignores the fact that the world often refuses to be like our theory says it should. It also removes any possibility of judging between theories, except perhaps on arbitrary political grounds. It is only a step away from saying that a theory creates its own world to saying that it creates its own rationality or logic. Each theory, then, is logical in its own terms. This introduces a particular absurdity into the position. The argument that there is no way of judging between theories is disagreeing with an argument that says that we can judge between theories—it is therefore implying that it is a better theory. The very act of arguing that we can't judge between theories contradicts itself by its very existence. This is the sort of spiral into which the logical trap leads us.

Two further logical hatchet blows have been dealt to Althusserian theory. The conception of 'relative autonomy' is one target. It is argued that *either* the political and ideological levels are autonomous *or* they are dependent upon and in some way 'caused' by the economic level. The latter would be crude economic determinism which doesn't work, so the former must be the case. I discussed the alternative to this in the last chapter: a closer analysis of the underlying structures and causal mechanisms at work at each level. However, the either/or argument removes any possibility of a causal relationship between the levels and in effect collapses the idea of the social formation, making any distinction pointless. We are left with a mixture of politics and ideology and are led back to the level of general meanings.

The next step is to remove any idea of causality altogether. In the Introduction I suggested that some notion of teleological causality was necessary to understand human action: it involves notions such as intention and project. The logical criticism here argues first that any relationship between cause and effect is teleological, since the effect must somehow be present in the cause, just as my intention is present at the beginning of the action that it leads to. The next step is to accept Althusser's argument against teleological causality, which is part of his general attack on traditional ideas of the subject. The result is that any idea of causality is outlawed, and it is argued that the most we can do is talk about 'conditions of existence'—we can say that, for example, parliamentary democracy has certain conditions of existence, and other things must exist if parliamentary democracy is to come into being, but we cannot say that it is caused by these conditions. Again sensitive, if sometimes ambiguous, distinctions are dismissed in favour of logical clarity. Logical clarity leaves us with no way of distinguishing levels or 'regions' of the social world, no means of identifying causal relationships, and no way of choosing between different theories; in other words it leaves us in a mess—*all* we can say is that there is a lot going on—we can't even add 'out there' since if there is anything out there, we will never be able to know.

It isn't quite as bad as this, however: it leaves us with just one level of social reality—that of 'general meanings', and when I talked about

Paul Hirst's discussion of the theory of the subject earlier, I indicated that he took a different course to the one I took. In fact he suggests that we must look at the 'constitution' of the subject, the creation of the subject at the level of general meanings, in what he calls 'signifying practices' or 'discourses'. For a while, Barry Hindess and Paul Hirst were themselves subjects of a sort of cult following amongst younger British sociologists. Their criticisms of Althusser, however, led them in the direction of the development of post-structuralist philosophy proper in France and attention passed from the English critics of Althusser back to the French philosophers who had gone beyond Althusser. The political background to post-structuralism becomes important here.

THE POLITICAL IMPETUS BEHIND
THE FRAGMENTATION OF STRUCTURALISM

Althusser's work grew out of the attempt of the Western European Communist Parties to adjust to post-war political and economic changes; in the course of this process, the uprising in France in 1968 were particularly important. They were mirrored more or less dramatically all over the Western world, the common spark being opposition to America's involvement in Vietnam. The intellectual development I am about to trace is again French in origin and given the scale of the 1968 'events' it is not surprising that it developed more quickly there. In Britain and the USA the same ideas did not really take root until the mid-1970s, losing much of their political content as they moved further away from France. In the USA they seem so far to have been confined mainly to the area of literary criticism, with some influence on feminist theory.

At the same time as the Communist Parties were adjusting to conditions of comparative affluence in the Western democracies, radical socialists inside and outside of the parties were becoming increasingly dissatisfied with the new policies. These policies seemed often to involve unnecessary compromises with parties to the right, and it also seemed (and I think there is much justification for this view, particularly in the French Communist Party) that the bureaucratic and authoritarian organisation that had grown up under Stalin was able to change the noises it made but unable to change its behaviour. During the popular uprisings in France in 1968, which originated in the universities but spread to many factories and offices, the Communist Party seemed to play a conservative role. The uprising seemed to be very different from—and more radical in aims and method than—the conventional protests; it was not about wages so much as peoples' rights to control their own lives at their place of work. Where the Communist Party was able to control the movement it tried to channel it back into conventional forms of protest; where it could not control it, it tended towards opposing it. Many socialists became finally disillusioned with the Communist Party and organisations well to the left of the Party grew in number and strength. This feature was reflected in most European countries including Britain where the Communist Party had never been strong.

On a theoretical level, this led eventually to a wide-ranging criticism of Marxism itself. It was argued that the conservative and authoritarian nature of Western European Communist Parties was itself a reflection of the conservative and authoritarian regimes in Eastern Europe and both were the product of Marxism, an authoritarian and conservative theory. I will return to this point shortly; for the moment I want to look at how this affected the reception of Althusser's work. Part of his appeal had been the return to the original works of Marx, and the implication of this was that Stalinism and all that it entailed could be explained as some form of deviation. Given the 'relative autonomy' of the ideological and political levels, for example, it might be argued that the transformation of the economic level in Stalin's Russia had not yet led to the revolutions in the political and ideological levels that would be necessary for the establishment of socialism. The return to Marx was a way of by-passing Stalin and associated evils. However, the inability of the Communist Party to maintain its radicalism, and in some places, such as Italy, its tendency to enter into alliance with conservative opposition parties, together with its failure to change its own internal organisation, led to the conclusion by some that the return to Marx made no difference. In the graphic words of Foucault reviewing a book by Andre Glucksmann: 'Those who hoped to save themselves by opposing Marx's real beard to Stalin's false nose are wasting their time'.[2]

Andre Glucksmann's own development is interesting. He produced the first systematic critique of Althusser's work (see Further reading), a very difficult piece aimed mainly at *Reading Capital*. The points he made were telling—so telling in fact that there was no direct reply and when the second edition was published (this was the one to

be translated into English) sections that Glucksmann had particularly savaged were simply ommitted. Glucksmann himself later
became associated with a group known as the *nouveaux philosophes*.
They adopted what is basically a traditional right-wing criticism of
Marxism—that any attempt to create socialism automatically leads
to dictatorship and concentration camps, this being built into
Marxist theory itself. I believe that it is misleading to insist on such a
direct link between a theory and a type of society. There is a case to be
made that Marxism is implicitly authoritarian, but this might be
because the world itself is authoritarian. By this I mean that the
authoritarian aspects of the theory, which indicate that a transformation of economic relations requires first a centrally organised and
strictly disciplined party, and secondly the capture and use of a
centralized state power, these aspects of the theory reflect certain
aspects of the world. In a situation of chronic underdevelopment or
of chronic and devastating economic crisis, an authoritarian one-
party state might be the only way out. There are two reasons why a
Communist state in this situation might be preferable to a right-wing
state or military rule. The first is that, with very rare exceptions, the
latter attempt to keep in existence the very conditions that produced
the original crisis, in other words they offer no way out; and secondly
despite its authoritarian aspects, Marxism also offers a vision of a free
society, and some minimal hope can thus be kept alive. Eventually
such societies are faced with a choice based in a calculus of death:
which authoritarian regime will cost less lives compared with a
continuation of the crisis. It is too easy for those who live in the West
and have never had to face such choices to produce blanket
condemnations of those who have chosen.

However, this right-wing critique is not the one I shall trace. There
is a leftist, radical version, best represented by Foucault himself,
which leads to a pessimistic anarchism. It is partly a criticism of
Marxism and partly an alternative. It abandons the classical Marxist
view that revolution involves the seizure of the state and thus of
power on the grounds that power itself is not centralized in the state.
The social world is seen instead as a kaleidescope of power struggles
which can never be surpassed. All that can be done is to encourage the
resistance that arises wherever power arises. In place of a revolution
we are confronted with an endless series of power struggles which
cannot be resolved because power is a necessary and inherent part of
any relationship. We are left with a picture of the world as a flux of

conflicts very close to the picture presented by conflict theory, but worked out in a very different terminology; hence the title of this chapter. It is in fact the way the 1968 rebellions appeared in France, as a series of localized power struggles in colleges, factories and offices, and many recent political conflicts in Western Europe generally may be seen in the same way. In the approach that has become known as 'post-structuralism', fragmentation becomes explicit both politically and theoretically.

Perhaps I should say at this point that I have difficulty with 'post-structuralism'. On the one hand the course of its development in Britain seems full of theoretical naiveties, although in France it has rather more firm philosophical roots. The more systematic the attempts to develop it as a rigorous theory, the worse the theoretical problems that arise. On the other hand, there are themes and ideas which have a personal resonance and which seem to me to be appropriate as existential statements, as expressions of dilemmas faced by those who take politics and theory seriously in modern capitalist societies. They can be seen as well as expressions of the way we experience our own lives in modern industrial and bureaucratic societies. Perhaps these two reactions are related to each other: it might be that the attempt to develop existential statements into a proper theory is mistaken, since such statements abandon theory and its constraints. In any case I do not feel confident that I understand much of the work, nor am I able to pass hard and fast judgements. I will simply outline the main concerns of post-structuralism rather than try any systematic account, and if the reader is left in mid air she might find some consolation in the fact that the space is shared by the author.

THE THEMES OF POST-STRUCTURALISM

Post-structuralist philosophy itself has rather firmer roots than the criticisms of Althusser I have just outlined. It certainly owes much to the German philosopher Nietzsche, who was writing at the end of the last century and whose philosophy has variously been described as nihilistic, anarchistic and existentialist. In his work we find themes that have reappeared in post-structuralism: the relationship between knowledge and power, the relativism of knowledge and the death of God. But these have been developed through the filter of structuralism.

We have already met the idea that a language creates its own objects and this idea has developed, particularly in the work of Derrida, into a theory of meaning. The starting point is that meaning does not come in any way through a relationship to something outside language; there is absolutely nothing to which we can look to guarantee meaning, to assure us that we are right. Another way of putting it is that there is nothing playing the role of God, there is no 'transcendental signified'. Yet another formulation of the same idea is that meaning is never *present*, it is always somewhere else. On the simplest level, we have learnt from structuralism that the meaning of a word depends upon its relationship to other words—meaning lies in between words rather than in the words themselves. We only know the meaning of 'dog' because of its relationship to other words in the relevant paradigm and syntagm, not because of any inherent quality of the word itself. Meaning, then, always lies elsewhere and it is not guaranteed by anything outside itself; and of course, the world we see is created in and by meanings. There are only meanings.

Now this undermines structuralism as I presented it in Chapter 7. The very term 'sign' implies something is 'signified', that there is something outside the sign even if the theory denies it; and the idea of an underlying structure leaves the impression of something firm and solid at the base of meaning. Post-structuralism abandons these ideas: there is only one level, a surface level. There are no hidden depths in the world, and in its primitive form the surface level is chaotic and meaningless—a kaleidescope. There is a variety of puzzling metaphors employed to describe this ('the body without organs' is my personal favourite since it leaves me completely mystified), but the idea of life itself as a meaningless chaos upon which we must impose some order has a long history in European philosophy.

Any order that there is, is seen as coming from a process of differentiation within the chaos—remember that meaning lies in the relationships between words, the differences between words. The 'process of signification' is the drawing of these differences. When we make a statement we bring a momentary order to the world—we define something according to its relationship with something else. A statement is often described as an 'event' and the term 'discourse' is usually employed to refer to a collection of related statements or events. The argument to which Paul Hirst is moving in his criticisms of Althusser's philosophy is that 'subjects' are created or 'constituted' by 'signifying practices', by the production of statements in discourses—discourses being what bring a general order to chaotic experience. No statement or discourse has a fixed meaning—its meaning always depends upon its relationship to other statements or discourses. This means that there is a constant movement or slippage: when we ask the meaning of one discourse we are referred to another and so on. This has a resonance with the insights of ethnomethodology but it is much more radical in the sense that it undermines any sense of order in the world. Hence the anarchistic colouring of much post-structuralist writing.

In the work of some writers, particularly those most relevant to social theory, however, other sources of order or at least points at which meaning becomes comparatively fixed, are employed. Lacan uses the analogy of the points at which a loose chair covering is fixed to the upholstery and for Lacan the fixed points in the sea of discourse come through the production of male sexual identity. Some of his ideas have been taken up critically by the more *avant garde* feminist theorists. Of more immediate relevance to the concerns of this book, however, is the work of Foucault: his points of fixation have to do with power.

Foucault does talk about an external world, an 'extra-discursive' order, the institutional structure out of which discourses develop and which embodies discourse; this distances Foucault somewhat from other post-structuralists. Discourses and institutions are both 'fixed' by the power relations inherent in them. He inverts, following Nietszche, the commonsense view of the relation between power and knowledge; whereas we might normally regard knowledge as providing us with the power to do things that, without it, we could not do, Foucault argues that knowledge is a power over others, the power to define others. Knowledge ceases to be a liberation and becomes enslavement. Thus, in his *History of Sexuality* he argues that not only was the Victorian period the opposite of what we suppose it to have been, a period when talk about sexuality was repressed, but also that the popular modern view, that talking about sex is a form of liberation, is wrong. The Victorian period was one in which a number of disciplines such as medicine and psychiatry developed their investigations into sexuality and this process of bringing sexuality under control, of developing classifications and treatments and techniques, has continued to grow ever since. A discourse embodies knowledge (or, rather, what it defines as knowledge) and therefore it embodies power. There are rules within a discourse concerning who can make statements and in what context, and these rules exclude some and include others. Those who have knowledge have the power to fix the flow of meaning and define others. The world is thus made up of a myriad of power relations and each power generates a resistance; the world is thus a myriad of power struggles—something illustrated precisely by the 1968 uprisings in France.

This rather rarified philosophical atmosphere in which the world is seen as created by language might seem strange; in fact we have already met the idea in a different way in the most recent variant of action theory, ethnomethodology. As far as post-structuralism is concerned there is, I think, a striking resemblance in the nature of the approach to conflict theory. As with conflict theory we have only a few real theoretical statements—about discourse and meaning and power—but at a much higher level of abstraction, that of philosophical metaphysics. As with conflict theory, these statements point to the variegated, kaleidescopic nature of the social world. The next step is to describe that social world, and the most interesting of Foucault's work comprises studies of the knowledge/power relations in the growth of different sciences, in psychiatric medicine, in the criminal law and in theories of sexuality. His methodological works can be seen as developing rules for studying the world in the light of the metaphysical-theoretical statements, just as conflict theorists produce a series of hypotheses and rules for studying role conflict. There is, I think, rather more to be gleaned from post-structuralism than there is from conflict theory, and I will return to this shortly.

WHAT'S THE POINT OF IT ALL?

I've discussed structuralism as a theory of general meanings, structuralist Marxism as a general social theory, and the fragmentation of structuralism. The process of fragmentation has been perhaps more obvious than it was with action theory since we have been able to watch the approach break apart around three different realms of social reality: societies, agency and meaning. The theory, however, is more difficult not least because it is to a degree alien to our culture. In both Britain and in the USA our commonsense philosophy is empiricist—summed up in sayings such as 'seeing is believing'. We have been examining a theory for which 'believing is seeing'. If this can be grasped then it becomes much easier to understand.

A combination of the difficulty of theory, the political implications that it carries and sort of intellectual work that it has encouraged has led to some virulent attacks which question the approach as a whole and would dismiss it, possibly even outlaw it in the intellectual community. I want to look briefly at one such attack—E.P. Thompson's *The Poverty of Theory*—in order to try to distil what can be gained from the approach, to try to defend it where it is defensible. Thompson is an English historian who has always worked from within a Marxist framework; he left the Communist Party in 1956, after the Soviet invasion of Hungary and he has always been a political activist; his arguments come from the point of view of a working historian and an active socialist.

He argues that structuralist Marxism is a sort of religious practice; it does not involve a direct approach to real problems of making sense of the world, understanding social and political events, but rather concerns itself only with the logical problems of theoretical analysis, working through the careful exposition of sacred texts. In much the same way, mediaeval theology concerned itself with biblical interpretation rather than with anything that was going on in the world at that time. In both cases, the practical concern is the same—the outlawing of heretics—empiricists, humanists and so on. The approach produces an 'epistemological terrorism', the work of others, Marxist and non-Marxist alike, is dismissed without examination or consideration on the *a priori* grounds that it was produced in the framework of an unscientific problematic. This cuts off all possibility of debate or argument; only those who accept Althusserian premises can be considered. Thompson makes this argument in association with one which seizes on one side of Althusser's political intentions, his defence of a sophisticated form of orthodox Marxism, and argues that what he is really doing is presenting a sophisticated version of Stalinism aimed at an intellectual outlawing of those who are not in agreement with him.

As well as taking us away from the investigation of real situations, it is assumed that knowledge comes only from the logical elaboration of concepts. There have been several examples in my discussion of the criticisms of Althusser: arguments about causality and relative autonomy are carried on in strict logical terms yet it is assumed that they refer directly to the real world and any attempt to look at the causal influence of economic organisations, amongst other things, is abandoned without any reference to an existing society. The conception of the subject as simply the bearer of structures—whether of economic structures or of discourses—also takes us away from the real world and peoples' experience. All this cuts off theory from the world in which we are all involved and thus makes it irrelevent. However we approach social theory, the eventual justification of the enterprise, what makes it more than an abstract game, is that it can contribute something to the alleviation of human misery. If it has lost its roots in that misery, or—perhaps less dramatically—in the problems of everyday living, then it has become pointless. Structuralism, in all its forms, does precisely that.

There is much more to Thompson's argument which does not concern us here. The point I want to make is that it is possible to accept all these arguments, but still identify a function and a place for the sort of theorizing I have been discussing in the last three chapters. The problem with structuralism, structuralist Marxism and post-structuralism is that they seal themselves off from other forms of investigation and the external world; they do so through a combination of what I've called their metaphysical assumptions and a theory of science, and these lead to all the aspects condemned by Thompson. If we can put these aspects aside and read these writers as trying to say something relevent about the social world (a strategy they would not agree with) then it is possible to learn something. I have already indicated what I see as the useful aspects of structuralism and of Althusser's work, but it is important to remember that this is not all there is to theory. Theoretical activity can be envisaged as building up a verbal model of the social world which tells us much more than we can actually see. Althusser (and Parsons) and the structuralists, are both working at the level of the skeleton organisation, they are trying to identify the bone structure of societies. I have already indicated the reasons I find Althusser preferable to Parsons at this level. The surface institutions may be taken as the brain and nervous systems and perhaps Parsons might be of more use here; the blood flow and the heart, what sets it all in motion, is agency and here action theory has so far contributed most.

This brings us to the criticisms of Althusser and post-structuralism. The criticisms themselves, although falling in to the logical trap, nevertheless illustrate the way a theory of one area runs into problems if it attempts to account for others. The points at which Althusserian Marxism breaks apart are the boundaries between the world of social structure, of meanings and of agency. Structuralism is a theory of social structures; paradoxically its development through to post-structuralism ends up, I would argue, telling us more about agency. To begin with it illustrates that a theory of agency cannot be eliminated. When post-structuralism attempts to talk about the way subjects are created in discourse it meets the same problem as the attempt to show that subjects are created by social structures. There is talk about subjects existing within and between discourses, but this 'space' has to be attributed some sort of independent motivation, and recently there has been some return to the classic philosophers of subjectivity—Hegel and Husserl in particular—to account for this. The important point is that it is steadily proving impossible to avoid the idea of the subject as the author of her actions. Beyond this, however, it suggests a deeper understanding of subjectivity than does action theory. All the approaches we looked at in Part II assumed a simple notion of the subject as the unproblematic author of choice and action. From the development of structuralism into post-structuralism we can learn of the individual as driven and torn by unconscious desires and conflicting ways of making sense of the world, as placed amongst 'discourses' which are independent of her. We can use this 'de-centered' view of the subject, but within this de-centering, there is still choice and action. The subject, and the experience of subjectivity, can be seen as a sort of flux. We are constantly buffeted and torn apart by forces beyond our control; they limit us and sometimes push us in directions we do not want to go. But at the same time we are constantly striving to control them; perhaps the best we can hope for is to ride them without falling off and being trampled underfoot. Post-structuralism, for all its difficulties, succeeds as an expression of the chaos and the conflicts that beset 'subjects'.

NOTES

[1]Hirst, P. (1976), 'Althusser and the theory of ideology', *Economy and Society*, Vol. 5.
[2]Callinicos, A. (1982), *Is There a Future for Marxism?* Macmillan, Basingstoke, p. 108.

FURTHER READING

General background
Callinicos is by far the best, covering all the political, philosophical and theoretical issues from a politically committed though rather orthodox point of view.

Callinicos, A. (1982), *Is There A Future For Marxism?*, Macmillan, Basingstoke.
Descombes, V. (1980), *Modern French Philosophy*, Cambridge University Press.
Hirsh, A. (1981), *The French New Left: An Intellectual History from Sartre to Gorz*, South End Press, Boston.

Critics of Althusser
Of the criticisms moving towards post-structuralism none are simple though the work of Hindess and Hirst is reducible to the logical either/or trap.

Burchell, G. (1977), 'Review of Hindess and Hirst', *Radical Philosophy*, No. 18, pp. 22–30.
Centre for Contemporary Culture Studies (1978), *On Ideology*, Hutchinson London.
Coward, R. and Ellis, J. (1977), *Language and Materialism* Routledge & Kegan Paul, London.
Hindess, B. and Hirst, P. (1977), *Mode of Production and Social Formation: An Auto-Critique of Pre-Capitalist Modes of Production*, Macmillan, Basingstoke.
Hindess, B. and Hirst, P. (1975), *Pre-Capitalist Modes of Production*, Routledge & Kegan Paul, London.
Hirst, P. (1976), 'Althusser and the theory of ideology', *Economy and Society*, Vol. 5, No. 4, pp. 385–412.
Hirst, P. (1976), *Problems and Advances in the Theory of Ideology*, Cambridge University Communist Party Pamphlet.

For a criticism of the critics, see:

Collier, A. (1978), 'In defence of epistemology', *Radical Philosophy*, No. 20, pp. 8–21.
Skillen, A. (1978), 'Discourse fever: post-Marxist modes of production', *Radical Philosophy*, No. 20, pp. 3–8.

E.P. Thompson's attack and the ensuing debate:

Thompson, E.P. (1978), *The Poverty of Theory*, The Merlin Press, London.
Hall, S. *et al.* (1978), 'Debate on *The Poverty of Theory*', in Samuel, R. (ed.), *People's History and Socialist Theory*, Routledge & Kegan Paul, London, pp. 376–408.

For a view from outside Marxism:

Parkin, F. (1979), *Marxism and Class Theory*, Tavistock, London.

Post-structuralism
Foucault has been most influential as far as social theory is concerned. I am listing his most important works and a couple of introductions. None of them are easy reading.

Foucault, M. (1967), *Madness and Civilisation*, Tavistock, London.
Foucault, M. (1973), *The Birth of the Clinic*, Tavistock, London.
Foucault, M. (1970), *The Order of Things*, Tavistock, London.
Foucault, M. (1972), *The Archeaology of Knowledge*, Tavistock, London.
Foucault, M. (1977), *Discipline and Punish*, Allen Lane, London.
Foucault, M. (1969), *The History of Sexuality*, Allen Lane London.
Gordon, G. (1977), 'The birth of the subject', *Radical Philosophy*, No. 17, pp. 15–25.
Sheridan, A. (1980), *Foucault: The Will to Truth*, Tavistock, London.

Part IV
SUMMARY AND PREVIEW: FROM
STRUCTURE *OR* ACTION TO
STRUCTURE *AND* ACTION

Introduction to Part IV

In Part III, I portrayed a process opposite to that of Part II. What began as a theory of social structures ended by breaking apart when it tried to encompass social action and agency within the same theoretical framework. The first problems arise in attempting to identify the relationship between the economic level and the political and ideological levels, and I suggested that Althusserian Marxism is unable to define this relationship clearly as it would mean granting some sort of autonomous reality to structures of action, which is precisely what it is trying to avoid. The clearest difficulty is the failure to show how our experience of being a subject is determined — the subject will not lie down and enjoy being determined. The various over-logical criticisms emphasise these difficulties and result in collapsing the model of the social formation to one level, abolishing any idea of causal relations, and portraying an essentially kaleidescopic social world. A third area of social reality — of what I called 'general meanings' — also became evident and I suggested that if structuralism could be stripped of its metaphysical assumptions it could provide a useful method of analysing this level. Both structuralism and structuralist Marxism were subject to similar processes of fragmentation caused not only by the theoretical difficulties on which I concentrated but also by political developments and conflicts.

Now both action and structuralist theory attempt to reduce the social world to one of its parts. There is a third approach which goes some way to avoiding this, recognising the independence of both structure and action although not in the way for which I have been arguing. The word 'dialectical' is often used by its proponents. It has an elaborate philosophical meaning which need not concern us here; often it is used to mean 'There are two contradictory things going on here and I don't know how to sort them out'. The idea of two contradictory tendencies is obviously appropriate. The name most commonly given to the approach is 'critical theory', and it, too, originated in the works of Marx, but starting from the early work which Althusser dismissed as 'unscientific'. If it has one clear origin it is in Marx's theory of alienation. I do not want to discuss the theory in detail, but a summary of its essentials will be useful.

The theory presupposes certain features of human life which distinguish it from other animal life. The basic feature is that human beings are able to transform their environment; they have continuously and systematically transformed the face of the Earth whereas kangaroos, for example, follow much the same daily round from one century to the next and have had no such impact. This process of transformation is a collective effort, it involves humans working in groups, and as they transform the environment, so they transform themselves. As people change their social environment, so they must change themselves: industrial society is populated by a different kind of person to pre-industrial society; driving a car develops a different set of qualities to riding a horse. Put crudely, people produce societies and societies produce people. Now the most general way of defining alienation is when the social environment, the social structures established by human beings come to dominate those who produce them. Marx identified a number of aspects of this which are appropriate to capitalism—people are separated from what they produce, they have no control over the result of their labour; they are separated from each other and the collective nature of work becomes obscured, and they are divorced from their own capacities to work and make decisions—rather it seems as if they are forced to work by other people and, in fact, this is often the case. In fact alienation is a matter of people becoming the puppets of social systems that they produce.

The term 'critical theory' is built into this schema. It is based on the idea that there is something which is essentially human, the ability to work together to transform our environment. This provides us with a measuring stick, a means by which we can judge existing societies and criticize them. Societies which fragment our social relationships, which in one way or another prevent us from working co-operatively, which take away our ability to make choices and decisions in co-operation with each other, can be subjected to a systematic criticism; they are oppressive, unfree societies. There is a further related basis for social criticism to be found in critical theory, stemming from

Marx's philosophical forebear, Hegel. Hegel was, par excellence, the philosopher of consciousness and rationality. Part of what enables human beings to transform their environment is that they possess a rational awareness of the world, which for Hegel meant that each of us could come to know the world as a whole; we were each capable of achieving an 'absolute knowledge'. In fact he saw history as a long process through which this rational knowledge developed. 'Rationality' is a sticky word, and means different things to different people. The point here, however, is that whatever we mean by 'rational', the possession of rational faculties is also a defining feature of being human. Thus, any society which prohibits people from developing and employing those faculties can be criticized—it is, in fact, an irrational society. In this respect, critical theory is significantly different from either action theory or structuralism. The latter approaches are primarily concerned with cognition, with establishing what is or is not the case, even if they then go on to derive some form of political practice from the theory. Critical theory is also concerned with cognition, but insists on an intimate link between the way the world is, and the way it ought to be. This is often taken to the extent of arguing that we cannot understand what the world is until we have some idea about what it ought to be, that a value judgement about the ideal society underlies any social theory. Thus it might be possible to make a case (although there is no space to do so) that action theory is based on the implicit judgement that a liberal capitalist democracy is an ideal society, and structuralist Marxism is based on a view that a technocratic, bureaucratic society is the ideal form. Proponents of these approaches would certainly disagree, but the main point is that critical theory emphasises the value judgements or the moral drive behind social theory and at least this encourages us to look at other approaches with some suspicion.

Now if critical theory combines both a form of action theory and a form of structuralist theory, you might well ask whether it doesn't provide a solution to the problems of the other approaches: we could work in the other areas of the social world that we have come across in the argument, and there's the answer. Unfortunately it is not quite so simple. Although a combination of the two approaches is attempted, it does not view each as dealing with an *ontologically* distinct area of social reality, as separate 'materials' different from each other. At root, it sees social structures, however alienated and independent they might become, as having their origins in human action; this is so despite the fact that the relationship is seen as more complex than it is in Parson's action theory. The differences will become apparent in the following chapters; for the moment it is sufficient to say that it sees structures in the sense in which they were discussed in Part III rather than as systems of roles. Paradoxically, critical theory runs into the problems of both of the other approaches rather than solving them, so it too has an in-built tendency to fragment.

Perhaps to begin with, it is better to call it an oscillation rather than a fragmentation. It is possible to emphasise one side or the other of the dialectic—the creative ability of human action to shape the social world, or the oppressive and deterministic nature of alienated social structures. In Chapter 10, I will look at the work of Georg Lukacs, perhaps the master of Hegelian Marxism, who is concerned with the optimistic side, the power of human action to break out of its social straitjacket; in Chapter 11, I will be concerned with those theorists who most commonly fall under the label 'critical' and who congregated around the Frankfurt Institute for Social Research in the late 1920s and early 1930s—the 'Frankfurt School' where the term 'critical theory' originated. These writers by and large represent the pessimistic pole. The writers I will be dealing with in these chapters are primarily philosophers rather than social theorists, although the distinction becomes blurred; they are not however systematic theorists like Parsons, Althusser and Poulantzas and I will be concerned with drawing out the main themes of their work rather than attempting brief and systematic expositions. Then in Chapter 12, I will look at the work of a contemporary descendent of the Frankfurt School, Jurgen Habermas, who tries to break out of the circle by attempting a more systematic social analysis, but in doing so he produces an analytic system somewhat similar in principle to Parsons. Rather than identifying causal connections between levels of social reality, he seems to be concerned with general relationships between different parts of the world on the same level. And in the same way that action theory developed towards ethnomethodology and structuralism towards discourse analysis, so Habermas moves towards problems of communication and language, drawing this time on the hermeneutic tradition of European philosophy.

10 Georg Lukacs: the world of the revolutionary optimist

INTRODUCTION

Georg Lukacs was a Hungarian thinker whose life followed closely the course of Eastern European history. He came to Marxism in the years around the Russian revolution, having been intellectually productive for some time. He had produced what has been described as the first major existentialist work of the century (*The Soul and Its Forms*) and a major work on literature (*The Theory of the Novel*). The work which will concern us here, *History and Class Consciousness*, was published in 1923 and can be read as a sort of philosophical autobiography, in which Lukacs moves through criticism of Kant and Hegel in developing his own particular form of Marxism. He was also a political activist, who (like Althusser forty years later), was concerned to make Marxism a more subtle method of analysis. He too argued against the cruder deterministic forms of Marxist theory, but unlike Althusser, he was concerned to assert that consciousness—agency—has an independent role to play. Although his arguments are extremely abstract and difficult, they are infused with a passion which is far beyond Althusser at his best. The reason for that, perhaps, is that Lukacs was a political activist in a more direct way. He held a ministerial post in the short-lived Hungarian revolutionary government in 1919 and was arrested for a short period during Stalin's lifetime.

The fate of his political activism in fact illustrates the optimism of his early theoretical work. That work was appropriate to, and inspiring, in the years after the Russian Revolution, when much of Europe was in turmoil and revolution seemed imminent in several countries. As the revolutionary wave subsided, however, Lukacs' politics came into conflict with the new Stalinist orthodoxies and he withdrew from direct political writing. He became famous as a major literary and cultural theorist, and while there are many debates about the extent to which he 'gave in' to Stalin there is a case to be made that he trod a careful course saying nothing that would bring him into too direct conflict with the regime but at the same time offering, in his literary theory, a coded criticism of Stalinism. However nothing in his later life has the vitality of *History and Class Consciousness*, nor its originality. He did return to writing philosophy but at a much more abstract and rather schematic level.

History and Class Consciousness is the work of a man who believed that socialism was capable of healing a divided and war-torn world, and that it was a real possibility in the near future. It is no surprise, therefore, that his work was read again during the 1960s, when many political radicals also believed once more that history was on their side—perhaps more naively than Lukacs, who at least had the evidence of the Russian Revolution before its loss of purity. His work influenced the American left directly and indirectly, since the American new left tended to focus directly on the issue of consciousness. In Europe he has had a more lasting influence through the presence of Lucien Goldmann at the Brussels Institute for Sociology. For many years, Goldmann drew on Lukacs' early work to develop a sociology of literature, but during the late 1960s, he began to publish his own philosophical and political analyses, often attacking structuralism head-on. As I said in the preview, my concern here will be to draw out the main themes from Lukacs' work; in fact there is little substantive social theory to be found there; he is more concerned with the nature of theory as such, its relationship to the social world and the consequences of that relationship for political action.

HISTORY, THEORY AND PRAXIS

All the views of theory we have met so far have tended towards one or the other of two opposite poles. Either theory is seen as producing knowledge which, until disproved, is valid everywhere and for everybody, so that, for example, $2 \times 2 = 4$ for the President of the

USA, a Vietnamese peasant and the person whose car I can hear in the distance; or it is always relative, depending upon a particular person's point of view on a particular situation. Symbolic interactionism comes closest to this second version. Lukacs attempts to produce a rather difficult combination of both views: on the one hand he argues that our knowledge depends upon our historical (rather than individual) situation: different societies at different historical stages of development will produce different forms of knowledge. On the other hand, it is not the case that any one form of knowledge is as good as any other. We can choose between different theories and say that one is better than the other. Over-simplifying, the basic criterion for choice is comprehensiveness, one theory is more inclusive than others.

This presupposes two things: first, that adequate knowledge is a knowledge of a whole rather than of different parts; and secondly that there is some logic of historical development which moves us towards being able to gain adequate knowledge. Taking the first presupposition, it is not possible to say that I know what a room looks like by knowing what the different parts look like. I can have a good idea of the chairs and the table, the colour of the carpet and walls and so on, but I only know the room if I know the ways in which all these parts are related in the whole (again, note the importance placed on relationships rather than the elements related). Thus, knowledge of society should take the form of knowledge of society as a whole rather than knowledge of different parts of it. I cannot know the nature of the family until I understand its relationship to the economy, the state, the education system and so on; and I cannot discover these relationships by looking at the family and the economy and the state separately, I have to take them as a whole. At one point Lukacs says that the concept of totality is the most important concept of Marxist theory.

Turning now to the second presupposition—that there is some logic of historical development which enables us to grasp the whole of the social world—it would be wrong, I think, to argue that Lukacs saw the whole of history from the beginning of time as moving towards the attainment of total knowledge, which might be the case with Hegel's philosophy. Rather, it is the development of capitalism that makes it possible for us to gain a knowledge of society as a whole, because capitalism is itself a 'totalizing' system, it possesses a self-expanding mechanism which eventually embraces all societies (otherwise known as colonialism or neo-colonialism). The possibility of knowing the social whole depends upon capitalism as an expansionary system. Our knowledge changes as it becomes integrated into a larger system of knowledge. This means that we cannot say the knowledge is true or false in any absolute sense. It always has aspects that are true and aspects that are false. If we move from the grandiose level of the development of world history to the more modest level of our own lives, then perhaps the point becomes easier to understand. If we are lucky we find out more about ourselves as our life progresses, but this does not necessarily invalidate what we previously knew; rather its meaning is changed. When I was fifteen, I knew I was ugly, now I know I am not ugly (however, only occasionally do I go as far as saying I am the most beautiful person in the world). On the face of it, these pieces of knowledge are contradictory—my looks might have changed but not that dramatically. But there is a sense in which both are true and both false. At fifteen, I *was* ugly, I still think so when I look at my photographs, but it was not, as I then thought, some judgement placed on me at birth. Perhaps it was my fear of my own growing sexuality which made me make myself ugly, emphasise the least attractive aspects of my appearence. Now I think I am more attractive, but I still have the same ugly features—rather more in fact, since I have become distinctly flabby in places; nevertheless I have more attractive features which I can emphasise. Thus my knowledge of myself as ugly was not wrong, it was partial and my history has enabled me to see that partiality, and at the same time recognise other features of myself.

Returning to society, the link between historical social development and our knowledge is *praxis*, another difficult concept the meaning of which can slide from one use to another. At its most general it would include all forms of activity—long-term projects, the practical actions taken to realise those projects, thinking, conducting relationships with others. Any form of action in the world gives us an experience of what the world is like and knowledge, theory, is the articulation and working out of this experience. I will return to this link between experience and knowledge later. For the moment, I want to emphasise an important difference between this approach and action theory which lies in what we mean by action. For all the approaches dealt with in Part II, 'action' was seen primarily as something to do with meanings, and social systems were congealed meanings. 'Praxis' embraces not just meanings but our practical physical relationship to nature (i.e. it embraces labour), and this enables critical theory to develop a view of material economic structures closer to those considered by structuralist Marxism than to the status role systems of action theory.

COMMODITY FETISHISM

Lukacs takes most of the Marxist structural analysis that I dealt with in Part III for granted, at least in general terms—the structure of the economic level in particular, although he would discuss it in very different terms to Althusser. He is most interested in the relationship between the economic and ideological and political levels of social structure. To approach this, he starts with the theory of commodity fetishism that Marx outlines in the first chapters of the first volume of *Capital*. Very briefly, Marx starts from the fact that dis-similar goods can be exchanged for each other (usually via money). We can say, for example that two books equal five beers. We make this equation all the time if we live on a finite income: buying one thing means foregoing another—something economists call 'opportunity costs'. Conventional economists would explain each equation in terms of supply and demand—how much of a good is available and how many people want it. These two forces determine price and that enables us to equate dis-similar goods.

Marx's analysis is rather different. Price is seen as a not necessarily accurate reflection of the *value* of a good. He distinguished between use value, which is entirely subjective—I hate getting drunk but I enjoy a good book, whereas my friend takes the opposite view—and exchange value, which is the value of one good measured in terms of another, one book equals two-and-a-half beers. Now, he argues, if we can equate different goods, they must have something in common. What they have in common is the amount of labour expended on them—this is the much argued about labour theory of value. Of course, it is not as simple as this. If it were, the labour I've expended in producing this book would give it sufficient value to keep me in reasonable comfort for several years; as it is, I'll be lucky if a get a short family holiday from it. There are various qualifications and distinctions which Marx makes to overcome the obvious difficulties which do not concern us here. The main point, as far as commodity fetishism is concerned, is that the amount of labour expended in producing different goods, thus determining the values at which they exchange for each other, is part and parcel of a complex of social relationships. The division of labour in a society, the way the society allocates its labour force to different tasks, is a network of relationships between people. The market system of capitalism turns this into a network of exchange relationships between things—the comparative values of different goods reflect a network of relationships between people. Now the word 'fetishism' can be used in two contexts: a fetish is an inanimate object that is worshipped by a society, an object often believed to be inhabited by a spirit, and it is an inappropriate object of sexual desire—a shoe fetishist gets turned on by shoes. Both uses are relevent. In the same way that human sexuality is essentially social, concerned with another human being, so is the process of production; just as the social activity of sex becomes diverted to an object, so does the activity of production become diverted in exchange relationships between objects. We talk about 'the market' as if it were a living thing which determines what we do—it becomes a power which dominates us. Here again we have the idea of levels of society: an underlying level of social relationships and a surface level of market relationships, relationships of exchange value, which hides and dominates social relationships.

REIFICATION

Lukacs develops these ideas in several ways, all united by the term 'reification'. Perhaps the best definition is 'thingification', the way in which human qualities come to be regarded as things and take on a non-human mysterious life of their own. This produces a powerful moral criticism of capitalism which is seen as turning people into things that can be bought and sold. In marriage—a favourite example—I buy the sexual and other services of a woman in return for keeping her usually somewhat above subsistence level but not by any means in luxury. It can be argued that her value depends on her physical attractiveness, her submissiveness, her ability to cook or the money she will inherit from her father. Similarly I sell myself as a commodity to my employer.

Lukacs, however, is more interested in other aspects of reification. He is particularly concerned with looking at its effects on theory and knowledge. We have seen that the social world comes to appear as a world of objects, it comes to appear like the natural world. Society becomes a 'second nature', it seems to be as independent of human action as the laws and phenomena of nature and it comes to seem that we could no more change society than we could stop the sun shining. This is not only an 'appearance', the processes involved in commodity fetishism and reification do create external social structures of which human beings become puppets.

There is more to it than this, however. Social life and social relationships are matters of process: they develop and change, giving rise to what we call history. Reification hides that process from us. Instead of seeing everything in movement, we see only static objects in fixed relationships to each other. Thus the social sciences model themselves on the natural sciences, looking for regular relationships between different phenomena which can then be seen as laws of society. We might claim, for example, that in the same way that a metal expands when heated, so a society with full employment will suffer inflation. Beyond this there is a further tendency to break a social whole into its separate parts and develop different sciences for each: sociology, psychology, economics, history, geography etc. The hidden reality of the social world is that all these different parts make up a whole in a constant process of development. Reification prevents us from grasping this. It has more concrete effects where social activities are concerned: thus legal institutions are separated from welfare institutions, or have only limited connections, or medical services are separated from industrial production despite the prevalence of industry-based diseases. This process of fragmentation has real effects on social organisations as well as knowledge. The world is split into separate parts.

EXPERIENCE AND THEORY

So far little I have said has anything to do with revolutionary optimism. Lukacs has described the opposite: the way in which society solidifies around us, the way in which human beings turn into objects and the way in which the world appears to fall apart, to be fragmented into various distinct separate objects. As it stands, the argument can also be taken as a crude economic determinist account. Commodity fetishism is a result of the structure of capitalism, and reification is the spread of commodity fetishism through the non-economic structures of society. Lukacs' crucial argument, however, is that this fragmented 'second nature' which seems to control us can be changed, it can be seized and transformed. It is this which requires the intervention of consciousness and praxis as independent factors. The possibility for social change is built into the structure of capitalism, despite its oppressive nature, but the realisation of this possibility is not an inevitable result as some Marxists might claim.

In exploring this possibility, Lukacs argues at two different levels, about as far away from each other as it is possible to get. On the one hand he talks about the most abstract levels of European philosophy and at the other the most immediate experience of the worker at the point of production. One of the effects of refication on the major philosophical systems to emerge with the development of capitalism, from Kant through Hegel, was to separate the subject of action from the object (precisely agency from structure in the terms of this book). It seemed impossible to conceive a relationship which brings the two together without effectively dissolving one into the other (as action theory and structuralism do in different ways). This 'antimony' is associated with a number of others which are not relevant here but which create contradictions in each philosophical system. Lukacs argues that Marxism is able to solve these contradictions, and it does because they are solved in reality, or at least reality contains the possibility of their solution.

The reality he refers to is the experience of the worker in the capitalist economic enterprise: she experiences herself as a subject and an object at the same time in the course of her work. On the one hand she transforms a raw material into a finished product, or at least participates in that transformation: she is a subject acting on the world. At the same time she is organised into the production process as an object, an adjunct to the machine. She is treated as such by the management, and even by conventional economics, which sees her as another 'factor of production' alongside land and capital. This contradiction is manifested in its results: it causes an internal tension in the worker which in turn can result in explosions of spontaneous industrial action. Marxism is able to understand this experience and turn it into theory: the experience becomes the realisation that the 'object', in this case social and economic structures, is a human product, and that human beings are in turn produced by their products, formed by the societies they have produced.

It is at this point that the independent role of consciousness and praxis comes into play, through the revolutionary party, the Communist Party. The Party has a theoretical grasp of the mechanisms of capitalism based originally on understanding the experience and actions of the working class. Through the Party, the theory is brought into contact with the people whose experience the knowledge is based on; they become conscious of the meaning of their experience, that they can transform society, and they organise themselves to do so. At the same time, the theory itself is brought into contact with the world and is constantly revised and changed through that contact. The Party contains both intellectuals, theorists, and workers and they feed each other's thoughts and actions. The implication, as the French philosopher Maurice Merleau-Ponty points out in an excellent but difficult article[1] is that the Party should be a model of democratic, unbureaucratic and unoppressive relationships.

THE FAILURE OF LUKACS' OPTIMISM
AND THE LEGACY FOR SOCIAL THEORY

The basis of Lukacs' optimism was the central assumption behind his work that it was possible for human beings to collectively control social organisation and mould it to their desires; that agency could regain control over structure. Given Lukacs' view of the historical nature of knowledge, the way in which historical developments enable us to revise our knowledge of the world, perhaps the most telling criticism we can make comes from history since Lukacs. It is not just that socialism as he envisaged it has not been established, but, most tragically from the point of view of his own life, the Communist Party, the organisation that was to make all this possible, has tended towards the opposite form to the one implicit in his ideas. Communist Parties have been authoritarian, intolerant and highly centralized, and Lukacs and his work suffered directly. The theoretical gap in his work is oddly similar to that of symbolic interactionism: there is nothing which emerges directly from his arguments which enables him to engage in the analysis of either social institutions or social structures. Rather he takes a more-or-less standard Marxist analysis as given and goes on to talk about experience, consciousness, knowledge, philosophy, ideology and so on. It is as if he surrounds a

Marxist structural analysis with a theory of agency but does not stitch the two together. It is as if in the heady days after the Russian Revolution, Lukacs' philosophy of praxis could cover and hide the solidity and resistance of social structures, but it soon began to fall away, leaving those structures as solid as ever, and that is where the pessimism of the Frankfurt School takes up the story.

This does not mean that Lukacs' work is only of historical significance, the theory of reification providing the basis for later and more developed critical social theory. It is true that except in the work of Goldmann, Lukacs' work finds little resonance amongst modern social theorists, but there are, I believe, some useful and interesting ideas still to be found there. There is a theory of knowledge which goes beyond simple juxtapositions of right and wrong, true and false and which offers the possibility of on-going constructive criticism rather than destructive conflicts in theoretical matters. On a more down-to-earth level there is a phenomenology of workers' experience which goes a long way to explaining tensions and explosions in industrial relations. Beyond this, however, his idea of experience itself provides us with the nearest we have yet come to a link between structure and agency. The experience Lukacs discusses is framed by structural relations but at the same time feeds into consciousness and agency. As it stands it is too simple but it could be little else if my argument throughout this book is correct. Before it could be developed any further, more satisfactory theories of agency and structure are required.

NOTES

[1] Merleau-Ponty, M. (1974), 'Western Marxism', in *Adventures of the Dialectic*, Heinemann, London.

THEORY READING

On Hegelian Marxism
Agger is by far the clearest and is pitched at an introductory level.

Agger, B. (1979), *Western Marxism: An Introduction*, Goodyear, Santa Monica.
Howard, D. and Klare, K. (1973), *The Unknown Dimension*, Basic Books.

Lukacs
I'm including Lukacs' political writings from the early period only since these
are the most relevant to what I have discussed in this chapter. The most
important is *History and Class Consciousness* and the most important and
extremely difficult essay is 'Reification and the consciousness of the
proletariat'; it might be best to start with 'What is orthodox Marxism?' and
'Class consciousness'. Whereas Lukacs' work on literature was, perhaps for
political reasons, less innovative and exciting than his earlier philosophy, the
Goldmann references are based on some central ideas of *History and Class
Consciousness*. Goldmann's work on social theory is more disappointing and
not included here. The *Conversations* cover Lukacs' later views, shortly
before he died.

Lukacs, G. (1971), *History and Class Consciousness*, Merlin, London.
Lukacs, G. (1972), *Lenin*, New Left Books, London.
Lukacs, G. (1972), *Political Writings 1919-23*, New Left Books, London.
Lukacs, G. (1974), *Conversations with Georg Lukacs*, Merlin Press, London.
Goldmann, L. (1970), *The Hidden God*, Routledge & Kegan Paul, London.
Goldmann, L. (1977), *Towards a Theory of the Novel*, Tavistock, London.

Secondary works
Jameson is good but difficult; Lowey excellent in bringing together Lukacs'
life and theory; Lichtheim and Parkinson are both reasonable introductions;
and I am very fond of my own paper. Stedman-Jones's is the central critical
article of recent years.

Arato, A. and Breines, P. (1979), *The Young Lukacs*, Pluto Press, London.
Jameson, F. (1971), *Marxism and Form*, Princeton University Press,
    Chapter 3.
Lichtheim, G. (1970), *Georg Lukacs*, Fontana, London.
Lowey, M. (1979), *Georg Lukacs—From Romanticism to Bolshevism*, New
    Left Books, London.
Merleau-Ponty, M. (1974), *Adventures of the Dialectic*, Heinemann, London.
Meszaros, I. (ed.) (1971), *Aspects of History and Class Consciousness*, Merlin,
    London.
Meszaros, I. (1972), *Lukacs' Concept of the Dialectic*, Merlin, London.
Parkinson, G. (1970), *Lukacs*, Weidenfeld & Nicholson, London.
Craib, I. (1977), 'Lukacs and the Marxist critique of sociology', *Radical
    Philosophy*, Vol. 17, pp. 26-37.
Stedman-Jones, G. (1977), 'The Marxism of the early Lukacs', in *Western
    Marxism: A Critical Reader*, New Left Books, London, pp. 11-60.
Lowey, M. (1977), 'Lukacs and Stalinism', in *Western Marxism: A Critical
    Reader*, New Left Books, London, pp. 61-82.

The journal *Telos* Nos 10 and 11 (1972) carried a number of very difficult but
interesting articles on Lukacs.

11 The Frankfurt School: there must be some way out of here

INTRODUCTION

The themes of Lukacs' work sit easily beside much non-Marxist work of the nineteenth and early twentieth centuries, often lumped together under the label 'Romanticism'. Much of this work is not just anti-capitalist, but anti-modern society. In modern, industrial societies, people are seen as isolated individuals or as a conglomerate mass, but in either case everything that is good about individuality is seen as having disappeared. The modern world is seen as a spiritual desert, any meaning attached to life as disappearing, and people are empty and lost souls in a world they cannot understand. These themes appear in different ways in the work of the founding figures of sociology, in Marx as alienation, in Durkheim as anomie and in Weber as disenchantment. In the work of the Frankfurt School, the bleak landscape has turned into a nightmare: the social world becomes an electronic monster feeding off its own members, manipulating and absorbing any resistance that may be offered. We can make sense of this at least in part by looking at the world in which the main writers developed.

The Frankfurt Institute for Social Research was founded in 1923 as a centre for socialist research. It was the year in which *History and Class Consciousness* was published and and already the revolutionary tide that had followed World War I was abating. The following years saw first the rise of Stalin and the decline of the principles behind the Russian revolution, ending in horrors that do not need to be recounted here. Ten years later the rise of Hitler led to further horrors, driving the members of the school into exile (in the USA) and causing the death of one of its more marginal but now increasingly popular members, the literary critic Walter Benjamin. After World War II the horrors abated in their more extreme forms, but as a social system, capitalism seemed to become firmly established and unchallengeable, supplying material goods but systematically destroying centuries of culture. It seemed as though the possibility of radical social change had been smashed between the twin cudgels of concentration camps and television for the masses.

A range of intellectual stars were associated with the school: amongst those which I will not discuss here but which you may come across elsewhere are Walter Benjamin, whom I've already mentioned, Leo Lowenthal, a sociologist of literature, Erich Fromm, a psychoanalyst and Karl Wittfogel, an expert on China. The three main figures, however, were Theodor Adorno, Max Horkheimer and Herbert Marcuse. All three are now dead and whilst there were differences between them, there are common themes to each. Perhaps the most evident difference is that after World War II, Adorno and Horkheimer returned to Germany whilst Marcuse remained in the USA. These three are major thinkers who have written more in their lifetime than many of us could hope to read: to deal with them in one chapter is even more absurd than previous discussions of other thinkers. Nevertheless I shall be absurd.

DOMINATION

I said of Lukacs that whilst he took a Marxist analysis of social structure for granted, his own contribution to Marxism did not enable him to engage in any original structural analysis. The same is true of the critical theory of the Frankfurt School, with the difference that they do not take Marxist structural analysis for granted. Rather they argue that the early forms of capitalism that were analysed by Marx and taken-for-granted by Lukacs have disappeared, but they do not provide an alternative structural *analysis*: they do discuss general trends and perhaps the general functions of different social institutions but no more. In later years Marcuse contributed more to the structural backcloth of critical theory than the others. He argued that the contradiction, discussed in Chapter 8, between the forces and relations of production was no longer a contradiction. The productive forces now produced such immense wealth that rather than come into conflict with private ownership, they could be employed to re-enforce private ownership; the wealth was employed to produce waste products and false needs—of which more later. The growth of monopolies and large-scale state intervention on a national and international level has led to peoples' lives being controlled in ever more sophisticated and successful ways. Despite this Marcuse remained the most optimistic of the three thinkers: he thought that the contradiction between peoples' real lives and the lives made possible by the available wealth might provide a focus for discontent. In the period in which he was writing it would have been possible, for example, for all the Western Governments to provide well-equipped free health services, yet wealth was spent rather on armaments, or on producing twenty three different brands of similar washing powder where one would suffice. Health services remained non-existent or set about with restrictions. He also argued that even if the working class could no longer initiate social change since it had been bought or manipulated into the system, certain other groups not so well integrated could provide the spark which would awaken others: intellectuals, students, minority groups, Third World nations. It is easy to see why Marcuse was to become popular during the 1960s—the Vietnam War, the civil rights movement and the student revolt all spoke for his theory.

However, the bulk even of Marcuse's work belongs to the pessimistic side of the oscillation. Whereas Lukacs was concerned with the spread of reification *and* the ability of the working class to halt and break the trap it set around them, the Frankfurt School catalogued the victory of reification, arguing that the theory needed to be extended and developed to account for modern conditions. The one consistent and uniting theme is *domination*. For reasons that will become clear shortly, they do not offer any clear definition of domination. Perhaps the best meaning is its commonsense one: if somebody dominates me they are in some way able to make me do what they want me to do. If I dominate my wife, she does as I desire, her personality and her freedom of action are subordinated to my life. If there were no domination she might lead a very different life. The Frankfurt theorists are concerned with the way the system dominates: with the ways in which it forces, manipulates, blinds or fools people into ensuring its reproduction and continuation. I want to look at three areas of domination dealt with by all three thinkers: the way of looking at the world which justifies the domination of people over each other and the system over the people: instrumental reason; the way in which modern popular culture integrates people into the system; and the sort of personality structure which not only accepts but actually seeks domination.

INSTRUMENTAL REASON

'Instrumental reason' is explored in a series of books, the most important being Adorno and Horkheimer's *Dialectic of the Enlightenment*, Horkheimer's *Eclipse of Reason* and Marcuse's *One Dimensional Man*. Instrumental reason is a logic of thought and a way of looking at the world. We have already seen how, for Lukacs, the economic level of capitalist society is such that human relations come to appear as relations between things, that people come to see themselves and others as objects and the social world comes to seem a 'second nature' as unchangeable and independent of our actions as nature itself. This is the heart of the Frankfurt School's conception of instrumental reason but its implications are explored in greater depth and it is seen as having a significantly different history from that assumed by Lukacs.

The term 'instrumental' carries two dimensions. It is a way of looking at the world and a way of looking at theoretical knowledge. To see the world as an instrument is to see its elements as tools, instruments by means of which we can achieve our ends. I do not see this tree for its beauty and the enjoyment it brings me, I see it as timber which can be processed into paper on which to print the book I am writing. I do not see my students as people engaged upon learning but as people who, if I impress them sufficiently, might be useful in furthering my career; I do not see my ability to understand other people as something to be placed at their service but as a means by which I can persuade them to do what I want to do. I will return to this dimension of instrumental reason when I look at its history.

We can also look at knowledge as an instrument, a means to an end. This is perhaps a more difficult idea because it so imbues our culture that an alternative might seem inconceivable. I will try to illustrate the distinction by looking at alternative views of philosophy. Most people do not think very much about philosophy in the normal course of events but those who do often see it as a way of thinking that enables us to try to divine the meaning of our lives, of life in general and our place in the world. It is a way of living, a way of becoming reconciled to life and nature. It holds out the possibility of a harmonious world of Truth with a capital 'T'. Truth is the ultimate value, rather as God and his will is the ultimate value for Christians. For the Frankfurt theorists, such a view of philosophy would not be mistaken: it is a way of living. If such a person went to university, however, this is not likely to be the sort of philosophy she would find being taught there. Instead of philosophy as a way of life, she would find philosophy as an instrument. The most common view of philosophy is as an 'underlabourer' to science: science produces knowledge, philosophy can help sort out problems that science runs into—conceptual problems, that is, difficulties with its theory. Philosophy is a sort of mechanic for the engine of science; the idea of Truth as a way of living is nowhere to be seen.

Instrumental reason, then, is concerned solely with practical purposes. Another way of putting this which takes us further is that instrumental reason separates fact and value. It is concerned with discovering how to do things not with what should be done. Science can provide us with the knowledge to produce electric prods; it does not matter to science whether they are used for controlling cattle or torturing people. It is often argued, particularly in the Western democracies, that science can find us the most efficient means to reach an end, but the end must be decided by others, by the democratically elected representatives of the people. If these representatives decide that inflation damages social organisation, it is then up to the science of economics to find the most efficient means of halting inflation. If we follow this argument through, it can be seen that this instrumental, 'value-free' view of science actually reduces the area open to democratic debate. Economic science might tell us that the most efficient means of cutting inflation is by drastic reductions in public spending; but reductions in public spending can lead to very high levels of unemployment, increasing poverty and everything that goes with it. Some people might argue that a certain level of inflation is an acceptable alternative to the strains and misery of unemployment and poverty. The most efficient means, then, is open to dispute on the grounds of value judgements—a less efficient means of producing inflation might be preferable. There are various types of instrumental reason but the Frankfurt theorists tend to lump them together under the heading of 'positivism'. This can be misleading since positivism is also a precise technical philosophical label, but it does have some justification. The man who coined the term 'positive science', Auguste Compte, also regarded as the first sociologist, was writing in the period of social conflict that followed the French Revolution. He thought that a science of society would tell us what society really is like, and thus would put an end to all the debates about what it should be like. This is precisely the attitude to which the Frankfurt theorists object. It leads to a passive attitude to the social world; it is not seen as a human product but as an external reality governed by laws as fixed as the laws of nature. We can deploy our knowledge in a technical way, to alter this or that, but we cannot bring about any fundamental change. By and large, we have to adjust to things as they are.

Instrumental reason is seen as the dominant way of thinking in the modern world, governing both the natural and the social sciences. When Lukacs described the effects of reification on thought, he was evidently getting at much the same thing. For the Frankfurt School, however, the roots of instrumental reason go much further back than the development of capitalism. Rather as Max Weber traced the origins of the Spirit of Capitalism back through Christianity to Judaic beliefs, so Adorno and Horkheimer find the origins of instrumental reason in Judaism. It came into its own in the period we call 'the Enlightenment', the period during which took place the revolutions in thought that founded the natural sciences. Over this period, the 'instrumentalization' of nature occurred. Whereas previously, people had seen nature as God's creation, entrusted to humanity to care for and preserve, they now came to see it as an instrument, a raw material, to be developed and exploited for God's greater glory. This view developed over the following centuries, up to the present day, first to society and social organisation, where the change is from seeing the social world as a source of support and security to seeing it as a basis for individual exploitation and advancement, and then to individual human beings who are no longer seen as beings with their own integrity, rights and duties, but as possessors of qualities and skills to be exploited for some purpose outside of themselves. I do not judge my colleagues on the basis of qualities such as warmth, sense of humour, depth of knowledge or intelligence, but on the basis of the number of books and articles they have published, their efficiency in disposing of teaching and administration, their use to me in my search for promotion. People get jobs on the basis not of their integrity but of the successful completion of tasks.

In this account, instrumental reason seems to be something that establishes itself throughout our history, coming to dominate one area after another. Adorno and Horkheimer (but not Marcuse) seem closer to saying that capitalism is a product of instrumental reason rather than that instrumental reason is a product of capitalism. Once Marxism loses its concern with praxis, as began to happen immediately after the publication of *History and Class Consciousness* the positivist aspects to Marx's work begin to stand out. In later years they became increasingly critical of Marx, seeing him as accepting the instrumentality of the natural sciences and especially in his later work, extending it to society. The regimes of Eastern Europe can be seen as the fruition of instrumental reason as much as the capitalist societies. Althusser's Marxism is, according to this view, clearly a form of instrumental reason. Society is portrayed as the opposite of a human product; rather it is the producer of human beings. Revolution and socialism seem to have nothing to do with human freedom, rather it is an updating of the machine, a new model.

There are however evident similarities between the view of the Frankfurt School and post-structuralism. For the former, knowledge, at least in the form of instrumental reason, is equated with power and domination, and there is a similar desire to undermine this domination in the very style of writing adopted by both schools. Both are often deliberately vague and elliptical, refusing to present definite statements about the world or even about their own approach to it. The difference seems to be that the Frankfurt theorists juxtapose another form of knowledge or reason to instrumental reason—critical theory. Each writer has his own variant, but the differences between them do not concern us here. Critical theory is critical in the way I described in the preview: it is able to show how existing society is irrational or oppressive in that it takes away or destroys basic features of human life: the ability to transform our own environment and to make collective rational choices about our lives. It also claims to show how in the past we have actually created this society, how it is really a human product even if it can no longer be recognised as such. In other words, it puts our present society and views back into their historical context, showing that they are not fixed for all time, but part of a long and difficult process in which we are still engaged.

The way in which this can be shown, however, differs from period to period, and here we come to the roots of the particular difficulties of the style of the Frankfurt writers. We saw how, for Lukacs, 'totality' was a central idea, referring to the possibility of a unified humanity and world and a rational knowledge of that world. For the Frankfurt theorists, present-day societies, East and West, are already 'totalities' in the bad sense of totalitarian; they are unified entities which absorb and remove all real opposition. The idea of totality is no longer associated with liberation but with oppression, the attempt to gain a total knowledge is precisely the aim of a totalitarian society. Against this frightening prospect, it does no good to oppose another total system of knowledge, that is to play the other side at its own game. Rather, we must undermine that system wherever we can, adopt a negative attitude towards it revealing its holes and contradictions. *Negative Dialectics* is the title of one of Adorno's most important books. The outcome of all this is that Frankfurt theory frequently takes the form not of long and systematic arguments but rather short paradoxical pieces which emphasise ambiguity and contradiction. The most accessible work of this kind is again Adorno's *Minima Moralia* and in the introduction he suggests that the only place we might now find truth is not in the whole, the totality, but in the more obscure parts of individual experience which escape the totality. At times it seems as if any direct statement about the world is a concession to instrumental rationality.

ONE-DIMENSIONAL CULTURE

When it comes to more direct social analysis, the historical perspective I have just outlined gives the Frankfurt theorists a distinct nostalgic air. They often seem to be looking back to a golden past that is no longer and can never be again. Paradoxically, this golden past often seems to be the early period of capitalism which is seen as a time of real individualism to be contrasted with the modern denial of the individual. This emerges in the school's analysis of culture.

It is not surprising that so much Frankfurt work has concentrated on culture: given that they see society as no longer riven by economic and structural contradictions, the successful integration of individuals becomes the major problem, and culture in the sense of the ways in which societies and individuals formulate their views of the world, the major way in which integration is achieved. Perhaps the clearest statement of the arguments can be found in Marcuse's *One Dimensional Man*, but there is also an analysis of the culture industry in *The Dialectic of the Enlightenment* and Adorno in particular has produced a vast amount of work on literature, music and popular culture. The analysis covers all forms of culture, from highbrow to lowbrow, and the central theme is already familiar: human beings have certain capabilities and potentialities which are taken away from them in modern societies. It seems to be generally agreed that the highest forms of culture, art, literature and music can be a product of our human abilities and a criticism of our present society, although how this works changes from historical period to historical period. They do not offer an economically based explanation of works of art but concentrate instead on their form. Whilst a crude Marxist might say that a Jane Austen novel, for example, is just a product and reflection of British middle-class life in the nineteenth century, the Frankfurt theorists would concentrate on the way in which it is put together, the relationships between characters and plot. The structural analysis of Western films was an analysis of form, but not quite the same as that found in Frankfurt work.

The period of 'early capitalism' is hard to pin down, but generally seems to cover anything from the end of the seventeenth to the end of the nineteenth century. During this period, it is argued, a work of art could, through the perfection and balance of its form, offer a vision of an alternative to existing reality. The works of Mozart or Beethoven, for example, hold out the possibility of a harmonious and ordered world, which can be contrasted with the existing disorder and misery on which they throw a critical light. With the development of modern totalitarian societies, such a function of art is being squeezed out. Modern societies insist that they are already harmonious. Mozart is played to cows to keep up their milk yield; Beethoven's Ninth Symphony is the anthem of the European Economic Community and white Rhodesia. Now the critical function of art lies in anything that challenges this supposed harmony, that makes us think, that it is difficult to understand: the music of Schoenberg for example. More and more, this type of art has become marginal, *avant-garde*, of interest to fewer and fewer, and the 'culture industry' has come to dominate.

Marcuse talks about the way in which the culture industry produces and satisfies 'false needs'. The idea of a false need is a difficult one, because it means that we should question an individual's assessment of her needs and in effect claim 'we know better than you what it is you need'. You might like the Beatles but you ought to listen to Schoenberg. At the very best it can lead to cultural élitism, even snobbery. At the same time, the possibility of people experiencing false needs is built into critical theory. A 'true' need is a need that can be defined as deriving from or expressing the creative and rational powers that define me as a human being; it is a need which if satisfied will enable me to extend control over my life in conjunction with others and to deepen and enrich my relationships with others. False needs can be seen as a perversion of true needs. The following examples are my own. One clear example is the way in which part of the impetus of the feminist movement has been diverted. Feminism is a social movement: a campaign on a number of different levels by people who have been excluded from large areas of social life, and social responsibility. Its message is one of social equality and freedom, of deeper and different relationships between women themselves (sisterhood) and between men and women. The way in which this movement has been or is being absorbed (not necessarily successfully) into the dominant culture is by the transformation of these real needs into false needs. The demand for equality becomes transformed into a demand for the right to pursue a career as men pursue their career; women too must become competitive, surrender their more intimate satisfactions and human qualities for the sake of success. That this involves not deepening and different relationships but more shallow and exploitative relationships; and that instead of encouraging real collective control over our lives it encourages individual competition; these aspects go unnoticed. The modern woman of the advertising industry is as shallow, as plastic a figure as the modern man. The success of a recent book by Colette Dowling entitled *The Cinderella Complex: Women's Hidden Fear of Independence*[1] reflects the success of such a distortion.

A second example is the current concern in Western nations about health, manifesting itself in preoccupations with health food, jogging, self-righteous 'Thank you for not smoking' notices and so on. It is evident that health is not a false need, but it is a collective need. There is a great deal of evidence available about the links between social conditions and ill health and to change these social conditions requires a collective effort. The popular concern for health, however, is individualized and for that very reason, its real effectiveness is questionable. If lead pollution of the atmosphere remains high, jogging will mean that I absorb more lead. If I am a coalminer, no amount of wholemeal bread will give me the same life expectancy as a university professor. The further removed we are from real collective control over the major threats to our lives, the more enthusiastically we try to control the minor threats: I can do nothing about the possibility of a nuclear war but I can stop smoking. In similar ways, the true needs for freedom of choice becomes a need to choose between twenty three brands of similar washing powder and the need for freedom of speech becomes a need for a few rich combines to publish empty and ignorant daily papers.

The analysis goes further. Adorno suggests that the system still generates an economic insecurity—he was writing during the 1950s and 1960s—and we could also make the argument that any social system which denies basic human abilities creates insecurity. The feeling that we have a power we cannot employ is a frightening feeling. In any case, popular culture is geared to produce a substitute, false, security that is nonetheless effective. It does so in two ways, firstly through the standardization of its products. All aspects of popular culture from television soap operas to pop records to sporting events attempt in their various ways to emphasise the familiar and the secure. At the basic level plots, lyrics, rythms, the order of play, are the same and interchangeable with each other. If this were not the case, we could not have identified the basic plot-types of Westerns discussed in Chapter 7. At the same time these basically standarized products are given a gloss of false individuality leaving the impression of a freedom of choice and an individuality of meaning. We can argue endlessly about which pop song is the better, which football team is the better and all the time we are arguing about superficial differences and gaining a false security from the underlying similarities.

In a brilliant article, 'The stars down to Earth'[2] Adorno shows how this effect is achieved through the immensely popular press horoscopes. To begin with, astrology presents itself as a sort of science, it can lay claim to a (largely spurious) expertise which by itself represents a re-assurance. There is more to it than that though, as we can see without using Adorno's examples. My own horoscope in the London *Sunday Express* of 3 October 1982 makes the point equally well: 'Monday is a especially good day for trying out new ideas or dealing with officialdom. The week ends in fine style too'. I evidently have some thing to look forward to. I am a creative person, I 'deal with' officialdom, and the week is going to end well. The reassurance is obvious and the least important part. Most important is first the fact that the horoscope reassures me not only that everything will be OK, but that it is me who makes it OK despite the fact that it is written in the stars. After all, I am creative, I have new ideas, and I possess a certain degree of power since I 'deal with' officialdom. 'Deal with' is an especially nice touch since it can mean one of two opposite possibilities. If I storm into the tax office, point out numerous mistakes in my assessment, and come away having received abject apologies and a large cheque, I have 'dealt with' officialdom. If, on the other hand, I sit there through a series of embarrassing and humiliating questions and come away feeling acutely depressed, I have still 'dealt with' officialdom. I would suggest that most peoples' experience approximates to the latter, but the phrase 'deal with' adds a gloss to it, we can hope, or even pretend that the former meaning is appropriate. What the horoscope leaves at the end is an empty affirmation of my humanity by a pseudo-expert, empty because it has no tangible effect outside my own more ephemeral and less well understood feelings.

THE NEED FOR DOMINATION

Domination is not simply built into the culture industry, it requires a particular character structure, one that is not only receptive to domination but actually seeks it. This is the third major theme of the Frankfurt School, the way in which domination enters into the very heart of the individual. Much use is made of psychoanalytic theory, and Freud is frequently interpreted in a more orthodox way than Marx. I will try, however, to present an outline of this theme without assuming a detailed knowledge of Freud—my aim once again is to get across the general idea rather than the detail of the arguments. The best known works in the area are very different from each other. I will deal first with Marcuse's *Eros and Civilization* which is a work of speculative theory and philosophy, very influential during the 1960s, and close to the theme of the last section. I will then look, again in very general terms, at *The Authoritarian Personality* by Adorno *et al.* This is a large-scale study using a variety of empirical methods to investigate the claim that there is a correlation between personality structure and political and social attitudes. It was carried out in the USA at the end of World War II and was one of five 'Studies in prejudice' supervised by Horkheimer.

Turning first to Marcuse, we find the most general levels of Freud's work employed to develop a theory of sexuality in modern society. There is space here to deal with only the most basic of his arguments which has to do with the degree of repression necessary for society to operate. Freud's view was that civilization depended upon repression and thus necessarily involved misery. If we tried to gratify all our desires, sexual or otherwise, as and when they arose, society, civilization and culture would vanish overnight: life would be a chaos in which all we all used each other simply as objects of gratification, an immense non-stop orgy, ending in destruction. For some sort of ordered life to exist, we need to restrain ourselves, to repress our desires and direct the energy elsewhere, into socially useful activities. Freud seemed to see the level of repression as constant for all societies. Marcuse suggests that it can be different for different societies. In the earlier stages of capitalism, a high degree of repression is necessary to ensure that people spend most of their energy working, that profits are reinvested rather than enjoyed. Very few desires are allowed to emerge into consciousness and the pleasure-giving areas of the body are confined to the genitals. Freud can be seen as describing the processes by which this confinement takes place.

The growth of the productive forces in late capitalism means that such a high degree of repression is no longer necessary; a 'surplus repression' appears, over and above that necessary for modern society to remain in existence, and the tension this causes is seen as a possible force leading to social change, a 'de-instrumentalizing' of the world, so that we begin to see things for the pleasure they give us rather than their practical uses. The whole body would become eroticized. However, the system is also capable of manipulating this tendency to maintain itself, through what Marcuse calls 'repressive de-sublimation'. Sublimation involves the repression of a desire and the direction of the energy elsewhere: instead of being promiscuous I write a book on social theory. De-sublimation allows the desire to come into consciousness: I become aware of wanting to be promiscuous. Repressive de-sublimation persuades us to satisfy that desire in ways that are useful to the system. Commodities become associated with sex—naked women are draped over everything from

new cars to typewriter correction fluid as a way of selling them and at
the same time providing a vicarious sexual pleasure (this is almost
certainly true for new cars, although I'm not so sure about the
correction fluid). Books and films become more explicitly erotic, not
to say pornographic—a new 'opium of the masses'. There is a growth
in non-dangerous forms of sexual activity—open marriages, 'swing-
ing' and so on. A potentially dangerous development in human needs
is again turned to the benefit of the system.

The fundamental theory behind *The Authoritarian Personality* is
much less speculative and more down to earth, although it too is
concerned with the social manipulation of our inner drives. This time
the contrast with the early period of capitalism is more distinct. The
period of early capitalism is seen as one of individualism, where men
developed strong personalities, took decisions for themselves, and
adopted critical attitudes to the world. The strong private personality is in effect the second dimension to culture that Marcuse sees
as being lost in modern society—one way of summing up the whole
process is as the absorption into the public area of the private world
and the consequent stripping away of an independent basis for
judgement.

Such strong and independent personalities are seen as produced
through the processes described by Freud. It requires a strong and
independent father whom the son may use as a role model, as
someone to identify with, and at the same time develop through
engaging in conflict. The most basic conflict is the oedipal conflict
where the father and the young boy first clash over possession of the
mother. Simply because the father is adult and more powerful, he
wins; the conflict is repeated in different ways through adolescence.
The combination of identifying with and fighting the father produces
a son who is equally strong and independent in his turn. For the
pattern to continue, the requirement is for a strong father, a
patriarchal figure in charge of the household and with some power in
the world. As capitalism develops into corporate enterprises with a
strong centralized state, so both the role of the family and the internal
and external power of the father diminishes. The decline in the role of
the family is well documented: the state takes over an increasing
number of functions, primarily through the education system, the
family loses its productive function as factory production takes over
and so on. The father becomes an adjunct to the machine, separated
from home and family for most of the working day and as a

consequence his power diminishes and he becomes unable to exercise an independent judgement even in those areas where it still remains possible—the decreasing sphere of the family. This is reinforced by the son finding other bases for identification at school, and his earlier economic independence. He soon comes to realise the weakness of the father, and the battles through which his personality developed either no longer take place or take place in a weakened form. Late capitalism produces a weak 'narcissistic' personality, ridden by anxiety and seeking strong models with which to identify. Since the model can no longer be found within the home, it has to be sought in the outside world. It might be a pop star or a sporting personality, but in a more sinister way, it might be a strong political leader, a Hitler or a Stalin, or a strong political party. Since the personality is weaker, the unconscious drives are nearer the surface and more open to manipulation by such forces. *The Authoritarian Personality* was particularly concerned with investigating the relationship between personality structure and the support likely to be given to the mass irrational movements of fascism.

The first question that half of the readership might ask is 'What about women?' The answer is, in the work of the Frankfurt School, 'Not a lot.' There seems implicit in the arguments the idea that we need to return to proper patriarchal family relations. It sometimes seems as if the mother might offer a more gentle model for the child, but the mother is also stripped of her own rather different powers by late capitalism. There seems to be considerable difficulty in envisaging an alternative, and in the latest, most powerful book taking up these arguments, Christopher Lasch's *Culture of Narcissism*, the absence of an alternative to the more traditional family form is very clear. The implication is that we must put the historical clock back, not forward.

PROBLEMS AND CONTRIBUTIONS

Frankfurt School work has come under attack from two main directions: from those they label as 'positivist' social scientists and from Marxists. The most basic criticism from both sides is the same, although expressed in different terminology: critical theory is empty speculation. From the point of view of more conventional social scientists, critical theory has no foundation in the real world, it cannot be tested and confirmed or refuted against any external measurement, it is often put in deliberately obscure terms which indicate not so much profundity of thought or the complexity of the problem under examination, but rather the self-indulgence of the authors; much of it is logically meaningless even when we can translate it into intelligible terms. The Marxist version is only slightly less dismissive: critical theory represents a return to classical idealist German philosophy; as such, it cannot provide us with knowledge about the world or an analysis of real social structures. Its generalizations are abstract and speculative, though they might be interesting as representing the attitudes of a particular group of disenchanted intellectuals. It is usually emphasised that critical theory is connected to 'high culture', is university based, and has no connection with practical politics.

All these points seem to me to have some validity, but also to miss something important. I have already suggested that the Frankfurt School can be seen as the pessimistic swing of the pendulum in the battle between alienated and reified social structures and human action. We can, of course, find discussions of social structure, they are ever-present in the work of all three thinkers; but they are generalizations rather than the careful analysis of relationships that we can find in Parsons and Poulantzas, and if the presupposition behind my argument is correct, then a proper structural analysis would involve the recognition that social structures are not a product of human action separated from their origin. In the case of the Frankfurt School, however, it is not that they cannot or do not engage in structural analysis; rather it often seems they *will* not. It often seems as if they think that to engage in a structural analysis is to surrender to instrumental reason. Adorno sums it up when he points out that economics is no joke: to understand it, one has to make oneself an economist. This does leave their social analysis with the quality of over-generalization. It is possible, without any great trouble, to point to the difficulties. Family structures, for example, vary from social class to social class, and what they seem to consider as the original family structure of early capitalism was arguably confined to the industrial and commercial bourgeoisie, the social classes whose members were Freud's patients. The 'private area' that provided a base for independent judgement was also arguably confined to the same classes, and perhaps more important, a similar function might be played at present by the working-class community or the ethnic community. The failure in the USA to integrate different national communities into a common 'melting pot', despite the use of all the instruments of the culture industry, is strong evidence that the process of domination is not quite as complete as much Frankfurt theory would lead us to think. Of the three thinkers considered here, Marcuse is most aware of this.

At the same time that it fails to engage in structural analysis, the approach does not allow the development of criticism in any practical direction. The conception of human action, or praxis, remains very general. A closer and more detailed analysis of both structure and action is necessary to bring the two together in a way that can lead to the 'practical criticism' of bringing about social change, or even to a full understanding of the present situation. Taking the culture industry as an example, we would on the one hand require to identify the significant institutions and their relationships to each other, and we would need some way of identifying the most and least important; we would also need to look at the internal structure of these institutions and understand the relationship of all of them to other levels of society. On the other hand, we would need to know the objectives, the intentions and choices of the people who work in these institutions, the way they make sense of the world and see their place in it. For this we have to turn to the empirical sociology that is an anathema to most Frankfurt thinkers.

Given these failings, there is evidence that their work is more than empty generalization. Its very persuasiveness suggests that their analysis can make sense of people's experience and that they are identifying real trends in the outside world. We do not have to accept that the social world is in its entirety a human product to acknowledge the possibility of a greater degree of human freedom and control than we have at present. It is certainly true that the work of the Frankfurt School articulates the feelings of many who recognise that possibility. In this sense it is a useful corrective both to structuralism and to action theory. In relation to structuralism, it affirms that human beings are not simply the puppets of the social machine whilst at the same time it recognises that for most of our history this social machine has dominated us and forced us along paths we might not desire. In relation to action theory, it emphasises especially in the work of Lukacs and residually in that of the Franfurt theorists, that human action is a collective and not just an individual matter and that the social relationships produced by human action can take on a dynamic of their own.

The positive contributions of the Frankfurt School are, I think, primarily on this general level. Beyond this, they provide us with what empirical sociologists might call 'working hypotheses', ways of looking at the world which we might find useful in explaining some but not all of the things we want to study. I hope some of my examples in this chapter have indicated some of the more useful practical applications. Finally, of course, the period of affluence that fed the theory of domination is over; new economic crises and new conflicts have developed during the 1970s and these have had their effect on the second generation of the Frankfurt thinkers. The work of the most important, Jurgen Habermas, is significantly different from that considered in this chapter. We find there, amongst other things, a new theory of capitalist crisis and a rather more detailed analysis, as well as a developed theory of social action. At the same time, the theme of fragmentation re-emerges and we find an analytic model of society in some respects similar to that of Parsons.

NOTES

[1]Dowling, D. (1982), *The Cinderella Complex: Women's Hidden Fear of Independence*, Fontana, London.
[2]Adorno, T. (1974), 'The stars down to Earth; the *Los Angeles Times* astrology column', *Telos*, Vol. 19.

FURTHER READING

Crucial works by members of the school considered in this chapter

Aspects of Sociology or one of the readers would be the best starting point; *Minima Moralia* by Adorno is a good source for the 'feel' of the later works.

Adorno, T.W., and Horkheimer, M. (1972), *Dialectic of the Enlightenment*, Herder & Herder, New York.
Adorno, T.W. *et al.* (1969), *The Authoritarian Personality*, Norton, New York.
Adorno, T.W. *et al.* (1974), *Minima Moralia: Reflections from Damaged Life*, New Left Books, London.
Adorno, T.W. *et al.* (1967), *Prisms*, Neville Spearman, London.
Adorno, T.W. *et al.* (1973), *Negative Dialectics*, Seabury Press, New York.
Arato, A. and Gebhardt, E. (ed.) (1978), *The Essential Frankfurt School Reader*, Basil Blackwell, Oxford.

Connerton, P. (ed.) (1976), *Critical Sociology*, Penguin, Harmondsworth.
Frankfurt Institute, for Social Research (1973), *Aspects of Sociology*, Heinemann, London.
Adorno, T. *et al.* (1969), *The Positivist Dispute in German Sociology*, Heinemann, London.
Horkheimer, M. (1974), *Eclipse of Reason*, Seabury Press, New York.
Horkheimer, M. (1974), *Critique of Instrumental Reason*, Seabury Press, New York.
Marcuse, H. (1960), *Reason and Revolution: Hegel and the Rise of Social Theory*, Beacon Press, Boston.
Marcuse, H. (1966), *Eros and Civilisation: A Philosophical Inquiry into Freud*, Beacon Press, Boston.
Marcuse, H. (1971), *Soviet Marxism: A Critical Analysis*, Penguin Harmondsworth.
Marcuse, H. (1964), *One Dimensional Man*, Routledge & Kegan Paul, London.
Marcuse, H. (1968), *Negations: Essays in Critical Theory*, Beacon Press, Boston.
Marcuse, H. (1969), *An Essay on Liberation*, Allen Lane, London.

Secondary works

Of the following, Agger is the most straightforward, Held the most complete. The non-Marxist criticisms can be found in the *Positivist Dispute in German Sociology* (above); the Marxist criticisms in Anderson and Therborn (below).

Bauman, Z. (1976), *Towards a Critical Sociology*, Routledge & Kegan Paul, London.
Buck-Mors, S. (1977), *The Origin of Negative Dialectics*, Harvester Press, Hassocks.
Anderson, P. (1976), *Considerations on Western Marxism*, New Left Books, London.
Agger, B. (1979), *Western Marxism: An Introduction*, Goodyear, Santa Monica, Chapter 4/5.
Howard, D. and Klare, K. (eds) (1973), *The Unknown Dimension*, Basic Books, New York.
Jacoby, R. (1975), *Social Amnesia*, Beacon Press, Boston.
Jameson, F. (1971), *Marxism and Form*, Princeton University Press, Chapters 1 and 2.
Jay, M. (1973), *The Dialectical Imagination*, Heinemann, London.
Rose, G. (1978), *The Melancholy Science*, Macmillan, Basingstoke.
Schroyer, T. (1973), *The Critique of Domination*, George Brazziller, New York.
Therborn, G. (1977), 'The Frankfurt School', in *Western Marxism: A Critical Reader*, New Left Books, London, pp. 83–139.
Wellmer, A. (1974), *Critical Theory of Society*, Seabury Press, New York.

12 Jurgen Habermas: back to the filing cabinet

INTRODUCTION

Habermas studied under Adorno for a number of years and is generally recognised as the major contemporary heir to the Frankfurt inheritance. Although there are distinct common themes between his work and that of his forbears, he nonetheless takes it in a very different direction. I compared Lukacs with Adorno, Horkheimer and Marcuse as optimistic and pessimistic representatives of basically the same theoretical framework; what united them was a passionate concern with human freedom, however remote the possibility of that freedom existing in the real world. Habermas, too, expresses the same concern but he seems to lack the passion, there is little fire in his belly. He breaks out of the swing from optimism to pessimism and instead devotes much more attention to the analysis of social structures and action than the writers discussed in the previous chapter. However, he does so at the expense of any attempt at a real causal analysis of processes on either side of the structure/action divide. Instead he returns to the analytic model I discussed in the Introduction, breaking the world down into its different parts and suggesting very general relationships between them. He develops another filing system, not as complicated as Parsons, but nevertheless a filing system: he has a particular penchant for arranging things in threes, from types of knowledge to stages of social evolution.

Habermas has not been a lifelong radical: it seems that after growing up in Nazi Germany, he only began to move to the left under the influence of Adorno. For a while in the mid-1960s he was a committed supporter of the student left, but later distanced himself from them, arguing that they were only developing new forms of domination. His work has often been taken up by the left, but it involves a radical departure from the forms of Marxism I have discussed so far. I will try to outline its main features by means of a contrast between it and the work of the earlier members of the Frankfurt School on the one hand and the work of Talcott Parsons on the other, looking first at his view of theory, then at his criticism of Marxism and finally at the centre of his analysis of modern capitalist society. I will not go into detail with his various classificatory schemes: they are more simple than Parsons but eventually I find them equally tedious. It is more important to get a sense of his overall views and method rather than its details.

HABERMAS'S VIEW OF THEORY

For Lukacs and the Frankfurt School theory was Reason with a capital 'R', a rational knowledge of the world and ourselves. The way in which Reason might progress was seen differently: for Lukacs it was progress towards a totalizing knowledge; for Adorno, it retreated into the individual's ability to avoid inclusion in the totality, but for both it was something in which we must have faith if there is going to be any possibility of a better world. Habermas, however, deals not with Reason but with rational thought and he is concerned with drawing fine distinctions rather than broad generalizations.

I have already indicated that he discerns three types of theory, all of which he sees as necessary to human development. These are in turn based on three 'cognitive interests'. By this he means that we always develop knowledge for a certain purpose, and the purpose provides us with an 'interest' in this knowledge. The idea is not dissimilar to saying that a student develops an 'interest' in a particular type of knowledge through her purpose of gaining a degree and then a job by means of it. The interests discussed by Habermas, however, are shared by all of us by virtue of our being members of human society. His argument is rooted in Marx's early work and we can find here the beginnings of his major criticisms of Marxist theory. It is, he suggests, not only labour that distinguishes human beings from animals and enables us to transform our environment, it is also *language*, the ability to use signs to communicate with each other—an idea not dissimilar to that of G.H. Mead. These abilities, to work and to communicate, give rise to a different type of knowledge. Work, or labour, gives rise to a technical interest, an interest in mastering and controlling natural processes and using them to our advantage. We all, for example, have an interest in the development and employment of electricity since we can all benefit from it. This interest gives rise to what Habermas calls 'the empirico-analytic sciences', what earlier critical theorists might have called positivism, and what both would label as 'instrumental reason'. Habermas, however, affirms the place of this type of knowledge in human life—even when it is applied to human beings—since we are all affected by natural processes outside of our consciousness and over which we have no control. The earlier critical theorists are much more dismissive of this form of knowledge. Each interest develops through what Habermas calls 'media'—areas in which the interest is put into practice. The technical interest is rooted in and developed through work, and the problem with instrumental reason is seen as being not so much that it is in itself wrong or leads to domination, but rather that in modern societies it has gained priority over other forms of knowledge.

The second means by which human beings transform their environment, language, gives rise to what he calls the 'practical interest' which in turn gives rise to the 'hermaneutic sciences'. The practical interest is concerned with human interaction, the way we interpret our actions to each other, the way in which we understand each other, the ways in which we direct our actions together in social organisations. Hermeneutics is the science of interpretation—several of the approaches considered earlier can be seen as hermeneutic: symbolic interactionism, ethnomethodology, the structuralist analysis of culture and post-structuralism are all concerned in some way with making sense of what people say and think and its connection with their actions. The term itself originated with the practice of interpreting sacred texts, of understanding God's message, but today it is a label attached usually to an abstract form of philosophical argument concerned with what we mean by 'understanding' as well as with how we understand. Hans-Georg Gadamer, a German, seems to be generally recognised as the leading hermeneutic thinker and Habermas has been engaged in a long debate with him around the nature of understanding. The practical interest develops through the 'medium' of interaction, and one of Habermas's central themes is the way in which interaction is distorted and confused by social structures: people can be wrong in their understanding of each other, they can be systematically misled and manipulated, systematically blind. In Gadamer's work, so Habermas argues, such ideological distortion cannot be understood.

The practical interest, Habermas argues, gives rise to a third interest, the 'emancipatory' interest. This is also connected with language, and can be seen as ridding interaction and communication of their distorted elements. It gives rise to the critical sciences, for which Habermas takes psychoanalysis as the model, and it is rooted in our ability to think and act self consciously, to reason and make decisions on the basis of facts known about a situation and the socially accepted rules that govern interaction. Distortion arises when the facts of a situation are hidden from some or all of the participants, and when the rules in one way or another prohibit people from participating fully in the decision making process. Habermas seems to think that it is the very nature of language and language use that gives rise to this interest: there is something about language which demands that we speak clearly and on an equal basis to each other. The critical science based on the emancipatory interest reveals and contributes towards correcting distortions in interaction and communication. This is the basis for Habermas's critical theory and the similarity with traditional critical theory is evident. The medium through which this interest develops is power—the struggle which exists in all social institutions the eventual end of which is seen as equal participation of all concerned in the decision-making process. Psychoanalysis is taken as the model of a critical science because it attempts to reveal to the patient the unconscious processes which determine her action and bring them under some conscious control in what should eventually become a relationship of equality with the analyst.

Theory for Habermas, then, is a product of and serves the purpose of human action. It is essentially a means to greater human freedom, progressing on a number of different levels, and thus taking us away from the later work of Horkheimer and Adorno and the post-structuralists for whom knowledge is associated with domination and enslavement. It also involves a development of Marx's early work, drawing the emphasis away from labour and towards language and communication. It is to Habermas's critique of Marxism that I will now turn.

THE CRITIQUE OF MARXISM AND
HABERMAS'S VIEW OF HUMAN EVOLUTION

For Habermas, as for the earlier members of the Frankfurt School, the productive parts of Marx's work have become buried in an instrumental or positivist concrete. He argues that the responsibility for this can be laid on Marx himself, and the over-emphasis that he placed on labour as the distinguishing human characteristic. Although Habermas sees labour, and instrumental reason, as an important dimension of human life, he argues that socially organised labour alone is not sufficient to distinguish human beings from other animals and in fact language and communication make the decisive difference. Marx's emphasis on labour led him and later Marxists into the trap of instrumental reason. Habermas suggests, in fact, that the economic level of the social formation is only dominant in capitalist societies, perhaps only in early capitalism; unlike Althusser, he does not cling on to any idea of the economic being determinant 'in the last instance'. Rather he argues that we have to look to some other factor, some other level of the social formation in order to understand the development of human society. It is here that Habermas begins to move closer to Parsons: he suggests for example that each type of society is governed by a particular institutional complex: it might be economic institutions for early capitalism, the state in the case of late capitalism and the kinship system in tribal societies. The institutions themselves, however, may be seen as embodiments of cultural values and norms which he sees as progressing to higher and higher levels of universality.

To make the same point another way, human society is seen as organised around certain ideas—values, norms or whatever; through history these ideas are developed to possess more and more general applicability. There is here a debt to Max Weber's notion of the historical process of rationalization. Habermas uses as a model the development of the individual. As children, we learn first to identify very specific objects and attach names to them; we label the family pet, for example as 'dog'. We progress from this to a stage where eventually we can use the term 'dog' to identify a wide variety of animals, not only those of similar appearance to the family pet but those of very different appearance. Although the application of this model to human society would seem to lead to the directly opposite view to that of Marx, Habermas does suggest that the mechanisms which lead from one stage of social development to the next are not cultural but economic—although critics argue that he does not properly identify these mechanisms. Each evolutionary stage in this process creates a new set of problems and possibilities and Habermas seems to suggest that change occurs when all the possibilities for human development have been exhausted yet problems still remain. In fact he refers to some 'unlikely evolutionary thrust' that moves society on to the next stage. However we look at it, that is not a very precise definition of the mechanisms at work.

His most thorough treatment of this process takes us to the ideological rather than the economic level of the social formation and Habermas employs the work of Freud in an interesting way. Freud shows us, he argues, that social institutions exist not only to facilitate and maintain economic production but also in order to repress desires that would make social life impossible. Rather like Marcuse, he suggests that the degree of repression necessary will vary from society to society and social class to social class. The repression necessary to live and survive in social organisations entails the distortion of communication and interaction, since we are not aware of the unconscious forces affecting or determining our behaviour. The evolutionary trend is towards less repression and distortion and in trying to trace this he again uses the model of individual development. He deals with this in three areas: the growing independence and autonomy of the personality, the increasing ability to make moral judgements and act on them, and the growing universality of moral and legal systems.

Habermas looks at the evolution of human societies from a number of other points of view, usually producing a three-fold classification. I do not want to investigate the detail of these so much as emphasise just how far critical theory has moved, in his hands, back to a more conventional form of action theory. Societies are seen as products of human action in turn structured by norms and values, and it is to the development of these norms and values that we must look if we are going to understand social change. The basis for social criticism lies in the goal towards which social development is moving, a universal rationality in which everybody participates equally, a situation in which communication is not distorted—an 'ideal speech situation' which Habermas attempts to outline. As with Parsons' work we end with little conception of levels of social organisation, beyond that provided by giving priority to the cultural, no grasp of causal mechanisms, and a general classificatory rather than an explanatory system.

HABERMAS'S ANALYSIS OF MODERN CAPITALISM

Habermas's discussion of modern capitalism lacks the passion of that of earlier members of the Frankfurt School. It is seen primarily as a stage in evolutionary development—a stage that might go wrong and lead to disaster, but nonetheless it is, for Habermas, a social system rather than an evil. Like the earlier thinkers, he emphasises the dominance of technology and instrumental reason and we can see as well a rather nostalgic look back at the period of early capitalism. During this period, he argues, we can find the beginnings of the formation of a proper 'public opinion'; in public places, cafes, and the comparatively large number of magazines and newspapers, a limited number of people could discuss openly and freely public issues about which they shared information. In Britain this period could be dated approximately as ending with the eighteenth century, and it approximates to an 'ideal speech situation'. The operative word, however, is 'limited': the class structure of early capitalism made participation in the formation of public opinion a privilege, and the development of the economic system and class structure upon which such public opinion was based in fact undermined the public realm. Habermas sees modern capitalism as characterized by the dominance of the state over the economy and other areas of social life. Public affairs have come to be regarded not as areas of discussion and choice but as technical problems to be solved by experts employing an instrumental rationality.

For Habermas, state intervention and the consequent growth of instrumental reason has reached a dangerous point, that where what he calls a 'negative utopia' is possible. The progressive rationalization of public decisions has reached the point where social organisation and decision making might be delegated to computors and taken out of the arena of public debate altogether; this is a situation which perhaps Parsons might have regarded as the final confirmation of his theory, but despite his similarities to Parsons, Habermas maintains his critical stance. Classical Marxist economics and sociology, he argues, with its emphasis on class struggle, is no longer adequate to understanding our new situation. Although there are still disputes about wages and conditions of work, the most important conflicts take place elsewhere in the social formation, and if we are to avoid the possibility of surrendering human control over social life, we must understand these new forms of conflict. This leads us on to what might be considered Habermas's most important contribution to the analysis of modern society: his theory of crises.

Before moving on to this part of his work as such, it is useful to make some preliminary points. To begin with, Habermas does not see the relationship between development from one evolutionary stage to another, and the decreasing of necessary repression as a direct one. Each stage sets itself new problems, new repressions and distortions, and sets in motion new processes of change. His theory of crisis tries to trace these processes through the development of capitalism. Secondly he employs a Parsonian-related terminology of social and system integration. As far as I understand it, social integration refers to the social relationships between people, it has to do with experience people have of each other and themselves. System integration refers to the systems of institutions in which people are related, the 'steering mechanisms' which hold them together and direct them in their relationships with each other: 'boundary maintenance' again becomes an important term. The word 'crisis' itself is used to refer to a change in the system, experienced at the level of social integration as a threat to one's social identity. These two 'levels', which are in fact the familiar ones of structure and action, should, according to Habermas, be studied together.

He identifies (inevitably) three types of crisis as being endemic to capitalism: each stage of the system's development brings a new type to the foreground, although the previous type has not necessarily been eliminated. His analysis of early capitalism is similar to that of Marx, with economic crises the most important. However capitalism can be seen as a combination of guess-how-many subsystems: the economic, the political and the socio-cultural, and the site of the crisis moves from one to the other as the system develops. Economic crises and the resulting conflict between labour and capital are seen primarily as system crises. The growing intervention and power of the state is a response to and an attempt to manage these crises, on the whole a successful attempt, although Habermas does not claim that economic crises have disappeared; indeed at the moment it would be difficult to sustain such a claim.

Increasing state intervention produces what he calls a 'rationality crisis'. This, too, is a system crisis which arises because the state has constantly to borrow to fulfill its functions and thus creates a lasting inflation and financial crisis. It is a 'rationality' crisis because the problems are eventually rooted in the inability of the state to reconcile the different and conflicting interests of private capital. The basic irrationality is what Marxists usually call the 'anarchy of the market', the idea that we can build an orderly society out of conflicting private interests. On the level of social integration, the rationality crisis appears as a 'legitimation crisis': if the state cannot find the right strategies to reconcile the conflicting interests that it tries to rule, then it loses legitimacy in the eyes of the population, it fails in its task and the justification for its existence becomes blurred. We can see both levels of the crisis simply by following the political rhetoric of the Reagan and Thatcher administrations, both of which justify themselves in terms of decreasing state intervention, state borrowing and inflation, and both of which see themselves as insisting on the legitimacy of elected authority.

If the rationality crisis can be managed in the political subsystem, then the scene changes to the socio-cultural subsystem, and the third type of crisis, the motivation crisis. If economic crises are crises of system integration, and rationality crises crises of system and social integration, the motivational crisis is a crisis of social integration alone. The increasing state power and technocratic control necessary to manage the other forms of crises has the effect of undermining people's motivations for participating in the system at all. The spur of economic competition is steadily removed, together with the 'work ethic', the inner necessity that people feel to work. It disappears because work becomes routinely and bureaucratically ordered and the economic system seems to be self-sustaining. An increasingly powerful bureaucratic state also undermines the possibility of participating usefully in decision-making processes via the usual democratic institutions such as political parties and elections. The label attached to the governing paty makes less and less difference to what actually happens. Some modern social movements, the student movement for a while in the 1960s, and, more recently, the women's movement and the environmentalist and anti-nuclear power movements may be seen as symptoms of a motivation crisis.

I hope I have been able to give a general idea of Habermas's approach to theory, his view of social development and his analysis of modern society; I want to turn now to drawing the issues together in the light of the criticisms that have been made of his work.

CONCLUSION: FROM MARX TO PARSONS

The standard criticisms that seem to be emerging centre around two issues. One has to do with his failure to identify clearly the mechanisms of social change—or, as Anthony Giddens has pointed out—the mechanisms by which a society is reproduced in the same form over time. The second, coming generally from the more orthodox Marxist camp, is that Habermas in effect reduces politics to a matter of communication: it sometimes seems that if we could just manage to understand each other better, then everything would be all right. Once again the life and death struggle that makes up much political action is avoided in his theory.

It is, I think, possible to make sense of these criticisms in the framework of the general theme of fragmentation, although it is difficult because of the complications in Habermas's work. Once again the central divide is between action and structure, but Habermas adopts two different ways of handling the divide. Sometimes, when he is discussing social evolution, and especially when he is developing his theory of crisis, he tries to hold the two sides together. This brings him closest to the work of the original Frankfurt theorists—there is a similar tension between a dominating and alienating social structure and human action which has freedom built into its structure. Unlike the earlier theorists, however, he does not swing from one side to the other, but rather tries to hold the two sides together, employing the critical terminology of David Lockwood's discussion of Parsons: system integration and social integration. All he manages to do is hold them together: the mechanisms by means of which, for example, a rationality crisis becomes a legitimation crisis seem to me obscure. To try to identify the mechanisms relating the different levels, or those relating the different subsystems to each other, or the mechanisms by means of which a society changes, would involve making judgements about priority, deciding what is cause and what is effect. On these grounds I think the critics of Habermas are clearly right.

Of course at other times, Habermas does make judgements of priority. He argues clearly that language is more important than labour in distinguishing human beings from other animals, and equally clearly that apart from the stage of early capitalism, we can understand different social formations not by looking at the economic level but by looking at their cultural norms and values and the ways in which these are brought to life in different institutional complexes. His theory remains analytic: it breaks the social world down into different components and develops classifications. The nearest we get to an explanatory theory is the granting of priority to the socio-cultural subsystem for most types of society, but since he does not identify the mechanisms connecting different subsystems, he has no real theoretical reason for granting priority in such a way. Neither do the more orthodox Marxists have any reason to maintain the opposite. What we are left with is a less complex classificatory system than we can find in Parson's work (but he would have to be a true obsessive to outdo Parsons) and a way of looking at social organisation which adds something to Parsons. What it adds is a critical dimension: the theory of ideology, of distorted communication is not present in Parsons who assumes an unproblematic link between action and structure. Habermas keeps that link problematic, even if he does not identify it clearly. 'In the last instance' however it is again social action which is eventually responsible for the very existence of social structure and Habermas does tend to generalize from what he sees as the structure of social action to the structure of societies: the use of models of individual development in the understanding of social development is an example of such generalization.

Habermas, then, stands astride the division with a severe list to one side. Like the conflict theorists he is at times half-way out of the circle, only to fall back into it, and he ends by concentrating on language, speech and communication. This must by now be a familiar ending point: whether we have started from action theory, from structural analysis or from critical theory, language and communication have been the final destination, as seen by ethnomethodology, by the post-structuralist philosophers or by Habermas. It is now time to ask what this might mean.

FURTHER READING

Habermas's own work translated into English
There is no easy starting point in Habermas's work; it is best to choose the work which deals with the issues in which you are most interested.

Habermas, J. (1971), *Toward a Rational Society*, Heinemann, London.
Habermas, J. (1972), *Knowledge and Human Interests*, Heinemann, London.

Habermas, J. (1974), *Theory and Practice*, Heinemann, London.
Habermas, J. (1976), *Legitimation Crisis*, Heinemann, London.
Habermas, J. (1979), *Communication and the Evolution of Society*, Heinemann, London.

Secondary and critical work
The best introduction is again provided by David Held; the widest range of critical essays is provided by Thompson and Held.

Bauman, Z. (1976), *Hermeneutics and Social Science: Approaches to Understanding*, Routledge & Kegan Paul, London.
Bauman, Z. (1976), *Towards a Critical Sociology: An Essay on Common-Sense*, Routledge & Kegan Paul, London.
Connerton, P. (1976), *Critical Sociology: Selected Reading*, Penguin, Harmondsworth.
Held, D. (1980), *Introduction to Critical Theory*, Hutchinson, London.
Keat, R. (1981), *The Politics of Social Theory: Habermas, Freud and the Critique of Marxism*, Basil Blackwell, Oxford.
McCarthy, T. (1978), *The Critical Theory of Jurgen Habermas*, MIT Press, Cambridge, Mass.
Kortian, G. (1980), *Metacritique: The Philosophical Arguments of Jurgen Habermas*, Cambridge University Press.
Thompson, J.B. (1981), *Critical Hermeneutics: A Study of the Thought of Paul Ricoeur and Jurgen Habermas*, Cambridge University Press.
Thompson, J.B. and Held, D. (1982), *Habermas: Critical Debates*, Macmillan, Basingstoke.
Giddens, A. (1977), 'Habermas's critique of hermeneutics', in *Studies in Social and Polotical Theory*, Hutchinson, London. pp. 135–64.
Howard, D. (1974), 'A politics in search of the political', *Theory and Society*, Vol. 1. pp. 273–306.
McCarthy, T. (1973), 'A theory of communicative competence', *Philosophy of the Social Sciences*, Vol. 3. pp. 135–56.
Therborn, G. (1971), 'Jurgen Habermas: a new eclectic', *New Left Review*, No. 67. pp. 69–83.
Woodiwiss, A. (1978), 'Critical theory and the capitalist state', *Economy and Society*, Vol. 7. pp. 175–92.

13 Conclusion: the future

INTRODUCTION

As a conclusion, I will try to do three things. Firstly, I will make some general comments about the current state of social theory and what we are likely to witness in the future. Secondly, I want to make a case for the continued study of social theory and some suggestions about how students might best employ theory not only in their thinking about sociology but about the world in general. Thirdly, I want to make some comments of my own about what I see as likely dead ends and ways forward in theoretical work, using as my starting point the end point of the three different traditions discussed in the course of this book: the study of language.

The future of social theory is unlikely to be influenced by anything I might prescribe here. My guess is that the present confusion and arguments will continue, with all the aspects I have criticized. The notion that somewhere there is the final theory, the overall inclusive answer, is always hovering in the background, and it is likely that there will be further premature attempts at synthesis. Despite what I have suggested throughout the book, I feel the unspoken obligation to offer my solution as a conclusion. Indeed it is not even unspoken: discussing it with a colleague recently, the conclusion was described as 'pulling the rabbit out of the hat'. The truth is of course that there is no rabbit and I have spent some 70,000 words trying to show that we have nothing that can even be identified as a hat. If I have a prescription at all, it is that we should live with the confusion and fragmentation of social theory and not try yet to pull it together. *De facto* this is anyway the situation and the current signs are that it will be more rather than less difficult to deny it.

There have been times over the last fifteen years when sociology has appeared to be going through a theoretical frenzy. Fashions have appeared and disappeared with a stunning rapidity and some arguments travelled very strange roads. Even if everything else remained the same, this would lead to a theoretical exhaustion, if not a turn away from theory towards more conventional forms of empirical research. Everything else has not remained the same, however. The economic crisis, certainly in Britain, has had direct and indirect effects on the discipline. The 'theory boom' of the late 1960s and early 1970s was in part a product of the expansion of higher education in general, and sociology in particular. Now the expansion is over and a contraction taking place, it is becoming more difficult to engage in theoretical work, not least because research money, if it is available at all, is likely to be available only for more conventional forms of empirical research, often connected with policy decisions. All this will have a possibly beneficial effect of slowing down theoretical work, and concentrating it in areas which have been most directly connected with empirical research.

At the moment three such theoretical areas can be identified. The first is conflict theory, now informed by the more sophisticated varieties of Marxism, and concerning itself with class structure and attitudes. The second rather more marginal area, is symbolic interactionism and some forms of ethnomethodology. At present the most important empirical areas here seem to be deviance and education. Finally there is now established a comparatively sophisticated Marxist research tradition, concerning itself with the nature of the present economic crisis, the role of the State and ideology. If the theoretical frenzy has succeeded in informing researchers of insight from other traditions, so that ideas can be used flexibly, then it will have had a beneficial effect. The arguments will continue, of course, not least because different types of research and different types of theory do have political implications, both at the level of policy making and of the general vision of the sort of society in which we want to live. If the nature of these arguments can be more clearly identified, then some of the excesses of the past fifteen years might be avoided.

Thus despite the likely continuation of all the bad features of theoretical work, there is some hope that, paradoxically, the restrictions now operating on such work, might direct it in more open and reasonable directions. I think that what remains certain is that at most we have only some of the material necessary for the hat and the rabbit is a distant mirage.

WHY STUDY SOCIAL THEORY?

If there is no rabbit, and no hat, but only a lot of hard work that sometimes turns out to be pointless, and if the tendency is towards more direct empirical research, then any sensible student must wonder: why bother?

The question must occur more readily in the presence of what seems to be a *bona fide* rabbit held out by real scientists. At various times in the past, solutions to sociological problems have been offered by psychologists, economists, linguists and others; at the moment the offer comes from biology and I want to make a short detour to establish the most basic reason for studying social theory.

Sociobiology[1] at its simplest draws direct parallels between human and animal behaviour: for example, animals stake out their territory and fight for it, so do human beings. In both cases the cause is the same, some sort of genetic patterning which makes us act this way and therefore we have an explanation of war and social conflict. There is also the attempt to show that there are universal features to human life other than aggression, which can be traced back to our biological makeup. Such ideas carry the authority of a 'real' science and have the additional and very special advantage of being straightforward. Why, then, should we not work with such a theory rather than the complex and unsatisfactory ideas I have discussed up to now? To begin with, I would not want to argue that biological factors make no difference to social life. Social organisation would have been very different if we had evolved wings, or if we had maintained the organs of both sexes and were able to fertilize ourselves. Our biological make-up gives us certain possibilities and removes others. The problem, and one of the standard criticisms, of sociobiology is that it can only make its case by underrating the variations in human behaviour and the different meanings which human beings attach to their behaviour. In this sense it is really a retreat from social theory rather than a contribution towards it. There are innumerable forms of social conflict and we should be suspicious of any argument that tries to see them as a result of one simple cause—particularly when that cause is so fundamental as our biological make-up and we can do nothing about it. Social theory emerged and remains in existence because when people live together we find 'emergent' phenomena—things that happen that do not stem from their biological or physical make up. These things come to comprise the most important problems we are likely to face together or as individuals: war, economic prosperity or poverty, the ways of life open or closed to us. The first reason for studying social theory, and the most basic reason, is that it addresses these problems, and one of the reasons that theory is so difficult is that the problems are so difficult. If the sociological rabbit is a distant mirage, the socio-biological rabbit comes close to being a fraud.

At the most abstract level, then, social theory can offer a deeper understanding of what is at stake in political conflicts and social conflicts: it provides an opportunity to become what might be called 'better citizens', more aware and with a deeper understanding of what is going on around us. If it does not provide answers to problems it enables a better understanding of their complexity and difficulty. There are, however, more personal and immediate reasons for the study of social theory and I hope I have demonstrated these with some of the examples I have used. There is a sense in which anything new we learn changes us on a more personal level and we are not always immediately aware of it. If the different theories discussed in this book have been thought about as openly as possible, or if you have become enthusiastic about and followed up one particular approach rather than another, then the change might already be noticeable. Every time your view of the world shifts, however slightly, you begin to see things you did not see before; the connection between such shifts and action might be obscure but it is nonetheless there. If, for example, you begin to think of mental illness as a result of social processes; or the strikes as built into the relationship between employer and employee; or of the education system as an ideological apparatus, then your reactions are different when you come into contact with them. Theory has its effect at a much more personal level than might at first appear to be the case; the theoretical thinking I described in the introductory chapters is a way of deepening and extending yourself as well as of thinking about the world.

HOW TO USE SOCIAL THEORY

Some time ago Paul Feyerabend, an American philosopher of science, published a book on the natural sciences called *Against Method*.[2] He argued for what he called an anarchist theory of knowledge based on the principle 'anything goes'. What we normally regard as the scientific method is, he argued, restrictive, and if we look at the history of science we find all sorts of peculiar things have contributed to its present state. He suggests, for example, that Galileo was able to persuade people that the Earth moved around the Sun not on the basis of scientific evidence but because he was a more imaginative propagandist than his opponents. Feyerabend is concerned to encourage the wilder ideas of science; no old theory should be abandoned and no new theory rejected; they should be worked with, played off against each other and played with.

I would like to encourage something like this in the case of social theory, but with some modification. A thorough-going anarchism is self-contradictory; if anything goes then a strict methodology is permissable as well; and Feyerabend would not have written his book if he did not consider that his case was better than others. So it is not quite true that anything goes—some things go better. There is in fact a broad framework within which anything goes. In Feyerabend's case, this consists at least of rational argument and his book is well and clearly argued. In the case of social theory, I have tried to distinguish a different type of framework based on the objects we study, a framework which is 'out there' in the world rather than part of our argument. I have argued against too rigid an approach, the attempt to embrace all features of the social world in the framework of one theory and theoretical explanation. Instead I have suggested that the social world is made of different types of phenomena and each type needs a different theoretical understanding and explanation.

The basic organising division is between social structure or society and social action or agency, and I have suggested that the attempt to move across this divide in the framework of one theory is responsible for much of the fragmentation in the area. Beyond these two areas, I have suggested there are others on either side of the great divide. Each needs to be understood differently and involves a different type of causal explanation. On the side of society, the most basic level is the underlying structure of the social whole. Of the theories I have looked at, structuralist Marxism seems to me to make best sense of this underlying structure, and it provides us with a way of distinguishing between different types of society (according to different modes of production) and different forms of the same type of society (according to different relationships between the three basic levels). I further suggested that there is a 'surface' level of social institutions, those organisations which we can identify clearly, work in and study more or less directly. These include such organisations as schools, political parties, churches, etc., and although some general features at this level might be explicable in terms of structural analysis, they incorporate human action in a very different way. The functionalist model, with its analogy between social institutions and the biological organism, is likely to provide some insights at this level, since it involves looking at 'congealed' structures of action. The conflict model will offer some insights here, too; despite its general theoretical limitations, it points towards the real complexity of such institutions.

In Part III, I came to place considerable emphasis on what I called a level of 'general meanings': networks of ideas or systems of thought, both commonsense and theoretical, which, like language, pre-exist each of us and into which we enter as we grow. Structuralism and post-structuralism can tell us something about the organisation and interplay of such systems, the way in which they form and delimit our views of the world. Whereas the structural analysis of societies employs a structural model of causality, and the functionalist and conflict analyses of surface institutions employ a teleological model, neither structural nor post-structural analysis seems to employ a developed idea of causality; the former deals with rules, the latter sometimes with rules sometimes just with the play of meanings.

This takes us on to the realm of social action proper. One level of social action is the deployment and use of general meanings in forming attitudes, intentions and actions, and this involves a clearly teleological explanation. Symbolic interactionism brings us closest to the detail and flow of this process, and ethnomethodology makes some steps towards identifying the rules followed. I suggested, without going into great detail, that there seems to be other levels of agency which are not dealt with by these approaches, and that we might reach these through psychoanalytic theory, and both structuralism and critical theory move in this direction. It is critical theory that comes closest to recognising the distinction between society and agency but fails to hold them apart properly and eventually collapses the former into the latter. However, it does make explicit the ideal or critical impulse that must lay somewhere behind any attempt at theorising.

How, then, does a modified form of 'anything goes' fit into this as far as the sociology student is concerned? The first point that stands out for me from the summary is that the different approaches only come into conflict with each other when they try to account for something to which they are not suited, when they move into each other's territory. It clarifies the reason why so many arguments between different approaches have been sterile and destructive. Such arguments can be constructive but only when one side or the other is not laying claim to an absolute validity. When that happens, theory becomes a sort of football league, with onlookers and participants applauding points with varying degrees of dismay and pleasure. The arguments should concern themselves less with which is right or wrong—all theories are in different ways right *and* wrong—but with which aspect of some external situation or event may be understood by which theory in which way. 'Anything goes' in this respect means that we can play with a variety of theories—play in the sense of inventing and re-inventing explanations of the same object, picking first this side, then the other, then something not yet noticed, but drawing on all theoretical sources, even when they are not obviously appropriate. Thus to return to my impotence: in the Introduction, I suggested a sort of structural explanation employing the notion of patriarchy. But might there not be a structuralist Marxist explanation? My class position in the economic order brings me under various competitive pressures which reveal their destructive nature in my impotence. As a member of the new petit bourgeoisie engaged despite myself in the rate race for promotion, I am supposed to be afraid of failure, it spurs me on; and my fear of failure shows up in the most sensitive place as impotence. Perhaps in the private meanings I develop in my relationship with my wife, lack of stamina becomes defined as and turned into impotence. Perhaps I become impotent because I am aware of it as a possibility in the discourses surrounding sexuality in our society; if I had not heard of it, it would not have happened. Perhaps it is an effect of being dominated by a highly organised technocratic society which drains me of an energy which might otherwise be used against it. Perhaps it is a result of a temporary historical imbalance between the socialization and economic subsystems of the social system (in other words, I am working too hard). And finally, perhaps, to grant biology its place, perhaps it is an early sign of some nasty disease.

All these explanations might have some degree of truth to them even if in some formal sense they are incompatible. In thought and argument the rationalization process necessary to theory will take place as a matter of course; it will always involve some aspect of the traps I have discussed: crossword-puzzle solving, brain-teasing exercises and the logical trap. The last is most dangerous; I tried to show how the criticisms of structuralist Marxism disposed of the baby at the same time as the bathwater, in particular by insisting that something must be either this or the other. This sort of insistence originates in any claim to have a clear way of distinguishing between adequate and inadequate knowledge. It leads to a form of intellectual terrorism which manifests itself in the classroom and seminar as much as in the debates carried out in books. It is a way of outlawing ideas and ways of thinking in the same way that those who operate in their moral life with clear criteria of right and wrong would sometimes like to outlaw behaviour that others find quite acceptable and normal.

I want now to turn to some theoretical play of my own, as a rather limited example of what I have been arguing for. In the development of the three approaches one common factor has emerged; they each have tended towards the study of language. There is in this both a dead end and a possible way forward—not towards pulling out the rabbit, but to identifying one of the seams that might eventually make up part of the hat.

LANGUAGE AND THE WORLD

With ethnomethodology, post-structuralism and the work of Habermas we find a concern with and concentration upon language. There is to this a profoundly pessimistic and retreatist side. In a world in which human beings seem to be losing control over their own lives and their social worlds; in a world which itself seems to be fragmenting, in which international and civil tensions build up daily and in which there is a real and increasing dread of nuclear war; in a world which at its most benign seems to consist of large-scale bureaucratic organisations unable to recognise or cope with the personal and private qualities which for each of us are our defining and unique characteristics; in such a world it is easy to give up, to make the assumption that it can never be known, that human beings cannot be known beyond describing their internal chaos, or at best the only thing we can try to do is understand each other better. This is particularly true of ethnomethodology and post-structuralism. They do not enable us to make judgements about what the world is like, to choose rationally between conflicting arguments, or to gather knowledge of the world and act on it. With ethnomethodology, all we can do is point to the way in which people speak; we cannot make judgements about what they say, or what they mean. Any one statement is as good as another and serves only to create a sense of social order. In the case of post-structuralism, we are in the same position with a different jargon: all we can do is describe the discourses which constitute our world. There is nothing more than discourse and the play of discourse.

Habermas, too, at times, moves in this direction: I noted his tendency to suggest that understanding is a solution to conflict, to move away from the real battles of the social world and the resistance the social world offers to our attempts to change it. There are, however, saving features in his work, and what I want to suggest now is also an implicit acknowledgement of the value of critical theory and Habermas's work. The basic point I want to make is that if we confine ourselves to language we are in a hall of mirrors. This is recognised by structuralism: meaning appears only between words, we are moved from one meaning to another and back again. We cannot go anywhere. If, however, we can bring ourselves to see language as *also* identifying things outside us in the world, and expressing things that go on inside us by means of this peculiar self-reflecting structure, then perhaps new ways of looking at the relationship between the different types of theory might be possible.

The work of the Frankfurt School and of Lukacs is concerned directly with this problem of the relationship between the internal workings of the human agent and the external social structures in which they are placed, and I would argue that one of the most interesting features of the former is its employment of psychoanalysis. I want to suggest that a rather different employment of the same theory might contribute more, and we can see the beginnings of such an employment in Habermas's work. Psychoanalysis has been dubbed the 'talking cure' precisely because it attempts to enable the patient to put unconscious feelings into words and thus work through and gain some control over such feelings. In its theory it deals with:

1 The formation and working of unconscious drives and experience.

2   The relationships between these and patterns of action in the world.
3   The way in which these drives become attached to other agents.

The words in which we express ourselves are the nexus of the process, they articulate the inner workings and point outside at the same time. If I discover the depth of the anger I once felt for my father and become able to express it, then I also come to realise how that anger has influenced me in my everyday actions, political attitudes and so on.

The appropriate metaphor here is difficult to find but two do spring to mind. It is not a matter of saying that language is the place where everything happens and is resolved. Rather it is a seam or a sort of zip fastener joining different materials. It links internal and external processes, which in themselves are very different from and irreducible to each other. It is like a hinge, linking the teleological 'door' of agency to the 'structural frame' of society. Perhaps also a different type of machine metaphor might be appropriate. Whereas structuralist Marxism sees social structures as a sort of self-producing machine, making its own fuel, I would suggest that we separate machine and fuel. The fuel is human energy, intentions and actions, and it possesses the peculiar property of changing the machine into which it is fed, as well as enabling the machine to continue functioning. In this case we can see language as the fuel pipe, the passage through which the energy is fed into the machine, only it is a fuel pipe which can change direction and shape depending on the type of energy and intentions which move along it.

I suspect neither of these metaphors are clear, but they are the best I can manage at the moment. I am suggesting a further study of psychoanalytic theory, I repeat, not as offering a synthesis of the different approaches, but rather as indicating one of the ways in which we might be able to organise the approaches together. The fact that the idea is so schematic is a reason for regarding it with suspicion, but at the very least if it can avoid the trap of studying only language, then it will serve its purpose.

NOTES

[1] For a simplistic version of this approach, see Morris, D. (1967), *The Naked*

Ape: A Zoologist's Study of the Human Animal, Jonathan Cape, London; a more sophisticated account can be found in Wilson, E.O. (1976), *Sociobiology: The New synthesis*, Havard University Press, Cambridge, Mass. For counter arguments, see: Sahlans M. 1977: *The Use and Abuse of Biology* Tavistock Publications, London.

[2] Feyerabend, P. (1975), *Against Method*, New Left Books, London.

Index

Adorno, T.W., Chap. 11 *passim*; 203, 206. See also: Critical theory
Althusser, L., 16, 103, 106, 112, 113; Chap. 8 *passim*; 168, 170, 171, 175, 189, 207; English criticisms of: Chap. 9 *passim*. See also: Structuralist Marxism

Balibar, E., 134
Barthes, R., 106, 113, 114ff
Benjamin, W., 184
Berger, P., 88, 95
Bhaskar, R., 21ff, 124
Blumer, H., 72, 73, 74

Causal explanations, 24ff, 51ff, 130ff
Chicago school, the, Chap. 4 *passim*
Chomsky, N., 94
Cicourel, A., 92, 94, 95
Cohen, P., 59ff, 63
Comte, A., 106, 188
Conflict theory, 16, 29, 35, 49, 55; Chap. 4 *passim*; 141, 148, 155, 158, 213, 216, 220; and power/authority, 60ff. See also: Dahrendorf, R.
Coser, L., 50, 63
Critical theory and the Frankfurt School, 17, 29, 170, 175, 180; Chap. 11 *passim*; 203, 204, 207, 209, 212, 220, 223. Background to, 183–4; basis in Marx's work,

168ff; and cultural domination, 190ff; domination as a theme, 184ff; domination and the personality, 194ff; and instrumental reason, 186ff; problems and contributions of, 197ff
Critical theory (cont)., See also: Adorno, T.W., Habermas, J., Horkheimer, M., Marcuse, H.
Cutler, A., 148

Dahrendorf, R., 50; Chap. 4 *passim*; 139. See also: Conflict theory
Dawe, A., 18
Derrida, J., 106, 156. See also: Post-structuralism
Durkheim, E., 21, 38, 106, 110, 183

Engels, F., 134
Ethnomethodology, 9, 16, 35; Chap. 6 *passim*; 102, 107, 157, 158, 170, 205, 213, 216, 220, 222, 223. Background to, 83f, 90; criticisms of conventional sociology, 91; glossing, 92f; indexicality and reflexivity, 91ff; problems with, 94ff

Feyerabend, P., 218, 219
Foucault, M., 106, 153, 157–8. See also: Post-structuralism